Children of the Empire

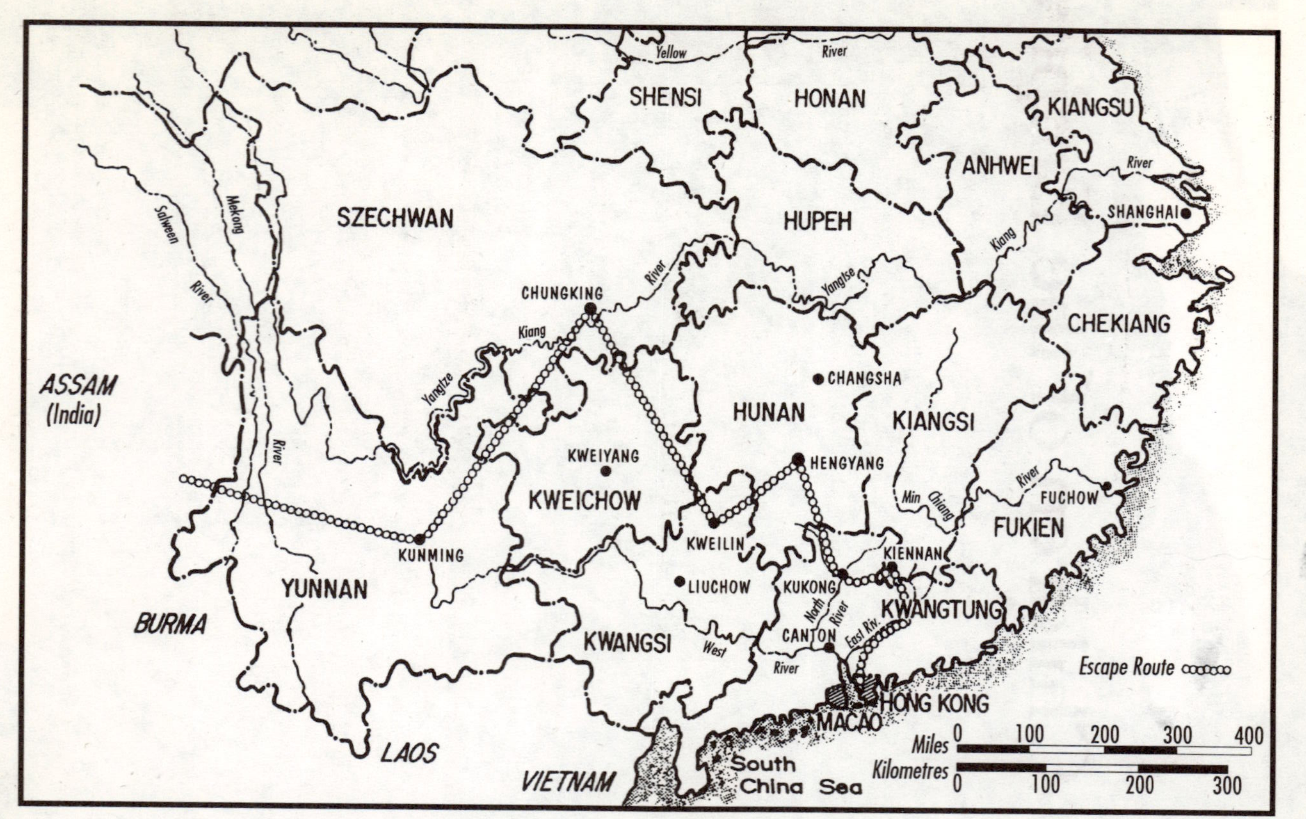

Tony Hewitt's escape route through China.

Children of the Empire

*

Anthony Hewitt

with a Foreword by

Hayley Mills

Kangaroo Press

By the same author

Bridge with Three Men
Across China to the Western
Heaven in 1942
(Jonathan Cape, 1986)

© Anthony Hewitt 1993 and 1995

First published in paperback by Kangaroo Press Pty Ltd
3 Whitehall Road Kenthurst NSW 2156 Australia
PO Box 6125 Dural Delivery Centre NSW 2158
Printed by Star Printery Ltd, Erskineville 2043

ISBN 0 86417 723 2

Contents

Foreword

When my uncle Tony Hewitt paid me the compliment of asking me to write the foreword to his book, despite my concern that I should do it justice, I accepted with alacrity.

It is an intensely personal story yet also encompasses much of the momentous times of our recent and most troubled history.

His childhood was in India during the last great days of the British Raj; as one of the outcast children of the Empire he was sent to the cold grey shores of England, to the unfamiliar constraint of shoes and boarding school and away from the love and security of his family, the colour and the freedom of everything he had ever known.

He tells of the world before the war with all its gaiety and innocence. The world observed through the eyes of the young officer in His Majesty's Army; the victories and defeats and the blunders of war. His great escape from Hong Kong prison camp across China to freedom. And all the time there is another life with so many parallels: that of a vibrant young woman, Elizabeth, now and then coming into focus until people or events pull them apart, but always there somewhere.

The different strands of their lives are held together with an unsentimental yet gentle touch, presenting it as it was, no more no less; like the arc of a rainbow.

This story is particularly special for me because of the light it throws upon lives and experiences of some of my family during a time and in a world that is not so very long ago but has now gone forever.

Hayley Mills

Prologue

The British Empire evolved children of a singular pattern. Kipling called them outcast children of the Empire. Their early years were spent in India or a Colony but eventually they were sent to school in England.

Distance, a relentless tyrant, prevented them from joining their parents for school holidays. In the 1920s and '30s a passage to India took three weeks; it took four to Malaya, even more to Hong Kong and almost eight to North China. Jet aircraft which could carry them to distant countries in a few hours did not exist. Letters took as long as ships, long-distance telephone calls were impossible and telegrams were the only means of rapid communication.

A lengthy sea voyage brought the children to England where they could remain for years. During those solitary years these waifs of imperialism yearned to return to the countries they first knew, to an enthralling life among the indigenous people, their laughter and cries, teeming bazaars, the smell of the Orient, tame and wild animals and jungles—even the heat and dirt. Once bitten by the lure of the East the children always returned, inveterate romantics.

These children believed the British Empire would last a thousand years. Many things supported their belief. On world maps a large proportion coloured red showed a remarkable assembly of Imperial territories, protectorates, possessions, colonies and dominions. Britain governed a quarter of the world's population. Government Houses, some of stately grandeur, dotted the huge colonial landscape from east to west so that 'the sun never set on Government House'. Everywhere in the Empire at sunrise a Union Jack was riding up a flagstaff, except at Lucknow where it had not been lowered since the siege of the Residency during the Indian Mutiny in 1857. The Empire was the greatest ever known; it eclipsed all ancient domains and recent Turkish and French empires. Its size and ubiquity fortified the children's belief in its permanency.

India was the crucial point of Empire. Vaguely called 'the Raj', a word which means 'rule', Britain governed the huge subcontinent except the Indian States ruled by Indian Princes. As a child I lived in British India. It was then a Kipling's India, full of soldiers mainly for defence against the Russians and the Afghan tribes on the North West Frontier and to assist the Indian Police in aid of the civil authority. The British and Indian Armies embodied the power of the Raj to keep India and with it the Empire.

I was six in 1920 when my parents sailed from India for eight months leave in England on board His Majesty's Troopship *Himalaya*. The ship filled its bunkers with coal in Aden where my parents had lived for a few years, patiently accepting the blazing heat and cruel conditions in this outpost of the Raj. Edwardians came from a hardy breed which readily endured immense discomforts for the sake of King and Empire. On that long sea journey British soldiers were ever apparent at Port Sudan in the Red Sea, at Suez and along the Canal to Port Said, at Malta and Gibraltar.

At sea the Royal Navy and the British Merchant Marine were even more prolific. The Raj depended entirely on the Royal Navy to safeguard the sea lines of communication with India and to afford the British merchant fleet virtual monopoly of the Asian trade. Huge battleships and cruisers lay at anchor at Portsmouth and giant British trans-Atlantic passenger liners crowded Southampton waters. I was convinced that the Empire was indeed great.

Elizabeth Hayley Bell was five in 1923 when she travelled with her parents from the Portuguese Colony of Macau to England and returned to Chefoo in North China. On those prolonged voyages the ship stopped at ports in British Colonies like Singapore, Penang and Colombo. In Chinese waters the halts were in Treaty Ports where trading rights had been granted to Britain as long ago as 1842. Amoy and Shanghai were of special significance to Elizabeth— her mother had been born in Amoy and her father in Shanghai. Everywhere a British presence was prominent. Elizabeth's parents extolled the importance of the Empire and she grew up naturally believing in its greatness.

Her beliefs were developed when her family moved to Hong Kong, a name sometimes interpreted as 'Fragrant Harbour'. At the Peak School she was made aware of the words of the Treaty of Nanking of 1842 which decreed that '. . . His Majesty the Emperor of China cedes to Her Majesty the Queen of Great Britain the Island of Hong Kong to be possessed in perpetuity by Her Britannic Majesty, her Heirs and Successors.' The definitive word was 'perpetuity' and it was supposed also that the New Territories leased by China in 1898 for ninety-nine years would remain perpetually beyond 1997. She believed the Empire was secure.

These convictions were but a part of the romantic legend of imperialism. The cost of victory in the First World War had almost vanquished Britain, her wealth squandered, her industry crippled, her finest men killed. A whole generation of young men born to rule who might have administered the Empire had died.

The First World War became a watershed in the history of the Raj. In 1914 India responded magnificently to the call of the King-Emperor to subdue Germans and Turks. Over a million Indians served in some capacity overseas; thousands perished. As a reward for their loyalty the Indians expected Britain to institute self-government rapidly but the obsolescent Edwardian-Georgian order of government failed to meet the need for political reform. The Indians. particularly the educated classes who anticipated political advancement felt betrayed. Mahatma Gandhi advocated passive resistance and the demand for independence grew, the consequence of which threatened the whole edifice of Empire.

In 1924 I was sent from India to school in England. I disdained English schoolboys who had never known the freedom of vast open spaces and galloping across the plains, or the beauty of jungles, but in an enormous Empire there were plenty of boys born overseas with whom I evoked like memories. Elizabeth was ten when she was sent from Hong Kong to school in England. Taken away from the love of her family and home on the Peak, she longed for her fond amah and Chinese staff, for the lively Cantonese people, and to live in a warm climate.

Our lives were to be highly influenced by the Washington Naval Treaty of 1922, which reduced the Royal Navy to equality with the United States of America and parity in the Pacific with Japan. Later, an Anglo-German Naval Treaty upset the balance of naval power and restricted the greater part of the Royal Navy to home waters, limiting reinforcement in the Pacific. Britain and the League of Nations were incapable of taking decisive action against aggressors and could resort only to sanctions when Japan invaded Manchuria and Italy attacked Abyssinia, and to appeasement with Hitler's Germany. Britain's role as the world's caretaker was being overtaken by the United States which incongruously was not a member of the League of Nations. British imperialism was still robust but it had lost much of its vigour and the impetuous romance of imperialism had faded.

This was the state of the Empire when Elizabeth and I responded to the lure of the East. The course of our lives was governed by the Empire and our future existence was drastically influenced by the course of events in China and Hong Kong, Malaya and Singapore. This is the story of two outcast children of Empire from 1914 to 1948—a corridor of time through which their footsteps echoed.

1

Macau

City of the Name of God

Elizabeth's childhood belonged to China. A baby in Shanghai, she grew up in Macau, Chefoo, Canton and Hong Kong, moving with her family to wherever her father, a Commissioner of Chinese Imperial Maritime Customs, was posted. Her life was an exciting adventure in an ever changing environment of different cities and houses and with varying kinds of Chinese people.

In Macau, Elizabeth lived in a colonial style Portuguese house on a high hill on the Roa da Boa Vista. Paved steps rose steeply from the road into a tropical garden full of colour, frangipani and bougainvillea and a profusion of flowers in green and yellow pots arranged along the garden parapet. Above the garden stood the antiquated house, two storeys high, with strong white pillars supporting an open verandah.

Views from the verandah stretched across the wide expanse of the Praia Grande Bay, its waters tinged amber by the mighty Pearl River unloading the silt of the East, North and West Rivers of South China. Venerable Chinese junks flying maroon sails rolled along the calm bay, disturbed only by busy steamers rudely marking their course with puffs of black smoke. Green islands, like pine-covered Coloane, rose from within the Bay and in the hazy distance lay a group called Nine Islands.

Voyages to Nine Islands in a Maritime Customs launch crashing through huge waves delighted the Hayley Bell children—Mary, Winifred, Dennis, Elizabeth and John. Once ashore they played on the rock-strewn islands amid palm and casuarina trees bent almost flat by wind from the China Sea. On humid summer days they lazed in the surf and listened to Mary, a born raconteur, relating tales of attacks by the Chinese pirates who abounded in these seas.

In safer waters, but not as exciting, the family frequently sailed in chugging *walla-wallas* to picnic on the white beaches of Coloane and played games in the sand or explored the island, often visiting the Church of Saint Xavier, which attracted the children with its mystic and archaic beauty.

Tall and slim, with delicate features and gazelle-like hazel eyes, Elizabeth was an intelligent and sensitive child, often excited by Mary's extravagant tales of pirates and other thrilling adventures. During the day she played with her brothers and sisters on the verandah and at night slept there. Her father insisted that the children always slept out of doors and remained out in all weathers, sure that such Spartan treatment would raise strong children.

It was a harsh rule for a small girl and Elizabeth often woke in terror to find herself out under the great stars of the China night; the aloneness seemed immense, the vast space above her hostile, the darkness terrifying. But in daylight she felt more secure in the love of her parents and with devoted Chinese servants, so kind and gentle, who stayed permanently with the family, moving with them to other cities or countries; and she was serene with the beauty of her home and its many flower-potted garden and with the thrill of exploring the ancient city in which she lived.

Officially founded in 1557 during the great era of Portuguese exploration, Macau was a city of friendly Portuguese and Chinese people, of curious narrow twisting streets full of many odours—burning incense, aromatic cooking and decaying rubbish. It varied from neat residential Portuguese districts to untidy closely-packed Chinese quarters. Solid terracotta colonial Portuguese villas, with flowers in window boxes and white shutters hinged open against pink walls, contrasted strikingly with ancient Chinese homes, sometimes hidden by large fig trees. Elizabeth loved to peep into courtyards through moon-shaped doors, at red-lacquered altar tables and little stone Buddhas standing demurely in the shadows. There were cathedrals, churches, temples, ruins; it was enchanting, so much to be discovered.

In stables nearby the family kept horses. Called 'Bom Jesus', built over an ancient Chinese temple, the place was haunted—a mystery that added to the fun. To the Chinese the stables were bad *fung shui*, or wind water, possibly because they were inconsistent with certain prescribed natural proportions. To protect the stables the *mafoos* (grooms) burned incense and made small offerings of fruit at the foot of the walls. There was much Chinese superstition: Elizabeth was forbidden to point at rainbows because it was unlucky to do so; everyone bowed nine times to a new moon, making wishes that must be kept secret. Perhaps the family did not pay enough attention to these superstitions, broke secret wishes, bewitched their dwelling places, or perhaps simply that the Commissioner's house had been built on bad *fung shui*, but one day a whole side of the house collapsed.

But nothing stopped the children from collecting their ponies daily from 'Bom Jesus' and riding through the tiny streets of Macau on their way to the Barrier Gate, an imposing stucco edifice crowned with the national flag of Portugal, and to the open country beyond.

There were no motor vehicles to avoid at this time in the 1920s but the narrow streets were congested with a jostling throng of pedestrians, rickshaws and sedan chairs. People in a hurry bustled through the crowd in a jog trot, wooden clogs clattering on the cobbles; others shuffled along in blue satin shoes, some carrying pet canaries in wire cages, a few stopping to read the big black or gilded letters on boards jutting out from shop walls; pretty little women with bound feet toddled painfully along the tortuous way; and everyone on foot tried to avoid rickshaws and chairs pulled by arrogant coolies who cleared a passage with raucous shouts. Of greatest fun were the people themselves, of many different colours and races: Asian, European, Catholic priests and nuns, Buddhist monks, Chinese mandarins, rich businessmen, poor coolies, beggars.

Elizabeth, her sisters and her brother were the only English children in Macau and as they rode through the heaving throng they were greeted joyously. Everyone knew who they were—the Hayley Bells. And as they cantered onwards beyond the Barrier Gate, they were in China, in Kwangtung Province of the Republic of China. The effusive Cantonese people greeted the barbarians with cries of joy and astonishment, amazed at Mary's red hair, a most ferocious feature in any foreigner. But Elizabeth was happy to be on Chinese soil because she belonged to China.

In the Church of Saint Joseph the Angelus commemorating the incarnation is said at morning, noon and sunset at the sound of the church bell. It chimed as Elizabeth and her small brother with their father, known always as Hayley, were walking in the Old Protestant Cemetery. It was a sound she loved, an inseparable part of Macau, as was the ancient cemetery where Hayley used to read aloud the inscriptions on the graves.

'Look,' he pointed, 'That says "George Chinnery buried in 1774". He was a marvellous China coast artist. And that one reads "Captain Lord Spencer Churchill of HMS *Druid*". He must be a relative of the Duke of Marlborough.'

The names were beyond Elizabeth but she liked being with her father whom she worshipped and who had such a profound knowledge of all things.

Born in Shanghai of silk and tea merchants, Francis Hayley Bell returned to China in 1891 at the age of fifteen after schooling in England and joined the Chinese Imperial Maritime Customs a few years later. His early service was in Central and Southern China and at the same time he was studying the way of life of the Chinese people. His periods of leave were spent walking across country from Shanghai to Foochow, from Canton to Nanning and Pakhoi, from Canton to Hong Kong. His knowledge of China was indeed profound.

Hayley spoke with a fine English voice, a musical voice of pure natural tones, probably a reason why he spoke Chinese so easily. Elizabeth loved the sound of his voice and never forgot it.

In the tropic dawn Elizabeth crept out of her bed on the verandah to watch the sun rise over the China Sea. The whole sky was filled with the majesty of the sun's blazing glory. Down below, among the banyan trees on the avenue winding along the shores of the sparkling bay, brightly clad Chinese people performed the balletic, trance-like *tai chi*, rhythmic exercises reputed to tone all the muscles and compose the soul. The entire scene embraced the lingering beauty of Macau.

The charm of the City of the Name of God and its venerable antiquity absorbed Hayley. Vasco da Gama had made a historic voyage to India at the end of the fifteenth century and early in the sixteenth century Portuguese explorers had turned east and north and set foot in South China in 1513. Macau was founded as a trading centre and a base for spreading Christianity to Japan and China. The history of Macau, its victories and calamities, is written in its archaic buildings and ruins. Hayley enjoyed showing these to his children.

He took them to the ruin of St Paulo, which was once described as 'the greatest monument to Christianity in all the Eastern lands'. Japanese artisans built it in 1602 but it was destroyed by typhoon and fire two centuries later. However a massive facade of four columned tiers remain with bronze statues and stone carvings, one of the Virgin Mary surrounded by only two kinds of flowers—peonies for China and chrysanthemums for Japan. Thereafter Elizabeth never forgot the national flowers of China and Japan.

There were many other places of interest on the Peninsula, known by the Chinese as 'the Water Lily Peninsula', some built centuries before the Portuguese first arrived such as the Temples of the Goddess A–Ma and the Goddess Kwun Yam. When the Dutch attempted to invade Macau in 1622 a cannon ball from the gigantic cannon of the Citadel of Sao Paulo Do Monte landed in the powder keg of a Dutch ship and blew the invading fleet out of the bay. This happened on 24 June, St John the Baptist's Day and St John was acclaimed patron saint of the city. The youngest Hayley Bell was John, so the huge cannon was much loved by the family.

One day nearing the end of Hayley's tour of duty in the Colony he gathered them for a final visit to the Temple of Kwun Yam, the Goddess of Mercy and Queen of Heaven. In the courtyard stood two fierce-looking stone lions each holding a round stone ball in its mouth. Suddenly grabbing a lion by its neck, Elizabeth turned the greasy stone ball three times to the left. 'It brings good luck!' she cried with a delicious little laugh. Chinese superstitions had become ingrained in her.

On an altar rested an image of Kwun Yam dressed in beautiful robes of a Chinese bride, serenely bestowing a blessing of heavenly mercy. On a wall was a figure of Marco Polo who had embraced Buddhism at the court of the Great Khan. To imply European origin the image was given a small curly beard, moustache, big nose and protuberant eyes. The sight was so comical that the children burst disgracefully into loud laughter. A Buddhist monk smiled and blessed the noisy children because they were so happy and because the people were distressed that the family was about to sail away from the beautiful City of the Name of God.

Macau was Elizabeth's first experience of living in a European colony. She learned that peoples of many races and creeds could live amicably together.

For four centuries the Portuguese have dominated the small peninsula at the mouth of the Pearl River, not far from Hong Kong, with a stringent yet benign rule. They brought trade and Christianity, European culture and art to the region. It provided a refuge for errant Japanese fleeing angry Emperors and for wretched Chinese escaping from the harsh rule of the Ming and Manchu dynasties and internal revolutions. Sun Yat-sen practised medicine in Macau for some years while sheltering from the Manchus. In World War II Macau became a haven for thousands of refugees fleeing the Japanese. The colony embraces a wealth of human kindness and relieves much suffering in China.

Father Manuel Teixeira of St Joseph's Seminary, a Jesuit Scholar and a world renowned historian, still remembers the English children. Many years later, in the 1970s, '80s and '90s, whenever Elizabeth stayed in Hong Kong she always visited Father Manuel, white-bearded, white-robed and sprightly, addressing her by her childhood name of Beattie. They met with Tony, her husband, in the Hotel Bela Vista opposite the Hayley Bells' old house, near the site of Bom Jesus and the stables. The Father, whose sandals know every cobblestone in Macau's six square miles, would lead them through the City of the Name of God and relate its history and that of the enormous Portuguese oceanic empire, the first global empire. Sadly, when Macau reverts to China in 1999, two years later than Hong Kong, the last remaining relic of that empire will crumble into history.

It was some years before Elizabeth understood why her father lived in China and why he was employed by the Chinese Government in the Imperial Maritime Customs. The 'Imperial' was a puzzlement to start with, because China had been a Republic since 1911, years before she was born.

Hayley said it retained a link with the Manchu regime which had opened five ports to foreign trade at the Treaty of Nanking in 1842 and permitted the appointment of foreign Consuls at each of those ports.

When more Chinese ports were opened Consuls were superseded by Commissioners, Deputy Commissioners and Assistants. Carefully selected foreign staff gave invaluable assistance to the Chinese Government, educating Chinese officials in diplomacy, shielding China from the ravages of foreign powers, forming an efficient National Post Office and supporting the economy and finance of the nation. Formed from almost every nation with men inspired with the ideal of loyalty to China and the furtherance of China's interests, the Chinese Imperial Maritime Customs became the first great international service in the world.

In 1911 when Hayley was serving in North China the total staff of the Service consisted of 1 345 foreigners and 5 885 Chinese. The Indoor Staff included one hundred and fifty-two British, thirty-eight German, thirty-two Japanese, thirty-one French, fifteen American, fourteen Russian, nine Italian, seven Portuguese, six Norwegian, six Danish, five Belgian, three Dutch, four Swedish, one Spanish, and one Korean. The cosmopolitan staff developed a remarkable international camaraderie which had no parallel elsewhere in the world. That was why Hayley enjoyed the Maritime Customs and being a servant of China's Government.

2

China

Chefoo, Hong Kong, Canton

Happy days in Macau ended abruptly when the family sailed away to England aboard a Japanese steamship, a voyage of eight long weeks. Elizabeth felt it would never end and that the dirty coal-burning ship would be her home forever.

England was weary, restrictive, cold and damp but at least she caught a bird!

Her sisters had chicken-pox and stayed in bed. Elizabeth was bored, had nothing to do, so she kept bothering them. With macabre interest in pox blisters, she demanded incessantly to see if any had popped. Mary became increasingly irritated.

'Go away, Beattie, get out, leave us alone, just go away!'

'What shall I do'?' she asked plaintively. '

'Oh, for heavens sake, anything—go catch a bird!'

Elizabeth ran into the garden and stood still on the lawn. A bird flew straight at her. She put up her hand and grabbed it. She had caught a bird! Excitedly she ran back into the bedroom.

'I did it, I've caught a bird. Look, a little sparrow!'

Mary sat up in rage and yelled, 'Oh hell, let it go!'

Freed, it flew round and round the bedroom hotly pursued by the entire family until it was chased out of a window. Then everyone made a fuss because according to Chinese superstitions it is unlucky to have a strange bird in a house. It means death may strike a member of the household.

Elizabeth, now seven, set out for China with her parents and John and Nanny Day. Separation from red-haired Mary, a vivacious girl, and from the quieter Winifred did not concern Elizabeth as much as she missed Dennis, a kind, sensitive boy.

Elizabeth enjoyed the long voyage; she loved the sea, its waves breaking away from the ship's bows with an angry roar, and she was not seasick, even in the notorious Bay of Biscay. At the ancient British colony of Gibraltar blue skies delighted her as did the warm Mediterranean in which she swam in the shadow of the imposing Rock, full of caves and Rock Apes. It was said that if the Apes abandoned the Rock the British Empire would fall.

The sky was even bluer at Port Said, a cerulean blue. Now she inhaled the inescapable musky fragrance of the desert, an effluvium made of camels' odours, dust and dirt. As soon as the big ship anchored it was surrounded by bumboatmen selling Turkish Delight, dates, poufs, tarbooshes, camel saddle-stools, beads, baskets. First on board was the gully-gully man, a charming dusky fellow who entranced Elizabeth with his ability to pull chickens from pockets, from under arms and out of ears, accompanied always with a fast patter of 'Gully-gully, gully-gully' as he performed astonishing sleight-of-hand tricks.

Forced away from her newly found Egyptian friend, Elizabeth was taken ashore to avoid the coal dust which swept through the ship in clouds. The dust was raised by almost naked wretches swarming up planks to throw coal into the ships' bunkers. On land, the Hayley Bells were pestered to buy trinkets and postcards by pedlars. A person in dirty red fez and gown pushed forward with the greeting, '*Sayeda, sayeda,*' and attempted to sell a lewd picture. Infuriated, her father shouted, 'Go away, you filthy beast! Out of my way! *Imshe, yellah*!'

To get away from the pedlars they walked along the pier at the entrance to the Suez Canal to the statue of Ferdinand de Lesseps, a French engineer who had opened the Canal in 1869. The Canal became a region of vital strategic importance to the British Empire and it brought major benefits to India and the Far East.

Before embarking the family went into Simon Arzt's gaudy store, well known to all travellers for the trash bought by newcomers to the East like spine-pads to prevent heatstroke, cholera-belts, shapeless topees and other useless paraphernalia.

Elizabeth and John clung open-eyed to the rails of the slowly moving ship, absorbing the sights of the Suez Canal. Swift lateen-rigged feluccas and other native craft sped past, along the Canal banks British troops waved at the passing liner, dishevelled *fellaheen* drove donkeys and herds of goats, and Bedouin led camel caravans across sandy wastes of the Sinai Desert. At Lake Timsah, where the ship anchored to permit north-bound vessels to pass, the sun set over the western desert in a blaze of glory like a picture painting, a typical Egyptian scene.

Old China hands like Elizabeth's parents well knew the term POSH—Port Out Starboard Home—and booked the family's cabin on the cool port side for the passage through the sweltering heat of the Red Sea. Even then the heat was excessive: in 1925 ships were not air-conditioned. Fans succeeded only in stirring up sultry air pumped through the ship's ventilation system or from scuttles stuck out of port holes.

The heat was worse when the ship lay at anchor coaling at Aden, a barren, torrid outpost of the British Empire, governed by the Raj in Delhi. It was cooler under way in the vastness of the Indian Ocean, where flying fishes race frothing waves and porpoises play Russian roulette with the ship's bows. At night for coolness they slept on deck but Elizabeth lay awake for hours gazing at phosphorescent waves breaking in the moonlit sea. Tropical nights revived memories of Macau and the fear of being alone amid a boundless sky but as she grew older she came to love the sky's extravagant beauty.

The vessel steamed out of the Arabian Sea, crept round India's Cape Comorin. Out of the horizon rose a green outline of hills, Ceylon, one of Britain's most treasured possessions. Then Colombo's magnificent harbour hailed the large liner as she glided to the docks.

The Hayley Bells rode into the city in gharries drawn by fine Arab ponies. Clean wide streets were framed by big white colonial government buildings and department stores like Whiteaway and Laidlaw where the children ate ice creams and the parents shopped. Soon they were in a large American taxi driving beside coconut beaches to the celebrated Galle Face Hotel to consume a hot-curry lunch of many dishes. They followed a routine adopted by most passengers from passing liners and they could not fail to notice the prosperity of the country. Within the Colony a sense of contentment flowed; the inhabitants flourished under the benevolent and stable rule of Britain; the white man moved with an accepted assurance among the peaceful people.

The ship hove-to briefly at Penang, passed through the Straits of Malacca and arrived in Singapore. Elizabeth was not to know the destiny that lay ahead for her in this equatorial island of Singapore, that this thriving Lion City would have a greater impact on her life than any other place. Here would be found adolescent happiness, boy friends, parties, picnics, dancing and the fascinating glamour and thrill of living in the oriental tropics. Here in womanhood she would be destined to meet her husbands and lover, give birth to a son, know the meaning of true love in a wartime romance fraught with impending disaster, suffer agonies of despair mixed with rapturous times of joy. Here she would endure the horrors of war, and finally be evacuated from a wounded Lion City in flames and about to be ransacked and raped by savage hordes of Japanese barbarians, losing her lover, friends and possessions.

Hong Kong was also to have a profound effect on Elizabeth's life, as a child and in marriage. However, the lovable No 1 Amah and the No 1 Boy and other servants from Macau joined her ship to travel to North China with them which, with the colourful Hong Kong scene, the Chinese and their sing-song voices and the prevailing smells, made Elizabeth feel she was home again.

Ten weeks after leaving England the family disembarked at Shanghai and stayed in their former house at 110 Bubbling Well Road in the International Settlement. Soon however they were sailing north again in a coastal steamer bound for Chefoo.

A squad of White Russians, survivors from the Russian Revolution, ex-Dukes and ex-Princes, armed with rifles and extremely long bayonets, protected the small ship. As a precaution against pirates, a steel grill confined deck passengers to the lower deck, more grilles secured the upper decks and cabins, barbed wire covered the ship's sides. Remembering thrilling tales of pirates that Mary, a gifted story teller, had told, Elizabeth hoped the pirates would attack. The handsome Russian aristocrats looked so strong and gallant that she was sure the wicked pirates would be defeated. Disappointingly, there were no attacks and the small globe trotters arrived safely at Chefoo.

Chefoo was different from Macau. Shantung people were pleasant, wore padded clothes and were taller than the Cantonese in the south. The intense cold turned Elizabeth's world into a winter wonderland of sparkling snow and frozen sea. Her home was the Commissioner's house where she was snug and warm beside a huge log fire, surrounded by her parents' lovely Chinese paintings, embroidered silk screens and blackwood furniture.

In spring a blaze of cherry blossom burst over the Shantung hills. Hayley returned from a Customs conference in Tientsin. The family met him at the railway station and rode home in palanquins carried by Customs men in wide brimmed hats and sailor suits who shouted the names and eminence of each passenger. The polite inhabitants bowed and clapped hands as the chairs passed regally by.

However, the people bowed and clapped with more enthusiasm at the glossy palanquins bearing august mandarins. Wearing ruby and coral buttons, peacocks' feathers on their hats and golden pheasants and white cranes on their long silk robes, they were a far more glamorous sight than the ugly foreign devils in dull clothes.

'I met P'u-Yi in Tientsin,' Hayley announced when they arrived in the house. 'He's about twelve years older than you, Beattie.'

Elizabeth was acutely interested as Hayley told them about P'u-Yi, actually His Imperial Majesty Hsuan-T'ung, the Son of Heaven, Lord of Ten Thousand Years, the Last Emperor of the three hundred-year-old Manchu dynasty. She asked, 'Why does P'u-Yi live in Tientsin?'

'A warlord known as the Christian General expelled P'u-Yi from his palace in the Forbidden City to a house in Peking and intended to execute him. P'u-Yi's tutor, Reginald Johnston, bravely snatched him from hostile guards and took him to the Legation Quarter where the Japanese protected him and his pretty little Empress. Then in 1925 the Japanese moved him to the International Concession in Tientsin. That's how he came to Tientsin. It must be sad for him, the last sovereign of the great Ch'ing dynasty, to have witnessed its fall.'

Hayley had also seen the demise of the Manchu Empire, hastened by greedy territorial demands of foreign countries and deplorable internal administration. Japan took Formosa from China in 1895; Russia occupied Port Arthur and lost it to Japan in the war of 1904-5; Germany seized Kiao-chou with its splendid harbour at Tsingtao; Britain obtained leases for territory at Weihaiwei and at Hong Kong, and France at Kuangshouwan. The Boxer Rising, the flight of the Imperial family from Peking, the desecration of Imperial treasures and palaces, and finally revolutions, warlords and anarchy throughout China, combined to bring about the fall of the Manchu Empire.

Elizabeth had heard many tales of the Imperial family and was sorry for the Boy Emperor. With their minds full of boy emperors, pretty empresses, wicked empress-dowagers and terrifying warlords, Elizabeth and John were put to bed. A happy Nanny Day told them, 'We're going to Hong Kong, a nice safe British place.'

A small Blue Funnel Line ship ploughed its way through the Yellow Sea and followed the heavily indented coast of China. Tsingtao, famed for its beer, stood beside an enormous harbour; a vast sea of brown water stretched eastward from the mouths of the mighty Yangtze Kiang, the fifth longest river in the world; further south the shorter Kiuling Kiang filled muddy bays at the stately island port of Amoy. Here Elizabeth's mother was born and raised by her Scottish-American missionary parents and here she first met Hayley, a young Customs cadet learning Fukienese.

The Blue Funnel ship *Jason* steamed her way through a myriad of vessels cluttering Hong Kong harbour: coal-powered liners and cargo ships from all over the world, busy ferry boats, chugging *walla-wallas*, sailing junks. In 1926 Hong Kong was the third port in the Empire. On the Kowloon side of the harbour, below the august Kowloon Hills stretched a substantial town. Its waterfront of docks and godowns was dominated by the towered terminal of the Kowloon-Canton railway and the many-storeyed Peninsula Hotel. Victoria on the island side was even more substantial with a waterfront of stately buildings such as the new Supreme Court and the Hong Kong Club. Above Victoria rose the green mountains of the Peak, dotted with white mansions.

Perched on a shoulder of the mountain at Magazine Gap stood the residence of the Chinese Imperial Maritime Customs, a huge red brickhouse with white angle stones, the only piece of land on Hong Kong island owned by China. Incongruously the Commissioners were Europeans, not Chinese. Elizabeth and John slept on the top floor of an octagonal tower attached to the house. The maroon tower resembled a castle in a fairy tale and John immediately named it 'The Red Castle', a name that remained forever.

There was no permanency in the children's young lives. Frequent moves were unsettling. Elizabeth never experienced the security of a family house. The only place her father owned was at Mokanshan in the Chekiang Mountains south-west of Shanghai, an ancient cottage called 'Chin Chia Shan' nestling on a mountain peak in a serene and beautiful environment. It was later destroyed during the Japanese occupation. Elizabeth came to live happily in many countries but she yearned for an enduring base, a house and tranquil surroundings. When she obtained a house of her own, however, she wanted to move on. Perhaps she was always seeking the cottage at Mokanshan.

Elizabeth and John were sent daily to the Peak School, a tiny grey house near Mount Kellett, about 2 000 feet above sea level, climbing to it by the winding mountain road lined with rhododendron and sweet-smelling jasmine, a delightful area with glorious views to the twisting shore and pretty bays below. The road was not navigable by motor cars and the only danger was rickshaws, bicycles and sedan chairs running fast downhill. Chinese and Eurasian children did not attend the Peak School. It was unusual for Chinese or coloured people to live higher up the mountain than May Road, about halfway, so European children seldom met Chinese children.

Elizabeth's parents spoke Chinese fluently, Hayley in many dialects, but they did not make their children learn the language. Hayley had travelled extensively throughout China, knew the people well and was at home with them, philosophising with them at wayside inns or wherever; Agnes as a young nurse in a Mission hospital had tended and cared for the Chinese as had her missionary parents. Yet despite their love of the Chinese they raised their children in the British colonial style, segregated from the native people.

Isolated from the Chinese, they played with Peak School friends, the children of *taipans* and colonial servants. They were carried in sedan chairs manned by stalwart Customs men to the nearest Peak Tram Station at Barker Road. If they ascended to the Peak Terminal with their mother and friends they would be treated to hot buttered crumpets in the luxurious Peak Hotel or they might walk with Nanny Day along tree-shaded roads named Harlech and Lugard encircling the Peak, a tranquil refuge from the palpitating city below.

Every Sunday the family rode downhill in the tram to St John's Cathedral. Elizabeth and John were well disciplined children and accepted the Sunday routines eagerly. In the Cathedral Close they met young friends and watched with amusement the spectacle of British troops being marched from Murray Barracks to the Cathedral with loud words of command: much stamping and a thunderous crash of hob-nailed boots on the paved aisle as the Tommies moved into their pews. The Hayley Bells sat serenely in the Commissioner of Customs' personal pew. Elizabeth loved the gracefully conducted service, the orderly fraternity and the hymns from the Ancient and Modern hymnbook sung enchantingly by a mixed European and Chinese choir.

After Cathedral Matins the family usually embarked in a Customs armed merchant cruiser and sailed away for picnics in one of the bays around the Colony. The children played on the beaches at Shek O, where there was a European Club, or at Repulse Bay, lunching in the Bay's voluptuous hotel. Chinese people did not bathe on the beaches in those days, wisely avoiding skin cancer and foreign barbarians, and did not frequent the lush hotels. It was an extravagant way of life but even as a child Elizabeth also felt there was something false with this segregated existence.

In cool winter months when sunshine and blue skies replaced the usual misty haze over the Colony the family took a train from Kowloon to Fanling on the Kowloon Peninsula, the land called the New Territories. It had been leased by the Manchu Empire to the British for a period of ninety-nine years beginning in 1898. By 1926 it had become the playground of the Colony and nobody bothered to think what would happen to the land when the lease expired in 1997.

Heedlessly Hayley rode with the Fanling Hunt, chasing foxhounds across the northern pastures, sometimes riding imprudently over the shallow eastern stretches of the Sham Chun River deep into China. An infringement of the frontier did not matter in those days. Afterwards the huntsmen assembled in the Hunters Arms, an ancient Chinese house in a walled garden, entered through a moon shaped door. Converted to resemble an English tavern, it preserved a nostalgic English atmosphere with jugs of frothing warm beer and enormous beef steaks.

The Arms was frequented by officers of the 1st Battalion The Queen's Royal Regiment, then stationed in San Wai camp close by. Into a hill above the camp they had carved the Regimental badge, the badge of the 2nd of Foot, formed in 1661 and the senior English Regiment of the Line, a Paschal Lamb gazing benignly at the soldiery.

Hayley had served in the Queen's in the Great War, joining the 10th Battalion in 1915 in France, where he was severely wounded at Flers near Passchendaele. Later he commanded the same battalion in Italy when his division was rushed to stem an Austrian attack after the disastrous defeat of the Italians at Caporetto. Returning to France, he was commanding the 10th Battalion when Ludendorff launched a massive offensive on the Somme between Arras and St Quentin on 21 March 1918 during which he was seriously wounded. He was twice mentioned in despatches and received the DSO.

Civil war spread over China; law and order dissolved. Sporadic attacks against treaty ports, international concessions and leased territories became increasingly violent and dangerous. France, America and Japan strengthened their military garrisons to protect their subjects and commerce. Britain reinforced the Royal Navy's China Station and hastily mobilised and dispatched the 1st Guards Brigade and the 13th Infantry Brigade to China. It was a powerful force of men and weapons, arguably the last time that Britain resorted to gun-boat tactics in China.

Among the infantry despatched in this so-called 'Shanghai Defence Force' was the 1st Battalion The Middlesex Regiment, the 'Die-Hards', which disembarked at Hong Kong in March 1927 and camped in tents on Fanling Golf Course. This splendid battalion of cheerful Londoners returned to Hong Kong ten years later and remained there to face the savage onslaught of a Japanese invasion in December 1941. Elizabeth was not to know the destiny that lay ahead for her with this Regiment which, as with Singapore, would affect the course of her life.

Just as civil war entangled life in China, problems arose in Mary's school in Dorset. Agnes hurried back to England to sort things out, taking yet again the long sea voyage via the Suez Canal. Elizabeth and John were left with their father and nanny. The children were delighted; life was much more exciting with the ever impetuous Hayley on his own—they never knew what to expect next. Nanny was also happy to have the children in her charge.

Thousands of terrified and bewildered people attempted to flee China, ravaged by civil war. They fled not from Communist or Nationalist ideology but from hordes of murderous bandits and heavily armed rampageous soldiers. They sought refuge in foreign settlements such as French Kuangchou-wan, Portuguese Macau and British Hong Kong. Some sailed down the great Pearl River aboard overcrowded vessels, ferry-boats, junks, *walla-wallas*, sampans; others struggled overland, shuffling along in an endless rhythmic step, carrying pathetic possessions in baskets hung from bamboo poles across their backs. Such was the plight of the poor and the peasantry, a never-ending flight from one or another predatory force. This time, however, their dilemma was worse because a boycott placed on foreign settlements prevented entry into them.

Foreigners on the island settlement of Shameen were besieged and denied entry into Canton, and Chinese Customs men were intimidated. The Customs Commissioner, Edwards, received a bullet wound. Hayley was called to take charge.

Impulsively, almost as if the old warrior was charging 'once more into the breach', Hayley set forth immediately for Canton taking with him Elizabeth, John, Nanny and the house servants. No doubt he thought a baptism of fire would be excellent training for his children and teach them to face danger with fortitude—after all, John wished to enter the Royal Navy and Elizabeth faced perils fearlessly and enjoyed them.

Sailing up the yellow waters of the Pearl River with a gunboat as escort, the convoy forced its way under fire from the Boca Tigre forts and tied up on the river side of Shameen Island, a flat oblong sandbank with straight paved roads and large European houses, separated from the seething mass of people and dwellings of Canton city by a creek but joined by a bridge at the southern end.

Elizabeth was surprised to find such graceful houses on the island, each with a well kept garden full of flowers. Her garden contained a sweet little white rabbit, much to her delight. It was not just another move to another place and house; this was much more exciting. When she, John and Nanny strolled along the Bund they were rudely jeered and stoned by a ferocious mob from the Canton side. They were not perturbed, assured in their rightful presence, but retired to the Customs House when shots were fired at them. Elizabeth and John had endured the baptism of fire!

Hayley explained to his battle-tested children that the island was completely besieged and that violent Nationalist rabbles could easily break into the settlement and attack them. If this happened, everyone—French, Dutch, Americans, Italians, Portuguese, Germans—were to assemble in the British Consulate, a fortified house and compound.

'It could be pretty nasty but we'll keep them off the island,' he said vigorously.

Daily Hayley policed the Bund, often under a hail of stones and bullets. With imperturbable courage he kept the Customs organisation together, demanding free access to food and freedom of movement for his officers.

When the Nationalists announced that they intended to take the settlement, Hayley was more active than ever, driving the riotous mob off the Bund and clearing the bridge. From the upstairs windows of the Consulate, Elizabeth and John anxiously watched their father—a tall slim figure, handsome in uniform, a 1914-18 steel helmet, khaki jacket emblazoned with medal ribbons, fawn breeches and riding boots, a 4.5 pistol in a holster—with pride and admiration, yet with terror and fear for him, at this moment standing courageously alone to face the ugly ferocious fray, a yelling, screaming mass of Chinese throwing missiles at him, armed with guns, swords and long poles.

Suddenly he was viciously attacked, brutally beaten with bamboo poles, his helmet knocked off, his head smashed by rifle butts, cut by swords, thrown defenceless to the ground, kicked and left there like a dead animal. Elizabeth never forgot the horror of it. Chinese Customs officers rushed to his aid, picked up the unconscious, frail, limp body and carried the bleeding man to the Consulate. For days he lay unconscious and temporarily blind, suffering greatly from severe head wounds.

Shameen was not seized by the Nationalists. Hayley's stubborn resistance and the example he set to other defenders deterred the mob.

The old warrior recovered, as he had from former wounds and hardship—a rugged campaign in 1905 with the Natal Carabineers in suppression of a Zulu insurrection, terrible battles and bloodshed in the Great War, arduous treks in primitive conditions in China.

But the fly-ridden island of Shameen did not spare Hayley easily. It knocked him flat with a bout of cholera contacted from a widespread epidemic in Canton. The children were untouched, mainly due to the care that Nanny Day took over domestic hygiene, insisting that all drinking water was boiled and that all vegetables, pots and pans were washed in potassium permanganate. Even then it was impossible to keep away the flies, which came in thousands from the filthy city of Canton.

The White Swan, an international hotel, now stands on the site of the Consulate. The episode of the siege of Shameen and Hayley's heroic stand on the Bund has faded away, yet the noble qualities of character displayed are as relevant as ever. However, the incident showed that the fire of imperialism was dying, that aggressive characters like Captain Elliot who raised the Union Jack on Hong Kong Island in 1841, only eighty-six years previously, did not exist. Moreover, before the Great War a siege of Europeans on a sandbank in the Pearl River would have been relieved immediately by a Royal Navy gunboat. And now that the Republic of China did not inhibit its xenophobia the future of the leased territories and the perpetuity of Hong Kong began to quiver.

Back in Hong Kong, safe in the Red Castle, Elizabeth and John related their extraordinary experiences to their sceptical yet envious small comrades, especially to the Clementi children. Hayley had developed a lasting friendship with Sir Cecil Clementi, the Governor of the Colony. Both men were sinologists with a deep love of China and both were speakers of Mandarin and Cantonese. Hayley Bell's wide knowledge of China was of value to Clementi and they held similar opinions on the future of the Colony and Empire: that European dominance in China was declining but that the British would never relinquish Hong Kong.

In 1929 Hayley was given leave and the family embarked for England, this time to place Elizabeth and John in boarding schools, a future utterly dreaded by Elizabeth.

3

England
Educating Tony

Huge trees with dripping leaves lined the drive to the Headmaster's house. The trees were horse-chestnuts. I kicked a conker on the ground trying to scratch my brand new shiny boots, bought on the way to England in Marseille, as was my French overcoat, adorned with a grey fur collar, opening down the middle with buttons on the wrong side. I clutched a small Indian bag.

A forbidding oak door faced me. I knocked and a maidservant, in a starched white apron and with a linen tiara on her head, answered.

'I am wanting headmaster Sahib,' I announced in a squeaky penetrating voice. 'I am Tony Hewitt.'

She stared at me in astonishment, as if I was something out of another planet.

'Pardon?'

The Headmaster came. 'You should have gone to the tradesmen's entrance, boy. This is my front door.'

Abashed by his haughty manner, I forgot I was in a white man's country and replied, '*Acchha* Sahib!'

He gave me a look of disgust and handed me quickly to Matron, an impersonal creature, who led me below and showed me my bed and locker. At Ahmednagar, Drummer Boys in army barracks slept in far better rooms than this cold dungeon.

Then I met the boys, who fell about in raucous laughter at my French overcoat with girl's buttons, pulled the fur collar, called me 'Mummy's darling', and roared at my French boots of patent leather and pointed toes.

Standing forlornly amid the little brutes I prayed for rescue. Suddenly, a boy beyond the rabble yelled out: 'Hewitt, Mummy wants you!'

I turned instinctively towards the voice. A horrible roar of jeers, mockery and laughter hit me. It was cruel; my mother was in India six thousand miles away and I was missing her desperately.

I was ten and strong for my age from living in the Indian sun, riding horses and playing games; few boys dared to bully me. I had little in common with those who had only lived in England but I made friends quickly with boys from Britannic domains, outcast children like me with parents scattered throughout the Empire.

So I survived although I was always cold and grew revolting chilblains on fingers and toes and got pneumonia. I wore a starched Eton collar daily, a hateful thing which frayed my neck, and on Sundays an Eton suit.

Many hours were spent on the School's nine hole golf course, with an intriguing ninth, which I often holed in one by taking a niblick and driving the ball high up into the branches of an old cedar tree overhanging the hole, from which the ball would drop straight down and roll into it. And I liked all the games. I had played cricket in India and loved rugger and was soon in the first fifteen.

Called Cherry Orchard, the school occupied a dilapidated ancient mansion which had been sold to meet excessive death duties. The state of the mansion was symbolical of Britain as she suffered from the effects of war, her past strength scattered on Flanders' fields. Poverty and despair beset the people mourning lost heroes, remembered constantly by pathetic wounded soldiers roaming the streets in shapeless blue hospital uniforms. Unemployment was rampant, coalminers enforced long strikes and a painful General Strike added to the decline and despondency.

Although aware of the national depression and more intimately their parent's uncertain wealth, the young pupils were mostly concerned with life at school and their own behaviour. All under fourteen, their manners, politeness and courtesy to elders were exemplary, due mainly to impeccable breeding and school customs. Small boys would rush to open doors for teachers and guests, stand up when they entered rooms, address them respectfully, and at the dining table eat faultlessly. They were obedient but not subservient and expressed their views fearlessly without cheek or rudeness. Fond parents hoped their sons would retain these angelic qualities but were often disillusioned.

With my parents and sisters away in India, I grew apart from the family. An uncle, a clergyman, was my guardian. Unlike my father, he had not even served in the Great War and had none of my father's soldierly qualities I so admired. My aunt disliked the intrusion of another child in her household, so I spent school holidays staying with school friends. I had no home, no family life, no affection or love.

During my schooldays, my eldest sister Margaret married an English business man in Bombay. My parents were in Ahmednagar, where my father was Chaplain to the 2nd Battalion The Middlesex Regiment. My second sister Kathleen married an officer in that Regiment and went to live with him in Madras and Monica, the youngest, married an English engineer in Baroda. The family was now spread over India and I was really on my own. I became introverted, kept my problems to myself; I stood alone.

The Headmaster persuaded my father that I might become an able doctor of medicine and should be sent to Epsom College, a school mainly for doctors' sons, to turn them into doctors. I passed the Common Entrance Examination and at the start of the summer term I travelled alone to the School, was placed in Wilson House and was met by the senior house prefect.

'You will fag for Stewart. He's a School Prefect, 1st XV, 1st XI, Colours for swimming. Look after him well.'

I liked him. He gave me House colours for cricket in my first term, a feat for a new boy. He was tall, extremely handsome, the idol of the House. He looked like the film star which he became, changing his name to Stewart Grainger, and he grew famous.

I always wanted to be a soldier—years ago in India the *Dewan* had said, 'One day you will be officer sahib.' I did not wish to be a doctor even in the Indian Medical Service or the Royal Army Medical Services so after I matriculated I gave up science and spent two delightful years in the Literary Sixth mainly reading history and English until I was old enough to take the Army Entrance Examination for the Royal Military College, Sandhurst.

With Robert Nesham, who was also at Epsom, I passed into Sandhurst 30th on the list and became a Gentleman Cadet, gentlemen because our parents paid the fees, not the State, rather like Gentlemen Cricketers, who received no payment for playing for a County or England.

The Sandhurst entry for 1933 was restricted to 147 men by an impecunious government suffering from the Great Depression, an unwise decision when there was ample warning that war with Hitler's Germany was inevitable when trained officers would be needed urgently.

They entered Sandhurst as strong young men, carefree and adventurous, the flower of the nation, sons of families that had produced soldiers for generations. Soon they faced the realities of war. As troop or platoon commanders, they suffered heavy casualties. They learnt about death, progressed from youth to middle age in one year, sometimes in several minutes. Above all, they learnt the lessons of courage and fear, of suffering and comradeship. They fought in every theatre of war; some were captured during the withdrawal to Dunkirk, in Desert battles, at Hong Kong and

Singapore. A third were killed, maimed or incapacitated from ill-treatment in prisoner-of-war camps, especially those of the Japanese. Some of the survivors of the 1933 entry eventually gained great distinction—Michael Carver became a Field Marshal and a Lord—many were highly decorated and others became renowned artists or authors like John Dudley and John Masters.

The colossal pillars of the Main Entrance and the Waterloo cannon standing proudly on each side, welcomed me. Eagerly I reported to No 5 Company, 'Lovely five', an expression of praise used by Gentlemen Cadets to urge on the Company. Months later, on the fateful day my jaw was smashed in two places whilst playing hockey for the Company in a hard fought struggle against No 4 Company, a bitter rival, I learned what the cry of 'Lovely five', sung continuously in a weary drawl, really meant, as it urged me to stay on the field and help win the match.

That was much later. When I arrived I was met by an Irish Guards sergeant, a green band round his cap and with a red sash, and I was suddenly enveloped in a wildwind, a whirlpool, a roaring tornado of being rushed and ordered about without pause all day and half the night for the next nine weeks.

'There's never a free moment,' complained Robert Nesham. 'Never enough time to change clothes. It's fatigues, drill uniform, riding breeches, PT kit, fatigues again, uniform again, sports kit, patrols, gym kit—all day long! When are we supposed to eat and sleep?'

It was so. Shaving parade at dawn preceded drill on the sacred gravel of the Square, stamping boots, smacking rifles. Then in any sequence, equitation, jumping endless fences; physical training, to which we rode on bicycles dressed in red and white striped pill-box hats, scarves, blazers, white flannels—an archaic turn out; bayonet fighting and dreadful assault courses, tearing fatigues to pieces; drill again; a gracious hour in academic tutorials; then rugger, hockey or cross-country running.

In the few precious minutes left before dinner, you bathed, cleaned your rifle and bayonet, polished leather and boots, changed into blue patrol uniform. After dinner you laid your kit on the bed for inspection. Finally, throwing off patrols, you pulled on PT clothes, jumped on a bicycle and rode to the gymnasium for boxing. Sleep at last, but only for a few minutes before the bugles called reveille, followed almost at once with the 'On Parade', meaning fall-in for shaving parade.

We were the junior division, just plain Gentlemen Cadets. Some of the intermediates were corporals, a few of the seniors under-officers and sergeants. We came from every level of society; we had an Earl, a Marquis,

Viscounts, Baronets, Lords, Siamese Princes, sons of Indian Princes and just ordinary men, sons of mostly impoverished fathers for whom the fees of £300 were a shattering blow, particularly for an underpaid profession of arms which chanced death at any time.

Despite different backgrounds, we evolved into an egalitarian group, revolved by a bellowing cyclone, clinging together in a strong bond of friendship, defending ourselves against the common enemy—the warrant and non-commissioned officers of the staff, mainly from the Brigade of Guards. Our Company Sergeant Major was Giddings, Grenadier Guards. We feared his bulky stature, the red band round his cap, the huge Grenadier badge, his raw face which he was supposed to scrub with a brush to make him look fiercer; we were shouted at with abuse and vile oaths, but addressed first as Mr and finally as Sir.

'Mr Hewitt, you're like a bleeding actor with long hair, Sir!'

And to the Earl of Macduff, seventh heir to the throne, son of Prince Arthur of Connaught, grandson of the Duke of Connaught, who was about to inspect us: 'Mr Lord Macduff, you're as jerky as a flaming monkey on a barrel organ, Sir!'

Sometimes we hit back. The Irish Guards Sergeant shouted, 'Squad NUMBER!' Like the rattle of a machine gun, we yelled in turn, '1,2,3,4,5,6,7,8,9,10, JACK, QUEEN, KING, ACE!' . . . silence. In deadly silence, we stood perfectly still, not daring to move an eyelid. Suddenly there came the most frightful roar.

'Numbers one to ten, STAND FAST—Court Cards to the Guard Room, DOUBLE MARCH!'

The Siamese Princes were in deep trouble; they could not perform drill movements correctly, made constant mistakes. In desperation Giddings decided to march the squad off the square: 'Squad—SLOPE ARMS—Move to the right in fours—RIGHT TURN—QUICK MARCH—All except the two Chinese gentlemen in the rear rank, who can do what they bloody well please!'

After nine weeks the junior division was inspected by officers from the Brigade of Guards, splendidly turned out in dark blue frock coats, gold brimmed hats and swords in silver-plated scabbards, and we were deemed fit to attend parades with the other two divisions. Much more important, we were now given more time to ourselves, were free to go out of the RMC when off duty, even granted weekend leave passes.

The Adjutant, Captain Gwatkin, Coldstream Guards, mounted on a superb animal who seemed to move instinctively around the Square for his lordly, gold-spurred master, commanded the Saturday morning parade. He inspected us, we marched past him in slow and quick time, advanced in review order towards him and did it all again if it was not perfectly performed. Names were taken for the slightest mistake; a serious crime, like dropping a rifle, resulted in the victim being marched up the Main Entrance steps at the double and thrown into a dungeon in the Guard Room. The parade was sheer pantomime. The Adjutant would shout, 'Idle man front rank 5 Company!' A staff sergeant would reply, 'Got him, Sir!', or sometimes the cadet's name. One happy day the Irish Guards sergeant yelled, 'Got him, Mr Fowke, Sir!' Gerry Fowke normally stood next to me, but on this Saturday he was on sick leave, so on Monday morning we watched Company Orders with glee and the sad sight of the Irish sergeant being marched hurriedly to the Guard Room.

Life was much easier for us now. I had time to read economic history as an additional subject and for extra riding classes, taking the horses across country, jumping new fences. We went to the 'flics', to cafes and pubs in Camberley or Aldershot, took trains or buses to London, absorbed goggle-eyed variety shows at the Windmill Theatre, ate huge spaghetti dinners in Soho for only ninepence. As I watched traffic roaring round Piccadilly Circus and crowds thronging pavements, I wondered how Eros could stand the deafening noise and the ugly people. Would he ever launch his golden quivers and fly away on his golden wings to mother Aphrodite? Perhaps the oncoming war with Hitler for which we cadets were being trained might release him from his stone pedestal?

I was happy at Sandhurst and grateful to my father for paying the fees. In the 1930s, unlike today, cadets' parents paid for everything, including the uniform. I liked the army and its way of life. The cry of 'Lovely five' gave the Company a compelling atmosphere. I made many life-long friends— Nesham (Garhwal Rifles), Adams (8th Punjab), Fowke (Welsh Guards), Denaro (Leicesters) and others. 133 of us passed out of the RMC; Noel Gudgeon, a close friend, was 7th and I was 20th on the list.

I could not enter the Indian Army because my father believed Indian independence would prevent a full career in that army. I was commissioned on 31 January 1935 into The Middlesex Regiment, Duke of Cambridge's Own. My father paid for my officers' uniform purchased at an expensive military tailor. I reported with Noel Gudgeon to the Depot at Inglis Barracks, Mill Hill, North West London.

Noel was posted to the 2nd Battalion in Colchester, Essex, but I wished to return to the East, to escape the cold of old England and to feel the warmth of a strong sun again. I was posted to the 1st Battalion in Egypt.

4

England
Educating Elizabeth

Elizabeth lived in a large brick house called St George's. She had never been so cold or miserable. Damp air seeped through doors and windows, often in the form of mist or fog. An unbelievable coldness crept into her navy blue skirt, white flannel shirt, black stockings and shoes, quite inadequate protection against these frigid conditions, unlike the thick padded jackets she wore in Chefoo, where she was warm even in the freezing dry cold that swept southwards from Manchuria.

The thought of China renewed the bitter memory of parting from her devoted Amah, whom she had known all her life—there was no similar commiserating person here to whom she could confide her secrets and troubles. Worse still, Nanny Day had left to work for another family. Elizabeth missed her desperately; Nanny had cared for her ever since she was born and she had grown closer to Nanny than to her mother. She was bewildered by these sudden changes, homesick for China and embittered that she had been thrown so cruelly into this strange school.

Mary and Winifred were also at this school, Malvern Girls' College. They were much older than Elizabeth, in different school houses and, with typical adolescent selfishness, were too engrossed in themselves to help her. Before long the two girls left the school to travel with their mother to China and join their father in Tientsin. Elizabeth was alone; love and affection seemed to fade out of her young life.

John joined Dennis at a preparatory school in Surrey, where he was looked after by Dennis. Every term Elizabeth counted the days to school holidays, longing to be with Dennis and John. She was very close to John; she had shared his life in Macau, Chefoo, Hong Kong and Canton, shared his devotion to their father, taken part in his childish games. She was happy with John, loved his golden hair and laughing eyes and exciting spirit—

trying always for the great adventure.

Elizabeth and her brothers spent their holidays at a so-called Holiday Home, actually a large estate in Essex run by impoverished gentry. With eighteen boys and girls, outcast children of the British Empire whose parents were in India or China, they lived in a huge dilapidated mansion. Conditions were appallingly rugged, lacking the stability, comfort and affection of family life. The Home was virtually another school, except for the lack of supervision, which allowed the children to run wild, riding and shooting over the estate. The Imperial orphans were all in the same boat and made the best of their existence, helping each other.

In September 1933 John, aged thirteen, entered the Royal Naval College, Dartmouth with thirty-three new cadets and was placed in the first term in Gun Room 'Greynville'. There were eleven terms and 372 cadets at the RNC.

John settled eagerly into naval routine and wrote in detail a description of the start of a day:

> At 7.30 the stewards come in and wait until 7.35 when the chief steward shouts "Turn Out!" and we get out, take off our pyjamas, put a towel round ourselves, get into bath slippers and run to the bathroom where we jump into a cold plunge bath. Then we wash, do our teeth, return to the cabin and dress in vest, pants, socks, boots, flannel shirt, black tie, white flannel trousers, blue belt, uniform reefer, cap and lanyard. This is called working rig.

Browning wrote, 'O to be in England now that April's there.' For Elizabeth it seemed that there was something intrinsically frail and ominous about April, that its ever-changing weather pattern resembled an excessively beautiful woman, spoilt and fickle, capable of extreme evil. This April began hurtfully with the departure of Hayley to China; Easter was early, the holiday with John was short and she returned to school in the middle of the month.

Then suddenly it happened; her prediction that something terrible might occur in April was true—John was seriously ill and had been admitted to the Royal Naval Hospital in Plymouth. The illness which started with measles had caused a mastoid in the left ear. John was so close to Elizabeth, her happy and brave little companion, her true and only real friend, that she could not bear him to suffer.

'Please help, Jesus,' she prayed, biting her finger nails in anguish. 'Please, Jesus, make John better, please look after him.'

Elizabeth went to the hospital with her mother, sisters and brother. John was dangerously ill. He had now developed meningitis and pneumonia and the surgeons could not save him; there were no drugs such as penicillin in those days.

Elizabeth never forgot that pathetic small bandaged head on the white pillow and that awful feeling of utter helplessness and aloneness. She knew she could never again feel so unhappy. No one understood her now that John had gone. No one understood her deep love for John. Everyone was too immersed in their own misery to care or give a thought for Elizabeth.

After John's death, Elizabeth entered the Francis Holland School near Sloane Square in London. Here she met many interesting girls from a broader scope of society than Malvern, such as Vivian Mosely, daughter of Sir Oswald Mosely, leader of the British Fascists, and Peggy Jean Epstein, daughter of the sculptor. These new influences helped to relieve her grief over John.

Hayley had now retired from the Chinese Imperial Maritime Customs. 'I've got a new job!' he announced triumphantly. 'It's Singapore, I'm to be the Defence Security Officer, Malaya Command. It's terrific, just what I wanted. You'll be coming out to join me!'

It was the most marvellous news for Elizabeth. After all those long years in England, at last she would return to the East and the warmth; and she adored Singapore, remembering the many times she had passed through the Colony, and the lunch in Government House Domain on the way to Chefoo. It was green and lovely, and oh, so warm.

Her mother said, 'It'll be just like living in a hot greenhouse in Kew Gardens, humid and sticky-hot. They call it Sweatypore.' That did not deter Elizabeth; she yearned to return to the East and felt she would capture some of the happiness of her childhood there. She was forever seeking happiness— at heart she was a romantic.

Hayley went ahead to find a dwelling. Agnes, Winifred and Elizabeth travelled overland to Genoa and embarked in the Lloyd Trestino liner *Conte Verde*. Hundreds of young Italian soldiers lined the ship's rails and waved and shouted to a huge crowd on the wharf. Two brass bands played from opposite ends of the docks. Corpulent Italian officers in dazzling flamboyant uniforms stood apart from groups of obviously grief-stricken relatives and parties of priests and nuns. As the ship sailed the brass bands played conflicting marches or anthems, drowning each other and the cries of spectators. The military on the dock gave Fascist salutes, right arms stretched skywards like an ancient Rome salutation; but a palpable lack of enthusiasm showed that many were aware of the reality of war, that some of the conscript soldiers would not return, others would be maimed or lose their youthful zest for life.

The lower decks of *Conte Verde* were crammed with troops, dejected men in ill-fitting uniforms; but at night they filled the ship with song, captivating love-ballads, which became increasingly melancholy as the vessel drew further away from Italy. They were sailing to fight primitive

Abyssinians, a tragic war of white men in black shirts against black men in white shirts. The young Fascist soldiers disembarked unwillingly under the relentless heat of the Red Sea at Massawa and marched away under a burning Eritrean sun.

A fragrant exquisite scent, peculiar to Malaya, a redolent aromatic smell of damp rain forests, pervaded the graceful white liner as it glided through the calm Straits of Malacca. Verdant islands with luxuriant tropical vegetation that grew down to the water's edge dotted the sea passage and added to the sweet-smelling jungle scent. The scent, a balmy breeze, native craft and junks with huge coloured sails signalled Elizabeth's return to the East.

She hung expectantly over the ship's rails as it moved slowly into Singapore's Keppel Harbour with busy tugs pushing it alongside the wharf. There waving frantically stood not only her handsome father but surprisingly No 1 and No 2 Boys, the same that she had left in Hong Kong eight years ago.

A girl of eighteen, tall fresh-looking, fun-loving and attractive, Elizabeth's charm had won the friendship of the Italians on board, jovial happy people who waved goodbye as she rushed down the gangway to her father and the two Boys and shouted, *'Sei una bella raga—a ciá le gamhe lunghe veramente bellissima!'*

5

Orient

Sphinx and Lion

Giant ridges of sand formed up, then faded away in bewildering sequence, a persistent mirage in a golden landscape beneath a cerulean sky. Two paces forwards preceded one backwards in agonising repetition. Sandy particles crept into boots, clothing, eyes, hair, rifles, food—the sands of the Sinai Desert spread everywhere into everything.

Across the arid space, two camels raced towards me, two troopers from the Reconnaissance Platoon, with a brief message: 'Beware Bedouin raiders.' The message chilled my blood; Bedouin Arabs were reputed to mutilate bodies vilely before killing.

From a distant sandy hill came a flash, a dull boom, the rattle of a machine gun. Instinctively my empiric warriors threw themselves under cover while the vicious enemy continued to fire long bursts. It was my first ordeal under fire, a vital test. My platoon was leading the advanced guard to the Battalion, marching doggedly towards an invisible oasis, the only water within reach. Immediate action was essential. What should I do?

The platoon sergeant advised, 'Sir! When I start firing the Lewis gun, double off to those hills on the right with two sections and attack from there with a section, leaving the other to give you covering fire.'

The attack was a masterly success, the ferocious enemy was routed—not Bedouin, but Jocks from the Royal Scots Fusiliers—and the umpire congratulated me. I congratulated the sergeant, a 1914-18 War veteran, who smiled at me and said, 'You're our officer, we look after our officer.'

These soldiers were Londoners, some from a background of poverty and hunger in London's East End, others from families whose sons had served the army for generations; the fathers of many were killed in the Great War. They were long service soldiers, signing on for seven years with the Colours and five on the Reserve, often re-engaging for further terms; they joined to escape appalling penury and unemployment in the 1930s, or to continue family traditions, or for the adventure, enticed by 'Join the Army and see the World' recruiting posters.

For two years in Egypt and Singapore I commanded No 9 Platoon, C Company, 1st Battalion The Middlesex Regiment, Duke of Cambridge's Own. Sergeant Kruck, champion boxer Lance Sergeant Roseblade, the Corporals and Privates such as Arthur Ellis and others who had known my Padre father in India, all looked after me. They nicknamed me 'The Boy' (not to my face, of course), because I looked so young; they protected me from senior officers; they deemed it their duty to teach me about Regimental soldiering. They were proud of their cap badge, which was polished to an indecipherable smooth surface; its laurel wreath commemorates those who fell fighting Napoleon's armies at Albuhera on 16 May 1811, where the sobriquet 'Die-Hards' was earned; the fleur-de-lis and *Ich Dien* are for Princes of Wales, Colonels-in-Chief; and the Coronet and Cypher are for the Duke of Cambridge. I was proud of my command of forty tough old-sweats, rogues yet friends, and proud also to be a Die-Hard.

Pipers of the Royal Scots Fusiliers bade farewell to the Battalion as the troop train drew out of Ismalia station, leaving behind the wives and children. I was appointed 'OC Families' although the Colonel's wife and RSM's wife, a formidable couple, really controlled the hundred or more Middlesex Regiment wives and children, all remarkably well behaved, stoically resigned to constant moves from country to country. Since leaving England in December 1931, the families had occupied married quarters in Palestine, Cairo and Moascar, and now in March 1936 were heading for Singapore.

California, a red-funnelled Anchor Line troopship, lay at anchor in Suez harbour, laden with the entire Battalion, all hanging over the rails to watch with amusement the embarkation of the families. Some of the subalterns who had travelled from England in the ship teased me with hoots of mocking laughter as I shepherded the families aboard. Noel Gudgeon, my close friend, was there, thrilled with his first glimpse of the canal and desert. Also in the ship was Martin Weedon who had joined the Regiment from Sandhurst with Noel and me. He was born and had lived in Egypt so that the Eastern sights were not new to him.

California berthed at Colombo and the Band and Drums and the whole Battalion began to disembark for a route-march through the city. But unexpectedly the flow of hob-nailed boots clanking down the swaying gangway was abruptly halted to permit three Indians to ascend. I was standing close to Colonel Tidbury, waiting to join the parade, as the Indians reached the ship's deck.

'*Hazoor*, Colonel Sahib, *Salaam*, we are wanting Hewitt *chota* sahib!'

The Colonel pointed at me: 'There he is.'

They were my father's old servants, the bearer, second bearer and the aged *dewan*, my old friends. I recognised them at once. Making *namasti*, joining hands, palms together, they greeted me.

'*Ali cum salaam*, Sahib, *ali cum salaam!*'

I made *namasti* and replied. '*Salaam ali cum, salaam ali cum!*'

Garlands of sweet smelling flowers were placed over me, right over my solar topee. The *dewan* touched the single brass star on my shoulder. 'Now you are officer sahib. I told you so.' He laughed, tears of joy in his brown eyes. 'No longer are you my *chota* sahib.'

It was a moment of palpable emotion. My visitors were in tears, handing me presents, little brass ornaments, sweets. I appealed for help. 'What shall I do, Colonel? Am I to join the march?'

'No, Tony, of course not. Stay on board and look after them. They've travelled for many days and nights all the way from Bombay to pay respect to you. It's part of their loyalty to your father and family, it's a marvellous gesture. You stay here.'

They stayed with me until just before the ship sailed, talking about my parents and sisters and Ahmednagar. My Urdu came back and with it childhood memories of India. And gratitude for the respect, love and loyalty my father had earned in his long service in India.

I waved goodbye to the rather sad group while *California* drew away. The bugles called 'Dress for Dinner' which would be followed in half an hour by 'Officers' Dinner', remembered through its farcical words, 'Officer's wives have pudding and pies, soldiers wives have skilly!' by which time we should be ready to dine in full Mess Dress.

The Battalion was being sent to Singapore to increase the garrison defending the naval base. Although an urgent need for a naval base at Singapore was recognised by the British Conservative Government in 1922, subsequent Labour Governments twice abandoned the project, in 1924 and 1929. Inter-service controversy further delayed progress until alarming acts of aggression by Japan in China and an increase in the strength of the Japanese navy forced a decision in 1932 to accelerate the first stages of construction.

Japan invaded Manchuria in 1931 and created the puppet State of Manchukuo, enthroning P'u-Yi, the Boy Emperor. In early 1932 three

Japanese divisions landed north of Shanghai and drove the Chinese army inland; and the next year Japan occupied the province of Jehol and crossed the Great Wall into north China. Condemned as an aggressor by the League of Nations, Japan withdrew from the League and denounced the Washington Naval Treaty, designed to prevent a naval arms race in the Pacific, and began an intensive naval building programme. It was apparent, therefore, that Japan aimed at achieving complete control over China, military supremacy and the suppression of Western influence in the Pacific.

An Anglo-German naval treaty signed in 1935 gave Germany the right to build up to 35% of the surface tonnage of the British Navy and greatly affected the balance of naval power, so that the greater part of the British fleet was restricted to home waters. The Singapore base was now required to withhold an attack for ninety days until reinforcements arrived. Into this perilous situation of an impending Japanese assault and into an unfinished base with a limited fleet, the Middlesex Regiment made its entrance into the Far East, landing on April Fool's Day 1936, an omen that augured ill for the future.

Coconut and rubber plantations, stretching westwards and northwards until they dissolved into the blue-green of equatorial jungle, surrounded the newly built Gillman Barracks which the Battalion occupied. Three-storeyed concrete blocks were perched on red laterite hills with delightful views of the Straits. Never before had British soldiers been placed in such palatial barracks, modern and clean, so different to wooden huts in Palestine and bug-ridden barracks in Cairo; far better than the old barrack lines at Tanglin now occupied by the Royal Inniskilling Fusiliers, the only other infantry battalion in Singapore in 1936.

Noel and I learned our military duties quickly because the Company Commander delegated the complete training and administration of the Company to us. We wrote training programmes, supervised section and platoon training and exercises in the nearby jungles, led route marches, organised weapon training and musketry practice on firing ranges, paid the men, attended drill and ceremonial parades, guards of honour, carried a Colour, arranged games and played in company teams.

Young subalterns were unconcerned with promotion. Hitler's paranoiac ravings or Hirohito's lust for war would either bring rapid promotion in battle or a fatal bullet, and a rule forbidding officers to marry before reaching thirty dampened marriage prospects. We predicted, mournfully: 'As infantry soldiers destined to be slaughtered by thousands, we'll be dead before they let us marry.' Sadly, many of us were killed in battle or died in prison camps, too young to gain permission to marry.

Terrible consequences faced a bold young officer who married without permission. He might be required to resign his commission, or transfer to a service or ordnance corps, or vanish with a colonial force into darkest Africa. Understandably, he was terrified of becoming closely involved with a girl. Married women were safer, preferably Catholics. In Singapore there existed a 'fishing fleet' of highly delectable young girls striving diligently to make a catch, but, woefully, most of us were too craven and too poor to become entangled in the net.

A second lieutenant's pay in 1936 was 9s. 8d. a day, out of which he clothed himself in uniform and plain clothes, paid for a Chinese servant, paid numerous subscriptions to the Mess for his food, polo, drums, silver funds et cetera, and notably mess guests. All visitors were offered food and drink, the cost of which was divided equally among the members and charged on mess accounts as 'mess guests'. On Guest Nights, when the band played sonorous martial music, distinguished guests such as the Governor, the Colonial Secretary, the General and Brigadiers fed and dined royally at our expense. Hence the ditty:

> Have another port, Brigadier,
> The subalterns will pay; they get ten bob a day,
> Have another port, Brigadier.

As construction of the naval base progressed and newly built accommodation became available thousands of military and civilian people sailed into the orderly little Crown Colony, the established domain of Sir Shenton Thomas, Governor and Commander-in-Chief of the Straits Settlements of Penang, Malacca and Singapore. Its character began to change. The graceful town of well-kept tree-lined roads, grass verges and flowering gardens of exquisite tropical plants was disturbed by new roads and houses. The white man, the *tuan besar*, lived in complete harmony with a cosmopolitan population of Asian, American, European, Pacific and Australasian peoples—but apart in traditional customs of behaviour, drink and food, of gin-pahits, whisky stengahs, dinner jackets and club life—even he recognised the change.

A boom hit Singapore and reflected into Malaya; Chinese and Indians flowed in to meet demands for builders' labourers; godowns on the docks were full with tin, palm-oil and rubber waiting for shipping. Imported European and American motor cars and domestic commodities were dumped ashore in large quantities. Large trading houses like Boustead, Mansfield and Harper Gilfillen increased staffs to ease the demand, as did the Hong Kong and Shanghai Bank, the Chartered Bank and the Straits Settlements Police.

Overcrowded troopships steamed through the sticky heat of the Straits to join the most frequented shipping crossroads in the world and to deposit pale sailors, soldiers and airmen on the wharves of Keppel harbour, often accompanied by bewildered wives and querulous children unable to tolerate the oppressive humid climate, the noise of yelling Chinese dock coolies and pungent Chinese smells.

Sailors joined the naval dockyard and ships' complements of the valiant old monitor *Terror* or the aircraft carrier *Hermes* and county-class cruisers, the submarine depot ship *Medway* and other ships. Airmen reported to the RAF Station, Seletar as crews for Torpedo Bomber Squadrons, General Reconnaissance Squadrons and Catapult Squadrons. Heavy gunners, members of Heavy Artillery Regiments, not weighty men as the term suggests, and anti-aircraft gunners filled new barracks at Changi and the small island of Blakang Mati.

The island was filling up, almost bursting at the seams; there was an exciting feeling of expectancy, eager young men mixed with experienced young rubber planters from up-country in the hotels, stately Raffles, the staid Adelphi, the unfettered Seaview. The exuberant Cricket Club on the Padang close to the sea overflowed with new members who played wild games of rugger and consumed quantities of Tiger Beer, a new taste. Travellers' palms at the entrance to the Tanglin Club greeted members to its cool dignified interior, to open verandahs where memorable curry lunches were served every Sunday, to its squash courts and the enticing swimming pool. Many young men joined the Bukit Timah Golf Club, an equatorial paradise among verdant fairways and manicured greens, shaded by giant rain-forest trees, with coloured shrubs and wild orchids and lakes covered with huge seductive water lilies.

Chinese, Malayan and Indian children, delightful little creatures wide-eyed with excitement, danced to the stirring strains of the kilted soldiers' pipes; and an admiring cosmopolitan crowd, thrilled by the vitality of the music, applauded them. To the tune of 'The Cock o' the North' the Pipers led the 2nd Battalion The Gordon Highlanders into the brand new Selarang Barracks, Changi.

Fortunately, the Scottish soldiers did not know it was their destiny to be imprisoned in these same barracks by the Japanese after the fall of Singapore on 15 February 1942; and to suffer terrible treatment, starvation and brutality from Japanese guards until released in late August 1945. Many worked as slave labourers on the infamous Burma Railway; many died in captivity.

I had two young friends in the battalion, Francis Moir-Byres, who survived a grim session on the railway, and Ivan Lyon, a 'Lovely five' cadet with me, who skilfully evaded capture, then led a daring raid in a vessel named *Krait* on Singapore harbour in 1943 but was killed in a subsequent raid in 1944.*

After dinner in Mess, the subalterns changed into white 'bum-freezer' jackets, the traditional civilian evening dress, and slipped into the 'Coconut Grove', a night club on a beach close to the Mess. A typical group of young officers would include the moustached 'Hippo' Beadnell, the animated 'Blanco' Whiting, the cavalier 'Fish' Fishbourne, the amiable 'Johnny' Peel, the handsome Noel Gudgeon and me. The 'Grove' was a rendezvous for friends, a buoyant place but if there were too few girls the atmosphere palled, and 'we happy few, we band of brothers' generally set out for the huge travellers' palms standing sentinel before the stately edifice of Raffles. Here would be more of the Regiment, the vivacious 'Flash' Chattey and the elegant 'Roly' Gwyn, now ADC to the Governor, often with 'Monkey' Stewart, a gallant major.

We drank gin-slings, whisky-ayer-suku-glass, whisky-stengah, danced to a splendid band, ate palatable late suppers with French wine at small candle-lit tables on the lawn of the courtyard under a tropic sky, paid for everything by signing a chit and blessed the valiant founders of the great British Empire for this extravagant way of life—and Sir Stamford Raffles.

Girl friends came from daughters of parents living in Singapore, nursing sisters and tourists. By boarding large passenger liners as they berthed, it was often possible to find delightful young women who readily accepted an invitation to dine at Raffles.

One blessed day we stepped aboard a US President Line ship and found to our delight a whole troupe of attractive young American actresses on a world tour, booked to perform for a week at the Victoria Theatre. We could hardly believe our luck, especially at their enthusiasm to join us after their first performance. That evening we happy band of rogues took front seats in the theatre, a theatre which had acquired prestige when Noel Coward played *Journey's End* there in 1930 as Captain Stanhope, with John Mills as Lieutenant Raleigh. Sitting expectantly on the edge of our seats, wildly applauding every act of the stage show, each one wondering which one he would pair up with later in the evening. We were a little alarmed at the amazing acrobatic skills of the girls, especially the contortionist. 'Keep clear of the contortionist,' warned Hippo, 'She'll tie you up in knots.'

---

* *Krait* survived the war and may now be seen at the Australian National Maritime Museum at Darling Harbour, Sydney, where it is on permanent loan from the Australian War Memorial.

Backstage we drank champagne, more in Raffles' long bar. We danced and dined, but the girls were strangely out of place in the over-British atmosphere of Raffles, so we moved to the Swimming Club, cool and close to the sea, romantic under the Malayan moon. With acrobatic dives and shrieks of laughter the American girls plunged fully dressed into the large warm pool, then screamed and shouted, 'Come on, you Limeys, come on in!' and pulled and pushed until we were all in, fully clothed. In the turmoil I found myself struggling in the shallow end with the deadly contortionist. 'Kiss me!' she implored and grabbed me in her strong arms. Twisting and turning in tortuous rolls, her legs and body entwining me, we spun about the floor of the pool. I was drowning until she released her amorous grip and flung me ashore, to lie belching water by the gallon.

With no more Limeys to chuck into the pool the jolly girls then threw the chairs and tables into the water, with hilarious screams and yells and laughter until the party ended. Next day, shame-faced, we stood rigidly before the Adjutant and received an imperial rocket. The Secretary of the Swimming Club had reported us to the Colonel for unseemly behaviour.

The horror of drowning in the arms of a passionate contortionist forced me to discard poodle-fakiring for rugby. With the rugged Noel, an outstanding centre three-quarter, I played in the Army rugby team in the Malaya Cup competition at Singapore and Seremban, and in the final at Kuala Lumpur. It gave me a chance to see a little of the beautiful country of Malaya and the amiable people, blessed by exquisitely formed features.

The match at Seremban, the small administrative capital of the State of Negri Sembilan, was the greatest fun. Travelling there on the small gauge Federation Malay States railway the team arrived the day before the match. Our friendly opponents, colonial servants, policemen, rubber planters, tin miners and businessmen, led us firmly to the Sungei Ujong Club, which boasted a longer bar than Raffles, and poured gallons of beer into us. At last a kind host, a *tuan besar*, collected Noel and me in a car driven by a Malay *syce*, smart in velvet *songkok*, white *baju* and gaily coloured *sarong*, who drove us to a large white bungalow, surrounded by green lawns and an enchanting garden.

After a few stengahs we ate a five course dinner, washed down with quantities of French wines. The Negri Sembilan players were achieving their aim of making us utterly incapable of playing hard rugby on the morrow.

In the Sungei Ujong Club before lunch we were offered more beer, then an enormous and delicious Malayan curry, with many luscious side dishes. They were consumed with an endless flow of cold Allsopp's Pilsener, donated by Caldbeck's, the wine merchants, and finally, to smooth the hot spices and chillies, with *gula melaka*.

Noel and I enjoyed the marvellous curry; we ate like savages and the beer made us very happy. We had never been entertained like this, never met such friendly people as these Negri Sembilans, especially the rubber planters. We were only twenty-one; both sons of clergymen, we had led sheltered lives, Noel in a town in the Lake District. Each had learned the discipline of a public school, Noel at Haileybury, and both at Sandhurst and the Army. No wonder we were enjoying ourselves, forgetting we had to play rugby, due to start at 3.30 p.m. It was quite clear now that Negri Sembilan hoped to defeat us through the effects of their excessive hospitality. The Army players crept onto the green field like a bunch of zombies, bewitched by the god Bacchus, and stood in serried ranks for protection, awaiting the savage onslaught. Immediately the whistle blew, Negri Sembilan, with a fearful yell of defiance, led by the captain Hugo Hughes, a giant wing forward, smashed through the feeble Army lines with a succession of withering attacks, scoring tries with ease. But the pace was too much for them and the less fit members wilted in the 85°F heat, especially those from firms like Sime Darby, Caldbeck's, Borneo Motors and Bousteds; only the rubber planters kept going, used to walking and running long distances daily on plantations.

The Army team included a Scottish and an English international and top Welsh and English club players. Ashamed at our performance we rallied and were ahead in the score at half time. However, to revive themselves our opponents ordered brandy and ginger ale for their half time drinks, and the valiant Hugo led them again in another shattering assault, tearing through us like a dose of salts. But again they tired, so that we won the match. Magnanimous in defeat, our opponents entertained us yet again in the Club before pouring us into the night train for Singapore.

Hugo Hughes was a rubber planter, fit and hard, an outstanding player. In the war he joined the Malay Regiment and lost a leg in the defence of Opium Hill near Pasir Panjang in the last hours of the Battle for Singapore.

Japanese soldiers killed the staff and wounded in the Alexandra Military Hospital, but missed Hugo lying unconscious in a bed. Unattended for days, he survived nevertheless. In Changi POW camp he endured terrible agonies in ghastly conditions with only primitive treatment. After the war he worked again in Malaya as a Citizen of Empire, then retired to become a Citizen of Australia.

6

Singapore

Encounter

Singapore stood as a sentinel over world trade from the Indian and Pacific Oceans. Situated on the southern tip of the Malayan Peninsula and separated from Sumatra by the narrow Straits of Malacca, Singapore was the world's most frequented shipping lane. It was of immense strategic and commercial importance to Britain, after India a second corner stone of Empire.

Events of great historical consequence were happening in China and Japan at this time, early 1937. Mao Tse-tung's epic Long March had been completed eighteen months previously and an end to the civil war between him and Chiang Kai-shek was feasible. A united China might withstand Japan's aggression in the north and enforce the return of European concessions and leases, which might diminish Singapore's importance. Japan was named the 'Yellow Peril', yet the danger was decried because it was regarded as a Mikado country, its manufactured goods shabby, its military strength no match for European or American forces.

I wished to learn more about China and Japan. Hippo Beadnell had similar interests so we applied for leave to visit those countries in the spring. While we were waiting for approval for our journey, Hippo met the two young daughters of Lieutenant Colonel Hayley Bell, the Defence Security Officer for Malaya Command, and was highly impressed. 'They're a China family, the girls have lived in China and their father is an authority on Japan as well.'

I looked forward to meeting the Hayley Bells and learning more about China and Japan. I had been invited to a party at Flagstaff House and I knew they would be there. Flagstaff House was the home of the General Officer Commanding Malaya, Major General Dobbie, nicknamed 'Dhobi General' by facetious soldiery. He lived there with his wife and his son, Orde, who was his ADC. They were a religious family, Plymouth Brethren, and gave many pleasant non-alcoholic parties.

Mrs Dobbie said, 'Tony, come and meet Elizabeth Hayley Bell.' I had noticed her as soon as I had entered the drawing room, a tall fine-looking girl in a fresh primrose-coloured dress. She was obviously at ease in these surroundings, friendly and easy to talk to.

I asked her how she liked living in Singapore. She loved it, she said, she had often come ashore here on journeys to and from China before she had been sent to 'that dreadful boarding school' (as if she expected me to know naturally how awful were boarding schools); and it was 'sheer heaven' to be back in the East again, 'just like coming home'. How extraordinary that she had the same feeling about school and separation and the East as me.

'I know exactly what you mean. I'm a waif, semi-orphan of the British Empire, never saw my parents or sisters, a slave to British convention.'

'That's one way of describing us,' she said. 'Rudyard Kipling, who is a cousin, called the children of parents who spent their lives in outposts of Empire "outcast children of the East". It's fashionable to send us to English schools. You can't blame the Empire. My father worked for China, not the Raj, but still sent us to England.'

'I don't know why I didn't go to a school in the Hills of India. I suppose there are good schools in China?'

'Yes, of course, a marvellous one in Chefoo where we once lived. Anyway, that's all over now; it's lovely to be back in the East. I'm sure you like it.'

We talked about the Malays, gentle, beautiful and proud, how Singapore island had belonged to the Sultan of Johore until Raffles came in 1816, how the Chinese were not indigenous. 'It's still a Malayan Island,' she said.

I told her about my plans to visit China and Japan and she was most interested. 'You must speak to Daddy about your trip. He'll tell you all sorts of things to look out for; he's travelled all over China and knows Japan well.'

The *Strait's Times* that day carried an article about the Anti-Comintern Pact between Germany and Russia. 'It's very dangerous,' I said, 'Germany under Hitler and his thugs is highly explosive.'

'Do you think we are going to have another war, Tony? How awful. Daddy says the Japs are a real menace and they would be much worse joined up with Germany.'

'I pray not, Liz. The British Empire should be strong enough to resist the Germans and Japs. I hope the Empire goes on forever.'

We spoke as if we had met previously. We had much in common; it was indeed extraordinary. I very much liked this girl in the primrose-coloured dress with large brown buttons running down the middle. I could have fallen in love with her.

For the adolescent Elizabeth, early months in Singapore glided into a tranquil carefree existence in communion with the ecstasy of dwelling in an equatorial paradise. Living with her parents and sister in a large bungalow at Lermit Road, Tanglin, cared for by long-known servants, the treasured Numbers 1 and 2 Boys and the beloved Amah, she was happier than she had been since leaving China as a child.

The bungalow was close to the Botanical Gardens, full of exotic tropical flowers and trees, with gardenias and frangipani in profusion. Inquisitive small monkeys leapt in glorious abandon from the trees into Lermit Road to forage for food in daring raids. These cheeky little creatures delighted Elizabeth with their fearless acrobatic antics.

Ordinary daily activities also delighted her. Travelling by taxi along Orchard Road, home of meticulous tailors, or through city streets by rickshaw, she learnt to recognise at close quarters the people of many different races clothed variously in vivid coloured garments. She smelt the raw odour of damp streets and the stink of deep storm drains. Bargaining was fun in Change Alley, where anything could be bought, even household silver stolen only a few days ago. Then there was more sedate shopping in Raffles Place at big stores like Robinson's and Little's. Better still, one could gaze in amazement at the rapturous display at C.K. Tang in River Valley Road of glittering jewellery, ecstatic Chinese vases and delicately painted crockery, camphor wood boxes, doleful Buddhas, everything imaginable.

And then cool drinks, a swim and tennis at the Tanglin Club and evening walks with parents to the MacRitchie Reservoir, strolling on red laterite pathways along the reservoir banks, surrounded by the huge trees of the tropical rain forest; or to Mount Faber, where the views across the Straits of groups of emerald islands lying dotted in a blue-green sea were immensely wide and where everything that Elizabeth saw made for greatness and freedom—and unequalled nobility.

Elizabeth was given a morning job in the Church of England Zenana Missionary School in the grounds of Government House. Here she typed for Miss Lane, the Headmistress, a missionary with many years of dedicated service in the Far East. Elizabeth liked the Chinese schoolgirls, the beauty in their serious little faces, their wide brown eyes and straight black hair. She made friends with them, but recognised that she would never quite know or understand them; that an ugly barrier existed between Europeans and Asians which discouraged mixed friendships in those days.

At times Elizabeth travelled all over the green wonderland of Malaya with her father who, in his role as Defence Security Officer, Malaya, was for ever gathering information and seeking agents among the Eurasians, Parsees, Chinese and Tamils. Hayley's extensive knowledge of oriental languages gave him access to these people. From various sources Hayley established a store of intelligence which invariably pointed to the infiltration of Japanese agents into Malaya, all surreptitiously occupying respectable civilian occupations: in businesses of all kinds; many in photographic trades; as barbers; waiters in European clubs; Japanese restaurants; in the rubber plantations and tin mines.

World events in 1936 disturbed Colonel Hayley Bell, whose interests were global. Most people in the Colony preferred to swallow their fears with a Singapore gin-sling and forget Ethiopia, annexed by Italy in May, or the Spanish Civil War which had been blazing since July 1936 and was providing training for Nazi ground and air forces.

In October that year Belgium declared it would adopt a neutral policy; Germany and Italy established the Rome-Berlin Axis; and an Anti-Comintern Pact was signed by Germany and Japan. The British Empire was isolated.

Major 'Monkey' Stewart emphasised the critical situation in lectures to subalterns as study groups. John Gunther's *Inside Europe* was compulsory reading and made me realise that humanity was fading in Europe and the dark ages were returning. Jewish refugees in ships passing through Singapore bound for Shanghai told tales of concentration camps and other horrors. Inconsistently, I felt that I was too far away to be closely affected. Distance measured by travelling time was greater in those days—Singapore was four weeks away by sea from Germany and Europe was another world. My feelings were like those of many people in Malaya.

Later, I read Edgar Snow's epic novel *Red Star Over China* and became deeply impressed by the Chinese people's struggle for freedom from corrupt rule by the Koumintang. China was so much closer than Germany. Major Monkey accused me of being a 'roaring communist' but Colonel Hayley Bell approved my interest in China. He had received numerous first-hand accounts of the Long March from persons visiting him in his bungalow in Tanglin.

A constant stream of visitors flowed in and out of Lermit Road, old China hands on their way to and from China, and global friends of Hayley— Singapore was very much the crossroads of the world. Many of them brought useful military intelligence with them.

Hayley's agents reported categorically that the Japanese army intended to land in north-east Malaya and attack the Singapore naval base from the Malayan peninsula. A Eurasian, born and brought up in Japan, gave positive information of these intentions but, astonishingly, little of Hayley's diligently collated intelligence was accepted by Headquarters, Malaya Command at Fort Canning; all the sources were downgraded and the Eurasian Japanese was classified as a double agent.

In Singapore, as Defence Security Officer, Hayley Bell dealt with a professional military bureaucracy whose opinions on the defence of the Naval Base were dominated by superior authorities. For instance, Lord Curzon's committee in 1923 considered that the nature of the country would make an enemy advance through Johore exceptionally difficult. It ignored the traditional Japanese tactic of attacking from the land, as at the capture of Port Arthur in 1904 and Tsingtao in 1914; and adopted the premise that any attack on Singapore would be from the sea.

Then in 1928 the Chiefs of Staff Committee considered an attack from Johore unlikely and that the defences should be designed to resist a seaborne attack. Not even a report in 1932, at a time of crisis in the International Settlement in Shanghai, that the Japanese had been ready to embark a division and artillery to attack Singapore from the mainland, changed the view that the assault would be seaborne. In 1937 airfields were constructed on the east coast of Malaya at Kota Bharu and Kuantan but it was still assumed that any attack would be from the sea and that an air attack would be made by carrier-borne aircraft. No land defence was provided for the airfields. It was not surprising, therefore, that Hayley's reports fell on deaf ears. The professional staff regarded Hayley as an eccentric, 'only a war-time soldier', and foolishly ignored his vast experience of the East and his remarkable talent for intelligence.

Elizabeth, only eighteen, in those days a tender age at which possessive mothers diligently guarded their daughter's chastity, was not permitted to go out with young men unless she was accompanied by a chaperone. Her mother insisted that she should return to their home by midnight, an edict that had to be strictly observed.

One of Elizabeth's most frequent admirers was Martin Weedon. A good looking young man and a splendid cricketer, he had been at Sandhurst with me but in a different company. He first met Elizabeth at one of Mrs Dobbie's tea parties which the ADC Orde Dobbie organised into a scavenging hunt. Martin took Elizabeth on the search in his small open red MG. One of the items to be found was described simply as 'A Highlander' which caused an indecent rush to the Gordons' barracks at Changi and acute embarrassment to soldiers wearing the kilt. Martin and Elizabeth did not find a Highlander or many of the objects for which they were meant to search, but they got to know and like each other.

Martin, she discovered, was twenty-one, his birthday the same day as Emperor Hirohito on 29 April, an only child, third generation Harrovian, parents separated, mother in England, father in France; he grew a moustache and smoked a pipe.

This was the beginning of a thrilling and happy love affair, at least as much as it could be in the constant shadow of a chaperone. Although Elizabeth had many other men friends, it was Martin that she saw most. She watched him play cricket and rugger, and march with a big sword on ceremonial parades on the Padang. He was always most attentive, arriving at the bungalow with flowers and presents, wearing a white gardenia plucked from the garden as he passed. The parents came to know Martin and liked him; he went up country with Elizabeth's father after big game and shot a rogue elephant and a seladang (wild Malay bison).

It was a rich, celestial time for Elizabeth; she floated through loving skies with youthful joy, in a truly beautiful adolescent love affair, thinking only of the day, never of the future, hoping this paradise would last for ever.

In an exciting episode for the Hayley Bells, Mary suddenly flew into Singapore in a flying boat captained by Scotty Allan, a daring aviator, whom Mary brought to the house in Lermit Road. Mary had been in Australia for some months with Faye Compton's 'Tour of Australia', playing in numerous plays. Except for Dennis, now in the RAF, the family was united for a few days.

Meanwhile, in March 1937, Hippo Beadnell and I were granted leave to visit Japan. The ubiquitous Peninsular and Oriental Steam Navigation Company's *Rajputana* cruised into the cool waters of the China Sea with Hippo and me happily aboard. Daily it became palpably colder and drier, a refreshing change from the hot humid Malayan climate. In splendour, we dined in warm dinner jackets with black waistcoats and in the day donned long tweed jackets, extravagantly coloured waistcoats, grey flannels—clothes not worn since we left Egypt.

Five days after leaving 'Sweaty-pore' *Rajputana* glided through the mists of a March morning into the superb harbour of Hong Kong. The stately Peak, briefly clouded. towered above like a proud sentinel over the grey-green harbour frothing with warships, liners, cargo ships, small boats and venerable junks driven by huge maroon sails. The splendid sight thrilled me but caused within me a foreboding that this tiny Colony was destined to have an enormous impact on my life. It was an extraordinary prediction, a strange fantasy that came to me, that here I would find both contentment and desolation.

The arrival in Shanghai was in startling contrast to that of Hong Kong and its beautiful harbour. The Whangpoo River and Soochow Creek were murky and refuse-laden, cluttered with war and merchant ships and thousands of junks and sampans. People lived their entire lives in these fragile craft on those filthy waters. Thousands more dwelt in squalid slums or in the ruins of Chapei, destroyed by Japanese in 1932. Shanghai was a monstrous mass of miserable humanity, of appalling poverty and despair, except for foreigners living in luxury in international settlements.

Even in these Concessions the streets were packed with millions of Chinese. Crowds of people with horses, carts, cars, buses and rickshaws, jogged along the Nanking Road and Bubbling Well Road past the Park Hotel, the Cathay Hotel and Shanghai Club on the Bund, like swarming bees, swaying and bunching, forever moving.

A *taipan* friend entertained us in the Shanghai Club, which boasted the longest bar in the world. He predicted that China was on the threshold of great prosperity.

'For the first time in this century China is at last united. The Kuomintang and Communists combined should be able to resist further Japanese imperialism. China can develop its natural resources, industry and trade.'

He was referring to the Sian Incident, how Chiang Kai-shek had been arrested by the Reds but released on a promise of a truce in the civil war. The *taipan's* prophesy did not materialise. Four months later, on 7 July 1937, Japan deliberately started the Sino-Japanese War, originating in an incident at a marble bridge made famous by Marco Polo, near Peking.

The 1st Battalion The Lancashire Fusiliers were stationed in Shanghai. Hippo and I met many friends in the Mess of this famous Regiment. Regimental tradition imbued high spirits into its officers, who joyously escorted us on a hair-raising tour of Shanghai's night spots, resting at last in the glamorous 'Casanova', drinking champagne with fabulously beautiful Russian girls. They were White Russians, all claiming to be princesses or countesses. They told me how their regal aristocratic families were brutally driven out of Russia by the Revolution, and heartbreaking stories of terrible hardships experienced in Manchuria and China. Every girl I danced with praised the British Army and wished to marry a British officer. I was determined to marry one of them, at least until 'Casanova' closed at 6 a.m., when I was thrown into the darkness and a freezing cold dry sub-zero temperature and sobered up remarkably quickly!

Hippo and I disembarked from *Rajputana* at Osaka. In Singapore army intelligence had briefed us on various matters to observe in Japan. Intelligence funds would be provided to help our travelling expenses, to be paid bureaucratically in arrears, when we submitted a report. We were warned to be careful, that Japanese spy mania was rampant.

On landing we noticed immediately that we were followed wherever we went, always by the same man, in trains, buses, hotels—he even took the next taxi and chased after us. We did not try to avoid him; it was really highly amusing. In Tokyo, staying in the Imperial Hotel, we invited him to join us for a drink. He was an amusing man, with a pleasant sense of the ridiculous and excellent English. After a few cups of saki he unwittingly disclosed things for which we were searching. Strangely, we lost our shadow at a hotel near Mount Fujiama, where it had been arranged to meet an officer from the British Embassy, with whom we watched a Japanese infantry brigade performing a field firing exercise, with artillery firing in support—highly dangerous, but impressive and excellently carried out.

Back in Singapore I wrote a report about the exercise in which I praised excessively the high degree of training and efficiency of the Japanese soldiers. General Dobbie told me that as a very junior officer (still a 2nd Lieutenant) I had been over-impressed and that my report would go no further. It was customary in those days to undervalue the Japanese. The British Empire, the greatest empire in history, was supreme; Asians were 'a lesser breed without the law'.

From the start of the Sino-Japanese war Japan staged incidents in China which involved British citizens, designed to undermine Western influence in China. To protect British communities in treaty ports and concessions, the British government increased garrisons in China. The Lancashire Fusiliers moved north from Shanghai to Tientsin and Peking, the Seaforth Highlanders moved from Hong Kong to Shanghai.

In August most of the Middlesex Regiment were out of Singapore. The polo team were guests of the Sultan of Perak, the cricket team was in Kuala Lumpur, many were on leave in Malaya or Siam. Suddenly, out of the blue, like a thunderbolt, a despatch rider delivered an immediate message to Battalion headquarters:

'WARNING ORDER: 1MX WILL PREPARE TO MOVE TO HONG KONG.'

Panic reigned in Gillman Barracks.

7

—

Hong Kong
Gathering Storm

All Singapore came to see off the 'Midds', the Die-Hards, a much loved Regiment. Tearful pathetic groups of soldiers' families hung close together, sharing their misery and anxiety. Broken-hearted sweethearts wept openly, unashamed of their emotions. Elizabeth, unable as yet to believe that a regiment could depart so quickly, stood forlornly with her uniformed father, wondering if she would ever see Martin again.

As the dirty little Blue Funnel cargo ship drew away from the wharf, the band of the Inniskilling Fusiliers played 'Auld Lang Syne', and even those who had not yet wept burst into wild tears. The Cockney soldiers lined the rails of the only open deck, waved and tried to cheer up the people with banter and promises to return soon, and finally burst into song, 'Bless 'em All'.

The Battalion had embarked within four days of the order to move, quite a feat for a regular battalion weighed down with peacetime paraphernalia. It could have embarked earlier, but the SS *Menelaus*, a cattle ship formerly used to convey pilgrims to Mecca, was declared unfit to carry troops until it was cleaned and fumigated. Even then it was full of bugs. Battalion cooks had to prepare meals in old fashioned horse-drawn cookers lashed to the decks.

In the frantic rush to get everyone aboard, polo ponies were left in Perak and sold cheaply, cars were sold for ridiculous prices, bulky personal possessions were left behind, and officers who had been up-country only just made the boat by driving straight to the dock and leaving their cars there, unsold. On arrival in Hong Kong the Battalion marched from Kowloon up the Nathan Road to Shamshuipo to occupy Nanking Barracks, hastily vacated by the Seaforth Highlanders. Just over four years later the battle-weary survivors of this same battalion would march doggedly along the same three miles to Shamshuipo as prisoners-of-war, but still staunch Die-Hards.

The Battalion was placed immediately on twelve hours notice to embark for Shanghai because of the Japanese advance towards the International Settlement. To this restriction, and the fact that the barracks, lines of low wooden huts on reclaimed land surrounded by Chinese slums, were the worst barracks the Regiment had ever encountered, was added yet another discomfort—a typhoon, the worst that had ever hit the Colony, killing hundreds of Chinese. The barracks' church, four big dining halls and all the Quartermaster's ledgers disappeared into the night. The transport horses broke loose and careered through the camp into the slums. The typhoon was an evil omen for the Regiment's beginning in Hong Kong.

The Battalion then spent its time digging defensive positions on the Gindrinkers' Line, so called since it started in Gindrinkers' Bay, a favourite place to sail to, anchor, picnic and drink gin, which stretched for eleven miles along the Kowloon Hills to the sea. At the western end, overlooking a beautiful reservoir and the massive slopes of Tai Mo Shan, the Colony's highest mountain, a redoubt was being built, covering about twelve acres of defensive positions, wlth underground tunnels connectlng machine-gun pillboxes. Cheeky, homesick Cockneys named the tunnels after London streets—Piccadilly, Haymarket, Regent—but a year later the defence plan was changed and the Line was abandoned. The situation in Europe deteriorated further at the end of 1937 when Italy joined the Anti-Comintern Pact and left the League of Nations.

To brighten our dreary existence, Elizabeth arrived. She sailed in to stay with old friends of her parents, the Murdochs of Jardine's, who lived in a palatial house high up on the Peak. Martin was in ecstasy, leaving barracks as soon as he could, persuading friends to take his turn as orderly officer. He raced his small car through overcrowded streets, Chinese scuttling out of the way in the nick of time, happy that the mythical tormenting devil following close behind must surely have been run over. Leaving his car at the Star Ferry he crossed the 'fragrant harbour', rode up in the Peak Tram, and ran along the Peak roads to the *taipan*'s house and to his sweetheart.

I met Elizabeth often, at the 'Grips', the Gloucester, Jimmy's Kitchen, the Peninsula, or playing tennis at the United Service Club. She was nineteen now, a flower in bloom, with a striking loveliness and sensitivity in her well-formed face. Martin brought her proudly to Regimental functions, cocktail parties, cricket matches. Colonel and Mrs Tidbury welcomed her warmly; she became a part of the Regiment.

We wondered, is Martin going to pop the question? Could he marry despite restrictive army rules? Colonel Tidbury, a kind and humane man, might accept it. War was imminent, surely Martin would be allowed to marry.

But Martin did not pop it. And to everyone's regret, especially mine, because her vivacity and fun were so attractive, she sailed away to Singapore. However, Martin had in fact written to Colonel Hayley Bell, who was on leave in Malaya at Fraser's Hill. When Elizabeth arrived in Singapore a letter from her father was waiting for her.

> Darling Elizabeth,
>
> . . . I do not in any way consider you engaged, nor can it have our consent until we have talked the many things there are to talk over, and until both Mummy and I know Martin better. There comes the question first, not of being engaged, but of when he is able to marry you. A long engagement that is public I will not consent to . . . when a date is determined, then, perhaps you may have your engagement properly and decently accepted and announced . . .
>
> Lovingly Daddy

Martin was desolate. He remained in the ugly barracks, almost a permanent orderly officer as he repaid those who had stood in for him during Elizabeth's visit, or volunteered for those who had urgent social engagements that clashed with orderly officer duty. Martin became acutely tired of always wearing uniform, even a sam browne in the Mess, forever wearing a sword as he performed his duties. He never wanted again to mount any more guards or turn them out day and night, or inspect the barracks with the orderly sergeant, smelly stables, stinking latrines, cook houses, dining halls. He could not bear to watch poor wretches on defaulters' parades, men who had committed heinous crimes such as a dirty chinstrap on the Adjutant's Saturday morning drill parade. Martin's mournful face upset us and we were thankful when Colonel Tidbury advised him to take leave and go to Singapore.

Martin jumped on the next ship going south, armed with a lovely sapphire ring acquired at Sennet Freres in Hong Kong. An engagement was announced on 17 June 1938.

However, the announcement of Elizabeth's engagement was foreshadowed by Japan's invasion of China in which the Imperial Japanese Army revealed that it could be both cruel and brutal. With widespread indiscriminate bombing of civilians it advanced into the Yangtse valley like a titanic tidal surge, killing and devastating all before it.

On 12 December 1937 British and American gunboats were attacked, with the loss of the US gunboat *Panay* and oil tankers. On that same fateful day the Japanese stormed into Nanking. 50 000 troops were let loose for one month in an orgy of rape, murder, looting and general debauchery. 42 000 people were murdered. We wondered, what would be the fate of Hong Kong if the Japanese captured the colony?

In far off Europe rampant international piracy prevailed. On 13 March 1938 Austria and Germany were joined in an Anschluss. Britain and France quivered inactively against the intimidation of Czechoslovakia by Germany. When Germany sent an ultimatum to that country, a conference was held hurriedly on 30 September 1938 in Munich. Chamberlain and Daladier shamefully signed a pact with Hitler and Mussolini, dividing Czechoslovakia in two. Chamberlain returned to England with a message of 'Peace in our time'. The next day Germany annexed Sudetenland, then Poland annexed Teschen and a month later Hungary annexed Slovakian territory.

It was apparent to Japan that Britain and France were too involved with piracy in Europe to restrict Japanese expansion in Asia. The Anschluss and annexations had shown that occupation of other nation's territory was acceptable, even if disguised as an Anschluss.

Consequently, in May 1938 Japan extended the war to South China and occupied Amoy, 300 miles north-east of Hong Kong. In October 1938 a Japanese expeditionary force landed at Bias Bay, only thirty-five miles from Kowloon and, advancing westwards, occupied Canton by the 21st. Hong Kong was thus cut off from the Chinese National Government. Japanese troops moved up to the Colony's frontier, interfering with the passage of persons and supply of food from Kwangtung province. Later the Japanese landed on Hainan Island some 300 miles south of Hong Kong and used it as a training base for jungle and amphibious warfare for future operations against Malaya. With the Japanese Navy virtually in control of the China Sea, the isolation of Hong Kong was complete.

Before the Japanese landed at Bias Bay, the Middlesex Regiment moved into the New Territories to live under canvas at San Wai camp, from where it deployed to defensive positions along the frontier. From posts scattered among virescent hills of bamboo, sycamore or fir, we looked down on the murky Sham Chun River which rises in the Wu Tung mountains to the east and which is the border between China and the British Colony. Rice fields north of the river were renowned for providing the best rice in China, once especially favoured by Emperors in Peking. Peasants working in the green fields and driving buffaloes, and hamlets of ancient azure-tiled cottages sheltered by huge cedars provided a pleasant rural scene. From my platoon headquarters in Lok Ma Chau police station I enjoyed this lovely view until the Japanese army drove Chinese soldiers away and advanced into the British Colony.

For the next three years, until Japan declared war on Britain on 8 December 1941, the Japanese army sat on the other side of the Hong Kong border. In Sha Tau Kok village the British shared with the Japanese the main street down which ran the international boundary. Forever conscious of the hostility of the Japanese but powerless to prevent numerous acts of cruelty by them on the Chinese people, our soldiers came to loathe the Japanese troops.

The threatening presence of a hostile army, peering through binoculars, planning its assault, induced a feeling of claustrophobia in us. We were rats about to be caught in a trap.

Our hostile neighbours however did not deter us. Hong Kong was a festive place, a refuge for enjoyment. The top hotels and restaurants were the best anywhere, the night life exciting. 'The Grips', a nickname for the Hong Kong Hotel's restaurant, was a social centre point where dinner jackets were mandatory for dinner and dancing. Overlooking an exquisite coastline, the Repulse Bay Hotel with its old-fashioned style was the epitome of colonial living. In Kowloon, the Peninsula Hotel, another centre of social activity, was our nearest haven, only three miles from barracks at Shamshuipo. And everywhere restaurants served all types of delicious Chinese food.

Upon landing on the Island from a Star Ferry, each named for stars: *Celestial, Shining, Twinkling*, the sedate buildings around the statue of Queen Victoria impressed the visitor with their sheer solidity as if they had been placed there for perpetuity, which was of course exactly what the Nanking Treaty of 1842 had decreed: '. . . the Island of Hong Kong to be possessed in perpetuity by Her Britannic Majesty, Her Heirs and Successors. . .' The Hong Kong and Shanghai Bank skyscraper stood high above the other buildings, the Supreme Court, the Hong Kong Club and round the corner the Cricket Club, a delightful sanctuary for young men for cricket and rugger. It was all so compact, orderly and serene, so British, true *fung shui*.

Weekly, there were races at Happy Valley, highly social events with private boxes for *taipans*. It was all efficiently organised by the members of the powerful Jockey Club, who were also reputed to run the Colony.

The army spent much time in the New Territories, guarding the border and on manoeuvres. In the five years that I was there I came to know almost every mountain, hill, valley, track, blue-tiled walled village with Cantonese and Hakka peasants and their horse-shoe shaped ancestral graves. With golf and hunting at Fanling, I took part in every type of sport, ran the mile, three-miles and cross-country, captained the Battalion rugger team and later the Army team. I shared a boat, kept meticulously by a Chinese crew that lived in it at the Yacht Club. I crewed in a 3-ton yawl in long races through the Pearl River delta to Macau. It was a full life.

Changes took place in the Battalion. The much admired Lieutenant Colonel Tidbury left to command a brigade in Palestine and was succeeded by Lieutenant Colonel Newnham. Major ' Monkey ' Stewart returned from his post as British Military Attache in Siam and became second-in-command. Hippo Beadnell was seconded to the King's African Rifles in Kenya and Noel Gudgeon to the Malay Regiment. Intellectually superior to the average officer, Noel had passed out of Sandhurst high on the list as a prize cadet. A great lover of classical music, an ardent reader, he spoke German and Malay fluently. He was an outstanding rugger player.

On 24 June 1939 Elizabeth and Martin were married at Aston Clinton in Buckinghamshire. The Hayley Bells were delighted: the youngest of their three daughters was the first to be married. Naturally they assumed that Martin had received Lieutenant Colonel Newnham's permission to marry.

Early in June 1939 Martin had applied for two months' leave, saying that he wished to improve his French to gain an army language qualification by studying in France, where he would be staying with his father. Colonel Newnham approved the application.

Leaving his ship in Marseille, he spent a few days with his father before joining his mother in her cottage near Aylesbury. Martin made his arrangements for the wedding and a week before it wrote to Colonel Newnham saying, confoundedly, that 'by the time this letter reaches you I shall be married to Elizabeth'.

The first half of the honeymoon was in Cornwall and the second was to be on the south coast of France, but before that could happen an urgent telegram was relayed to the hotel in Cornwall: 'LEAVE CANCELLED RETURN AT ONCE.'

Elizabeth was utterly shocked. She had no idea that Martin had not obtained his Colonel's permission to marry. She had been deceived, she could not trust him.

Hayley Bell was absolutely furious. He had assumed that Martin had received permission. It was an obvious assumption on which he had consented to the marriage, although he considered Martin immature and Elizabeth too young. He was desperately sorry for her, knowing that the position of a new bride in a Regiment was not easy and that this faux pas would make it much harder.

With alarming speed a passage to Hong Kong was booked on the P&O *Rajputana* sailing from Tilbury. Numb with the swiftness of events, Elizabeth hastily packed her wedding presents and belongings in much-travelled trunks and despatched them to the London docks. She had a quick and confused parting with her parents, who were worried about the effect this sudden recall might have on the week-old marriage. A sad farewell was made to Martin's frail little mother, obviously terribly upset at the unexpected departure of her newly-married son. She was kind to Elizabeth, the beginning of a lasting friendship.

In Martin's smart Jaguar they raced to Dover to catch the car ferry to Calais, and ever onward through Paris and to Montelimar in the Ardeche where lived Martin's father. The exhausted Elizabeth was introduced to him for the first time, since he had not attended the wedding. She had no time to get to know him but did not like him on first acquaintance; nor did she see much of the beauty of the countryside for very soon they were speeding southwards to Marseille, where, thankfully for Elizabeth, they boarded the awaiting liner *Rajputana*.

Weeks later the ship sailed into the 'fragrant harbour', early on a hot August morning. An officer of the Regiment ascended the gangway with a message that Martin was to report to the Commanding Officer at 1100 hours. Martin thought it an extraordinarily peremptory manner in which to treat an officer. After all, as ordered, he had returned to Hong Kong immediately, with a terrific rush, and he now had a wife to look after, and had to see to their baggage and find somewhere to live.

Fortunately Elizabeth was well known in Hong Kong through her parents and not so long ago she had been a schoolgirl at the Peak School. Kind friends like the Dowbiggins and Whithams came immediately to the rescue and looked after Elizabeth while Martin shot off to the grisly Nanking Barracks.

Smartly turned out in uniform, Martin reported at 1100 hours to Colonel Newnham, who reprimanded him and said:

'As far as I am concerned you are not married. You will live in single officer's quarters in barracks!'

It was a shattering start for a young marriage. Elizabeth was ignored by the Colonel's wife and by some wives of 'arse creeping' senior officers, but the younger wives and single officers, including the valiant Monkey, now second-in-command, whose wife was in England, were kind and helpful to her. They called frequently at the boarding house where she lived, and took her out when Martin was orderly officer or detained with other duties.

The colonial community, the *taipans* on the Peak and in the Hong Kong Club, and long time friends of the Hayley Bells such as Dot and Jack MacGregor (Jack had been Hayley's best man), thought the Colonel's cruel edict outrageous. The great trading houses, like Jardine's, had rules for early marriage but dealt with the problem compassionately, not tyrannically.

Elizabeth was as happy as she could be under this extraordinary life of being 'half-married', with Martin waking to an alarm clock and rushing out of the boarding house to return to barracks undetected before reveille. It was a disturbing, upsetting existence, an idiotic nightmare. Even the outbreak of war with Germany on 3 September 1939 did not cause Newnham to relax the restriction.

Elizabeth became a sort of 'stateless person', not recognised by the army, not connected with any of the firms or colonial government departments. Army doctors or dentists could not treat her, she could not be admitted to the British Military Hospital like other army wives; not that this mattered since Dr Black, who had delivered her mother's last child in Macau and who was a life-long friend of the family looked after her. (Dr Black was murdered by the Japanese in a hospital at St Stephen's College, Stanley, on Christmas Day 1941.) If an evacuation of women and children from Hong Kong happened, her name would not be on the list of any authority. Elizabeth's father worried about these matters and the effect of this strange existence on such a new marriage. He wrote to General Grasett, the GOC China Command, for help but he replied rigidly that he could not interfere.

Liz retained her indefatigable spirit, however, and her lovely laugh echoed o'er the fragrant harbour. I admired her tremendously for her fortitude.

Ominous events had occurred in Europe during the drama of Elizabeth's wedding to Martin, the cancellation of leave, the hurried return to Hong Kong and Newnham's extraordinary behaviour.

In February 1939 Hungary and Manchukuo joined the Anti-Comintern Pact. Elizabeth was disgusted that poor little P'u-Yi, the last Emperor of China and now of Manchukuo, was no more than a puppet of the Japanese.

Then in March, Hitler had entered Prague and made Czechoslovakia the German Protectorate of Bohemia-Moravia, committing gruesome atrocities upon the people. Lithuania, unable to resist, ceded Memel to Germany, giving it a northern naval base in the Baltic Sea, and Spain now joined the Anti-Comintern Pact. Britain and France were encircled by members of this Pact.

In a desperate effort to redress the balance of power Britain now offered guarantees of military aid to Poland, Greece, Turkey and Rumania. Hitler denounced these and made claims for Danzig. It was clear that war with Germany was inevitable.

In May Britain decreed conscription. The order caused concern in Hong Kong but those who were fit and eligible joined the regular forces or the Volunteers, and others left to join up in England.

8

Fragrant Harbour

Year of the Dragon

In July 1939 I was granted leave . . .

Creaking Chinese junks, with worn and sun-stained batwing sails flapping in the breeze, glided gracefully across the harbour, indifferent to the sleek white *Tegelberg*, outward bound to French Indo-China. I had a passage to Cochin China on this charming Dutch ship, which floated over the silvery South China Sea to Manila and then to Saigon, the Paris of the Far East. Here Europeans, not natives, served at pavement tables on the grand tree-lined boulevards. The city was clean, orderly and civilised; but the manner in which the French colonists mixed with the natives and assimilated into the country was vastly different to a British colony. The French had come to stay, unlike the British who retired to Britain when their work was done.

The giant Mekong River took me into Cambodia. I stayed a little in the fascinatingly beautiful capital, Phnom-Penh, the most oriental of oriental cities, where stately elephants, startlingly decorated, led highly coloured regal processions through ancient thoroughfares. Gentle cultured people descended from an aged civilisation with enchanting statuesque features were warmly friendly. Cambodia was an earthly paradise, my Camelot, as yet untouched by war and destructive communistic ideologies.

Striking north through dark green jungles, I suddenly became aware of gigantic temple towers rising above a faintly vibrating forest. It was Angkor Vat, a dead city of a lost civilisation, its ruins only recently discovered and in1939 being gradually cleared by the French. I strayed through miles of damp empty streets, climbed hundreds of stone steps into bat-infested temples, wondering who had lived here and whence came their strength, industry and knowledge to build such enormous monuments. I felt that their spirits remained still, that they watched my every move. An eerie feeling came to me; I knew I should not stay here. It is wrong to disturb ghosts and graves long since buried by mighty jungle vines and massive trees, to upset their rest by seeking their hidden secrets.

In Siam I intended to trace on foot the route already surveyed by Japanese for a railway from Siam to Burma. Earlier in the year an officer in my Regiment, Anson, had tried but had been defeated by the monsoon. Now, in August 1939, Japanese and German propaganda had caused a wave of hatred against us, as a result of which the British Embassy directed me to abandon the attempt. This route was, of course, that which the Japanese used to build the infamous railway, employing thousands of British, Australian, Dutch and Asian slave labourers taking, it is said, 'a life for every sleeper'.

I abandoned also the smelly canals, the overcrowded city of Bangkok and the glory of its Royal palaces and temples, for another Dutch steamer which deposited me at Batavia in Java. Here the magnificent Hotel des Indes, reputed to be the superior hotel of the East, fed me a *rijsttafel*, a feast of many various hot and spicy Javanese dishes, enough in one meal to last a week. Addiction to this food no doubt accounted for numerous obese Dutch people, so ugly in comparison with the sleek attractive Javanese.

I flew to the mountain town of Bandung, gloriously cool in the equatorial climate; and I journeyed slowly eastwards through a stimulating, beautiful country, travelling second class in trains with delightful Javanese people, to whom I spoke in Malay, learnt while I lived in Singapore, and staying in clean Javanese inns. The friendly Javanese, happy, well-fed and clothed, accepted contentedly the benefits of stable government, peace, prosperity, education and medicine that centuries of Dutch colonial rule had brought them.

If they could not speak English, I spoke to the Dutch in Malay also. They attempted to teach me the differences between Malay and Javanese. Amicable and hospitable, they were colonial government servants, bank managers and shop keepers, many married to Javanese, for the assimilation here after three centuries together was extensive. These white or Eurasian people, some from families which had lived for generations in the Indies, were not averse to performing menial tasks with the Javanese. Most of them told me they could never return to Holland. In my travels I met the military forces but I was not impressed; they could not possibly defend this pearl in the crown of the Queen of Holland. Many nasty bodies coveted the glittering pearl: Germans, Japanese, Javanese revolutionaries. Spies abounded, including a German spy masquerading as a salesman for 4711 Eau de Cologne. Much to his annoyance, I had met him in Shanghai in March 1937, travelled with him from Penang to Aden on a journey in late 1937, and now met again in Batavia. The future of the Indies was fraught with peril.

Elizabeth as a baby in Shanghai, sitting in No. 1 Amah's lap.

Macau in 1920

The view taken from the house of the Commissioner of Maritime Customs of the Praia Grande Bay showing the Lighthouse on the hill in the distance. Now, in the 1990s, the area of the hill is covered with high-rise buildings, luxury hotels and casinos extending on land reclaimed from the sea. It is no longer the quiet and peaceful Colony that the Hayley Bell family loved so much.

The Commissioner's House in Macau.

The Hayley Bells: *(left to right, from back)* Father, Mary, Nanny Day, Dennis, Mother, Elizabeth and John

The Globe Trotters: Elizabeth and John looking at Chefoo.

Elizabeth aged five.

The Hewitt family and household in India a few years before Tony's birth.
Father, Mother, Governess and two sisters (the third and youngest has just vacated
the cane chair at the left) *See page 135.*

Tony at Ahmednagar

Hayley Bell *(centre)* on the Bund.

Elizabeth and John's "Red Castle" *(left)*, Magazine Gap, Hong Kong.

Elizabeth, Hayley and John, dressed for the hunt.

Royal Navy Cadet Hayley Bell.

Tony in Eton suit.

Elizabeth at the Francis Holland School, aged sixteen.

The Royal Military College, Sandhurst.

Gentleman Cadet Tony Hewitt, aged eighteen.

The Officers' Mess at Gillman Barracks, Singapore, with Tony 'at attention', probably the Battalion Orderly Officer of the Day.

REGIMENT'S FAREWELL

WITH MEN OF THE MIDDLESEX REGIMENT lining the railings the Blue Funnel vessel Menelaus left Singapore for Hong Kong shortly before 5 p.m. yesterday.

I found the ultimate paradise in Bali. Beauty was everywhere, in the hills, the tropical luxuriance, the flowers, the sandy beaches and, of course, the gorgeous people. I overstayed my time, missed my ship at Surabaja and wired for an extension of leave to avoid being accused of being absent without leave. I sailed by way of Balikpapan in Borneo and, weaving through the creaking junks, I was back in Hong Kong where my intelligence report earned a few dollars to help with expenses. The journey had been a refreshing interlude from regimental soldiering.

My report was not favourably received by Major General Grasett, GOC China Command, because of remarks about the Americans in the Philippines. I wrote that when independence of the Philippines was declared in 1898 the Filipinos became the first Asians to discard European colonialism for American imperialism.

I was having a dig at America for its constant criticism against the British Empire, particularly whenever a riot occurred in India. Most riots were communal and seldom against the Raj. India was a country where riots were the normal order of the day, as they still are now. I described the harsh occupation of the Philippines by the USA after independence, how in three years of a war supposedly against guerillas. One million Filipinos were killed of whom only 16 000 were actually guerillas. The hypocrisy of the Americans incensed me.

The General explained that if war with Germany broke out British forces would be contained in Europe. No reinforcement could be sent to the Far East should Japan declare war as bound by its Pact with Germany. The only relief Hong Kong and Malaya could expect would be from the USA, if it entered the war. It was important therefore that British officers did not make derogatory remarks about America.

The General's opinion made me realise that not only would we be caught like rats in a trap if Japan attacked, but that we were also just expendable forces. A sickening thought.

The European situation now deteriorated rapidly and it seemed Germany was rushing to start a war by the European autumn, before winter reduced operations. On 24 August 1939 a Nazi-Soviet Pact was signed and the next day Britain signed a mutual assistance treaty with Poland. On 1 September Germany invaded Poland.

With Japanese forces surrounding Hong Kong, I believed Japan would attack the Colony as soon as a war began against Britain, but general opinion was that if there was a possibility the USA would also be involved, Japan would not fight Britain and the United States simultaneously. In Hong Kong non-European residents were unconcerned about world events; their attitude was of indifferent apathy, even with the Japanese encamped on the border. Attitudes of many European residents were not dissimilar.

In the early morning officers were gathered round the wireless set in the Mess listening to Neville Chamberlain's historic and mournful announcement made on 3 September 1939 that Britain was at war with Germany. Silently we dispersed, attempting to assess the horror that lay ahead. I walked over to the barrack room and talked with my soldiers, all equally disturbed with the news, especially the Great War veterans. In a typical Cockney way someone remarked, 'It won't be no bloody picnic!'

Later I went to Hong Kong island with Colonel Newnham. He had been a prisoner of war under the Germans in the Great War and he spoke about the horrors of war, the brutality, how it dehumanised men, destroyed civilisation. Unashamedly, he wept.

Newnham was captured by the Japanese when Hong Kong fell in 1941, brutally tortured for months in Stanley Gaol and executed. He was awarded the George Cross for his gallantry under those terrible conditions.

Elizabeth lived at the Royal Court on Observatory Hill. She became used to Martin's early morning departures in an army greatcoat over his pyjamas—in fact, she began to feel quite wicked, as if she was a mistress rather than a wife. Martin was always amazed by the respectful greeting he received from the sentry at the barrack gate, who no doubt admired his stamina. But that sort of life palled after a while, so that she was glad when Martin was sent to the New Territories in advance of the battalion to organize San Wai Camp for annual training.

Mr Humphries of the Chinese Maritime Customs, a friend of Elizabeth's father, offered to put Elizabeth up in his house. He was a delightful man whom Elizabeth loved, as she did the old grey-stone Chinese house close to the frontier with China and the beauty of the surrounding countryside of the New Territories. She collected dogs around her and walked daily for hours over the lovely rolling hills. Most pleasing of all was the fact that the Commanding Officer was not near to ensure that Martin lived in the Camp. They were together at last.

Days spent with Humphries were full of adventure, moving about the border regions, in and out of quaint Chinese villages and being welcomed by the villagers, except when smugglers were about. Once, stepping stealthily along a cobbled village street, they were fired upon. Elizabeth dived into the open door of a cottage and watched a fierce fire fight, madly wishing she had a gun; and was disappointed when the smugglers surrendered to the customs men. Another blessed day, Humphries arrested a Catholic nun. Elizabeth was shocked; surely the arrest was sacrilegious? But she was soon laughing when it was found that the 'she' was a 'he', a frail tiny man, loaded with opium.

The Battalion came to camp in January 1940, all eight hundred of them. Led by the Band and Drums, a splendid body of cheerful Londoners marched from Fanling station. They swung along to the martial music and, as they entered Camp, to the Regimental March, 'Sir Manly Power'. Elizabeth was there to welcome all her friends; and was now at last able to entertain them in the home that Humphries had made for her. The Hunters Arms also became a great gathering place for all the young officers, where Elizabeth joined them for meals—always nostalgic English food.

Most of all she enjoyed long walks across the lovely russet hills near her home; she loved being out alone at sunset, standing on a hilltop with the wind blowing across China from Mongolia, cold and dry, filling the air with clarity—and over her head, to the west, watching a single star rising, like a silver point in a sky of citrine topaz. She felt so fit and strong and well.

However, shortly after Chinese New Year in February, Elizabeth started to be sick continually and could not keep down any food. Dr Black, the family friend, said she was pregnant. She and Martin were ecstatic; they wanted the now embryonic 'Mark', as he was already called. And a child born in the Year of the Dragon was supposed to have magical qualities to stir the imagination, to be decisive, maybe overconfident, but ever fearless.

March came with marvellous news. Newnham was posted to the staff, and command of the battalion was taken by Monkey Stewart, an inspiring leader, a humane and charming man, who immediately wrote a note to Martin: 'There is no room for you in barracks. You will have to move out.'

Thus ended the long and ridiculous ordeal of their marriage not being officially recognised. They were now free to live in a flat; and on the return of the battalion to Kowloon in April, they found one in Boundary Street. At last they became accepted members of the Regiment.

After the fall of France in June 1940, the Japanese became increasingly aggressive and redistributed their forces in south China to make an invasion of Hong Kong easier. In addition, the 'National Peace and Regeneration Army' of Chinese traitors led by Wang Ching-wei, head of the Japanese-sponsored 'puppet' government based in Nanking, planned to attack Hong Kong.

The situation was highly critical. Defensive precautions were carried out such as placing charges under demolition sites, making the frontier railway bridge over the Sham Chun River impassable, and demolishing the bridges carrying the Canton Road. An Indian infantry battalion was deployed in the

New Territories. Its task was to delay an invading force for forty-eight hours while demolitions were completed in Kowloon, and then to join the rest of the garrison on the island of Hong Kong. It was decided to evacuate European and Indian women and children from the colony.

The Government's evacuation order hit Hong Kong with a bombshell effect. Although it was a wise decision in view of what was to happen just over a year later, the order met violent opposition by some civilians. The sequence of disasters in Europe, the Nazi occupation of Norway, Denmark, Holland, Belgium, France; the destruction of the French and British armies and, locally, the encirclement of the colony by the Japanese, still did not awake the people to the danger of this situation.

Nor were the inhabitants even awakened by the ominous action of the Japanese who, when the evacuation order was promulgated on 28 June 1940, announced condescendingly that Hong Kong Chinese would be allowed to return to China on 1 and 2 July, after which the border would be closed again. The obvious inference was that Japan would then attack the Colony.

The evacuation order was mandatory for the armed forces' wives and children; all obeyed it. Exemptions were granted to civilian women employed in medical or health services and essential appointments in government departments. However, some civilian women did not register, others found excuses to remain, a remarkable number suddenly became nursing sisters or invaluable stenographers in commercial offices. After the fall of Hong Kong the women and children who had remained served a sentence of 3¾ years in a Japanese concentration camp at Stanley on the south-west of Hong Kong island. Those who had ignored the evacuation order had only themselves to blame for the dreadful hardship they endured.

The situation became extremely dangerous. Colonel Stewart moved B and C Companies of the Battalion to barracks at Stanley so that they were close to their battle positions, manning machine gun pill boxes on the island. Martin and I, both promoted Captain, were the Company Commanders.

Knowing that the Indian infantry battalion in the New Territories was not expected to delay a Japanese advance into Kowloon for longer than forty-eight hours, Martin moved Elizabeth to Hong Kong island and intended to rent rooms for her near Stanley. Meanwhile, she stayed with the governor of the Prison, Major Willcocks, and his family in a fine house overlooking the vivid blue waters of Stanley Bay. Her first home in Boundary Street had not lasted long, three months in fact, but she did not mind; she was glad to be out of hot and dirty Kowloon and to be in the safer, fresh and pleasant surroundings at Stanley, even though it was always raining, as if a typhoon was approaching. It was exciting, too, to be close to the Middlesex soldiers preparing the defences. In her pregnant state she felt defenceless, but more protected now that she was near to Martin and his work. I saw her often as I rode a motor-bike round the twisting narrow roads, visiting the pill boxes where we were storing ammunition and erecting barbed wire entanglements on the beaches. Once she came to my company headquarters, a cluster of concrete shelters secluded in a ravine, and drank a tin mug of dixie tea.

The evacuation order shocked Elizabeth when it reached Major Willcocks in the evening of Friday 28 June. It said that the wives and families of the armed forces were to be evacuated on Monday 1 July. Civilian families were to go on Friday 5 July.

The thought of leaving Martin worried and upset Elizabeth. Where was she being sent, for how long, where—and this troubled her most—would 'Mark' be born, who would be her doctor? A grain of hope appeared briefly, when it was found that Elizabeth's name had not been recorded on the list of army wives. This was a result of Colonel Newnham's stupid edict not to recognise their marriage. However, Martin demanded that her name be inserted in the list and insisted that she would go, because of the critical state with Japan and because he did not want Elizabeth and 'Mark' to be in a place under siege or—if the worst happened—to be subject to rough treatment by Japanese soldiery. He was thinking of the atrocities at Nanking in December 1937, where 42 000 Chinese people were murdered in an orgy of rape and debauchery.

Saturday and Sunday were days of hectic rush and anguish. The banks were open on Saturday morning only, as were some shops. On various errands Martin and Elizabeth raced back and forth to the city, grinding over tortuous roads through Wong Nei Chong Gap and Repulse Bay, the small car breaking down at times. Ming, the white chow dog, had to be taken to the vet. It was only constipation, but she knew something was wrong with her human masters. It was heartbreaking for Elizabeth to leave her.

They packed and repacked the one trunk and suitcase, all the luggage allowed, time and again. Elizabeth took whatever was essential for herself and 'Mark'; everything else—wedding presents, furs, clothes, treasures, books—she left with Martin, scattered between Kowloon and Stanley; another heartbreak.

'Blast the bloody civilians,' Elizabeth kept saying. 'They've a week to get ready, we've only forty-eight hours. I hate them and the bloody civilian government, they're so unfair.'

The Middlesex Regiment families, who had been trailing along with the Battalion halfway round the world for nine years through different countries, were staunch in adversity, stoically accepting their fate, but this time they were furious at the short notice to evacuate and at the preference in time given to civilians.

'Another flaming move!' loudly exclaimed a Sergeant's wife in a delightful London accent. 'We followed the blasted drum from Palestine to Cairo, Moascar, Singapore and Hong Kong and we didn't mind, but this time we're being sent off on our own and we don't even know where we're bloody well going!'

That was the problem. Kitty Hedgecoe, wife of 'Robot', the second-in-command, tried to find out. She was told only that they were going to Manila; but what then? Where would they go? Singapore? The Regiment had sent the silver there, an impregnable fortress. Or Ceylon or India, perhaps Australia? Surely not Australia, fit only for convicts, kangaroos and sheep.

This uncertainty of the future worried Elizabeth. Wherever were they going? Luckily in Manila she had a friend, Betty Herridge, who cabled on Sunday, promising to meet her.

On Monday 1 July, 1 646 service families, with a few Americans and other persons, assembled at the YMCA in Kowloon with pathetic pieces of luggage and were transported by lighters to the *Empress of Japan* lying midstream. The ship, so ironically named for an evacuation from danger caused by Japan, had been stripped of all its interior peacetime fittings. These had been replaced by long trestle tables and benches. Cabins were converted to hold five times the usual number of persons. Even so, the numbers to be carried on this voyage were excessive, which resulted in the stewards going on strike, a shameful act in this emergency.

Martin accompanied Elizabeth on board, saw her into the tiny cabin she was to share with nine women and children, and ate bully beef sandwiches with her sitting at a rough wooden table. There was nothing to say, the pain was too deep. They just sat in misery, sharing it. At 3.30 p.m. husbands were ordered ashore. The ship sailed at 5 p.m.

I watched the ship fade in rain squalls into the stormy sea of an on-coming typhoon. Martin's face was white and drawn with grief. I took him to the Peninsula Hotel for a drink and dinner. I felt terribly sorry for him and sad that the battalion as one big family was finished; the families would not return.

The *Empress of Japan* steamed into Manila in a rain storm on the morning of Wednesday 3 July. It had crashed through a typhoon, throwing the women and children around in overcrowded cabins, causing sea-sickness, injuries and miscarriages; but the women combined unshrinkingly to help each other in their distress. Elizabeth was 4½ months pregnant, 'Mark' had just moved so her sickness had stopped and she was able to cope and help others in need.

Peacetime conditions in Manila contrasted strikingly with those in Hong Kong; there were no minefields in the harbour, no defensive preparations. Hitler's and Hirohito's aggression was ignored.

US Army men and wives came on board to welcome the refugees, offering generous hospitality, typically American. Elizabeth loved them for it. Betty Herridge, who had travelled with Elizabeth from England in the *Rajputana* and stayed with her in Hong Kong, took Elizabeth to her family home, a large house in beautiful gardens where she was received with kindness. She slept, recovered from the rough voyage, cabled Martin; but she wished to be with her friends, with the refugees who had been sent to Baguio, a hill station nearly 200 miles to the north.

Elizabeth rode by train into Luzon through a corridor of exotic vegetation, deep valleys and high mountains. The coolness was exhilarating. The US Army met her, tall genial young soldiers in boy-scout hats pinched in the crown, bemedalled tunics (although they had not been in a war), smart fawn breeches and long puttees with polished brown boots. They were so polite; the GIs called her 'Ma'm', but treated her as a social equal. She stayed in comfortable quarters in Camp John Hay, became used to American food, and was entertained in the officers' club; but she could not stay here for long and she worried about the future.

The Middlesex Regiment wives told her that they were to be sent to Australia. Elizabeth and two young friends, Nancy Hunt and Diana Forester, did not wish to go there; they did not know anyone on that vast continent; it seemed virtually the end of the world to them. They wanted to go to Singapore, which was not so far away from their husbands in Hong Kong, and if the situation with Japan improved, they might be able to return. However, there arose a major snag: for them, entry into Singapore was prohibited. Passages to Singapore could not be booked with the shipping companies. They decided, nevertheless, to 'have a go', and book tickets to a port in India on a ship sailing via Singapore, where they daringly intended to jump ship. Impudently, the three intrepid girls boarded the President Line *President Adams* in Manila, bound for Singapore and India.

As the ship entered Keppel Harbour, Elizabeth was elated, thrilled to be back in Singapore, where she hoped 'Mark' would be born, where she had many friends.

But would she be permitted to stay in Singapore? Would she even be allowed to step ashore?

9

Lion Island

Noel

A group of young women and children hung over the ship's rails, waiting in trepidation for the Singapore Customs men to come aboard. Their passports classified them as 'Refugees', which was stamped in bold print across a page. The refugees were Nancy Hunt, with Susie (5), John (3) and their English nanny; Diana Forester and Giles (2); and Elizabeth plus 'Mark'.

Innocently, they delivered passports and tickets to a Customs man who gazed solemnly at the documents, rather as if he felt sad for the plight of this pathetic cluster of refugees.

'You are going on to India, aren't you?'

'Yes,' they all lied, trying hard to look truthful.

'That's OK, then; have a good trip,' he said, returning the passports and tickets. He then left the ship.

The wicked refugees watched in astonishment as he walked away, quivering a little from excitement. 'We've still got our passports, we can go ashore,' cried Nancy. 'Come on, Liz, let's ring our friends.'

Frantic calls were made from the ship's telephone and soon officers from the Royal Artillery at Nee Soon collected Nancy and Diana, the children and nanny; and Colonel William Graham of the Gordons drove Elizabeth away to his house at Changi.

Jumping ship was easy.

After a month or so had passed, Headquarters, Malaya Command at Fort Canning discovered to its horror that three wives of British army officers had entered Singapore illicitly. They were illegal immigrants. The Headquarters ordered them to leave Malaya at once.

Elizabeth, now living in a boarding house, said her pregnancy was too advanced for sea travel, which excuse her sympathetic doctor, Jack English, supported. Nancy and Diana pleaded that they could not possibly leave Elizabeth, that it was essential to be near her and look after her, an extraordinary feeble reason that, surprisingly, was accepted without further question. So three cunning illegal immigrants remained on Lion Island.

Noel was now seconded to the Malay Regiment. He was a strong fine athlete, a keen soldier, but introverted, shy of women although his powerful handsome face made him attractive to them. He seldom joined mixed parties, seldom invited out a girl. However, Elizabeth had been in Singapore on her own for about six weeks and he felt he was bound to ask her out.

In England, the Battle of Britain raged in deadly ferocity. The morning wireless news worried Elizabeth. She prayed for her brother Dennis, racing his Hurricane into torturous battle skies, and for the RAF pilots fighting so valiantly for Britain. She hoped that when the sun reached England on this day, 15 September 1940, a decisive blow would be struck for Britain. All that day she thought about the battle.

In the evening Noel rang. Elizabeth was delighted. She had thought he never would, and hoped he would ask her to go out. But Noel was shy, apologised for not ringing before, and then talked about the great air battle.

It's marvellous news, Liz. They say there's been a great victory.' He continued to elaborate on the news. Liz saw her chance.

'How wonderful, Noel, let's celebrate the victory.'

Noel took her to a movie, but Elizabeth's big tummy embarrassed him. Tickets were half price for service families, and Noel ordered:

'One for me and one for army wife,' then, looking at her size, qualified his order, 'Not my wife!'

Elizabeth was still laughing when they had dinner at Cyranos in Orchard Road, celebrating the victory with wine imported from Free France.

'Mark's' approaching arrival into this tempestuous world brought Martin on leave from Hong Kong. Elizabeth with her amah was admitted by Doctor Jack English into the Singapore General Hospital and Mark was born at 3.25 a.m. on her 22nd birthday on 28 October. He had dark brown hair, blue eyes, weighed 8lb. 6oz. and was 22 inches long.

After leaving hospital, the proud young mother, her baby and the amah stayed in a large army bungalow at Alexandra. Martin returned to Hong Kong on 7 November.

Elizabeth missed Martin. He was so far away in Hong Kong. There were no telephones to connect them and communication was limited to letters which took a whole week, or cables. An immense tyrannical distance separated them. Mark compensated for her solitude. An adorable and good baby, he was cared for by a wonderful amah, a gentle little Chinese lady dressed always in immaculate white cotton jacket and loose black trousers. She was devoted to Mark; he might have been her own child. She never took a day off.

There were many family friends in Singapore, those whom Elizabeth had met with her parents, senior people like Sir Shenton and Lady Thomas (attended by Roly Gwyn from the Middlesex Regiment, the Governor's ADC), Sir Alexander and Lady Small, then Colonial Secretary, other colonial civil servants and *tuan besars* of the business world. However, her personal friends came from civilian and service couples, with whom she stayed like a roving gypsy, until she settled in a rented house shared with Rosemary Eustace, a Royal Marine's wife, at Pasir Panjang Hill.

Quickly regaining a slim attractive figure, Elizabeth renewed her zest for living and sprightly character, feeling strong and well, thriving on the tropical climate. She played tennis, swam and sailed, and joined a team of men and women to play football to raise money for the war effort. The match was played at the start of the Year of the Snake, a sinister reptile which witnessed stupendous events: Germany's invasion of Russia, America's entry into the war, Japan's conquest of Hong Kong and Singapore. Fortunately the young women in the picture could not foresee the horror that the Year of the Snake would bring upon them.

Normal peacetime conditions of life prevailed in Singapore; there was no rationing and no lack of anything. Food and drink were plentiful, the restaurants and hotels were probably the best in the British Empire at that time. The only scarcity was women on their own on an island full of young men, so Elizabeth was asked out constantly to parties, picnics, meals in restaurants; so much so that she seemed to be almost living in Raffles.

Noel, a lonely man, invited her out to concerts, the theatre and to meals whenever he came south from Port Dickson, the Malay Regiment's Depot. Elizabeth's merry personality dissolved his shyness; he even became quite possessive, telling her, for instance, not to play Rasket Football:

'You'll make an awful fool of yourself.'

In this blessed atmosphere, this Indian summer of pilfered time, war-torn England seemed so far away. Although people in Malaya were concerned about England and the war, there was little they could do about it—some hated missing the fighting, others were glad to be safe where they were. Elizabeth's family advised her not to return to danger with her small baby; moreover, England did not want more people to feed. So she stayed on, enjoying herself.

In February 1941, aboard the *Queen Mary*, the 8th Australian Division arrived to swell the ranks of lonely men. Formed up on the dock, a grand welcome awaited the Division as the enormous ship berthed: Air Chief Marshal Brooke Popham, Lieutenant General Percival, colonial servants, admirals, generals, air marshals, senior officers, lowly soldiers, the public—and military bands.

Swarms of bronzed diggers hung over the rails, waving and shouting; some heated pennies in coals and threw the red hot missiles from the top decks at the crowd below. Sheer pandemonium followed; stricken bodies dived for cover, topees and hats flew in all directions, coins shattered drum skins of the Loyal Regiment Band, amicably playing 'Waltzing Matilda'. Cries of anger broke from the crowd of waiting 'poms', damning the 'colonials' for their crude convict behaviour.

Elizabeth thought it was all very funny—she was not hit by a flying penny. But she was amazed at the fights that took place in the town between diggers and tommies. Streets were littered with crumpled slouch hats, bonnets, glengarries, topees, caps, web belts, torn clothing—and kilts. The Argyll and Sutherland Highlanders, some of whom were well versed in street fighting in Glasgow, joined their normal rivals the Gordon Highlanders and, combined with the Loyal Regiment and the Manchester Regiment, defied the rampageous Australians. The fights were evenly balanced but the Aussies excelled as vandals, painting every statue; poor Sir Stamford Raffles became a raging red demon.

The Australians were young, happy, friendly and exuberant; every man had volunteered to serve. There were no conscripts in the 8th Division; they wanted to fight and not sit around doing peacetime chores. They came from an egalitarian society, from all walks of life; some were sons of graziers, some had been educated in private schools, some were university graduates. They were used to entering any club, restaurant or hotel, irrespective of rank. In Singapore it infuriated them that some clubs, restaurants and hotels like Raffles were open only to officers. Soon the Aussies moved to Malacca, but encountered the same restrictions whenever they came to Singapore on leave.

Mark, now 5½ months, dressed in his father's christening dress, was baptised by an army padre in the lovely old Tanglin Garrison Church on Easter Sunday, 13 April 1941. In happy surroundings of beautiful Easter floral decorations Mark was very good, highly interested in the ceremony. He chuckled gleefully when cold water wetted his tiny head and kept a watchful eye on amah who stood close to the font. Blanco, seconded from the Middlesex to the Malay Regiment, his American wife Lillian, and Noel were proxy godparents.

For some months before Mark's christening Elizabeth had seen Noel frequently. He became possessive and hated her going to parties with other men, innocent parties with friends she had known for years. Elizabeth feared he had fallen in love with her.

In March he sent her a crazy letter, written hastily in Kluang Post Office on rough paper with an obsolete post office pen that dropped blobs of ink liberally over the paper so that the letter was indecipherable; but the message it held was that he loved her.

Elizabeth had known Noel ever since she had first arrived in Singapore in 1936, had seen him often at parties, rugger matches, ceremonial parades. They shared a common background over these years. She found him attractive and could easily fall in love with him if she stayed much longer in Malaya; but her parents did not wish her to go to England and women were not permitted to return to Hong Kong.

She was not sure how sincere Noel was for she knew that even at twenty-six he had never been in love before, had lived a lonely celibate existence, lacking affection. In her he had suddenly found how wonderful it was to have someone to fill his solitude, someone to offer affection. In that letter from Kluang he quoted:

> In your unhappiness you stretched out your hand
> And in my loneliness I took it

That described their growing relationship.

As a typist, Elizabeth worked in the headquarters at Fort Canning. A long-suffering RASC chief clerk readily accepted her terrible typing for the pleasure she brought into an otherwise dreary office. Her laughter rang through the solid building, inducing more errors in the typing pool; she was gregarious, made friends instantly with everyone, irrespective of rank or position; she vibrated with happiness—she was so obviously in love.

Noel was now living in Singapore at Normanton Camp with the Malay Regiment, which had been absorbed into the island's garrison, so Elizabeth saw him every evening. Their friendship had grown gradually but now Noel was insanely in love with her and Elizabeth found she loved him too, this tough, rugged handsome man, like his picture in khaki uniform.

Their love was a very splendid thing, a beautiful love of young people physically attracted to each other. It brought immense joy. They walked on air, no heaven exceeded their world of love, their happiness was supreme.

At times Elizabeth felt she was utterly enveloped in a whirlwind of Noel's intense passionate love and an overwhelming madness which prevented her from thinking clearly. She could not understand why she had fallen in love with Noel; perhaps destiny had ordained it to happen. She believed that if she could leave Singapore she would be able to think freely and assess her position in life.

So she wrote to Martin telling him truthfully what had happened, for she was not ashamed; her love with Noel was too beautiful to be shameful. Theirs was an open love, everyone in Singapore acknowledged it and most smiled benignly on the lovers. She hoped so terribly that Martin would understand and not be hurt. She implored him to obtain a special clearance for her to return to Hong Kong so that they could resolve the matter between themselves.

Within a few days Elizabeth wrote again, a happier letter, hoping more than ever that Martin would try to understand. In return she received a letter in which Martin made no reference to her request to return to Hong Kong but said he had been unfaithful to her. It was a childish reply, a tit-for-tat response which sickened Elizabeth. She would not have believed it if she had not been told previously by Hong Kong people passing through Singapore that Martin was having a 'good time' with a blonde called Yvonne.

What disturbed Elizabeth more was that Martin confirmed there was no longer a love between them. As her father had insisted, she was too young and inexperienced when she was married and Martin was too immature, living too easy a life, dismissing too readily any obstacles. His failure to request Colonel Newnham's permission to marry had started the marriage off on the wrong foot. The forced evacuation from Hong Kong had cut short their limited time together. It was a sad fact to face, but Elizabeth now realised she had made a mistake by marrying too early in her life.

While Elizabeth was waiting for a visa for Hong Kong, the Vichy government submitted to Japanese demands to occupy Saigon, Camranh Bay and Cochin China which they subsequently took on 21 July 1941. Thus, Japan was provided with an enormous harbour and airfields from which it could mount an attack on Malaya. Vichy France thereby signed Malaya's death warrant—and initiated the demise of the British Empire.

The Japanese occupation of Indo-China caused a considerable 'flap' in Malaya. Elizabeth expected war with Japan at any moment; she did not relish the prospect of being taken prisoner by the Japanese in Hong Kong but a temporary visa was granted and even though Japan ordered general mobilisation on 11 August 1941, the next day she sailed away with Mark and Amah in the SS *Van Heutsz*.

She spent an enchanted and unforgettable evening with Noel before she sailed. He gave her a gorgeous antique Malayan-silver bracelet, an age-old Malayan *kreis* and an exquisite silver powder bowl; they drank champagne and dined at the Tanglin Club, danced for long hours on the romantic dance floor at Raffles and returned to the happy atmosphere of the Tanglin Club to dance into the radiant dawn of that Sunday morning. It was a way to avoid the nightmare of the last few days and the awful parting about to happen.

Martin did not attempt to go aboard the anchored ship in the harbour, but waited at Blake's Pier for the forlorn little group of travellers to come ashore. It was a strained meeting; something had gone out of their relationship. They went to a flat in Argyle Street, where an airmail letter from Noel awaited Elizabeth, a love letter that ended:

> Come what may, in whatever guise and at whatever moment, I shall be eternally grateful to you for the happy times we had together, for the memory of your loveliness, for the privilege of being able to love you and for the most exquisite compliment of all—for having been loved at any rate a little in return.

I met Martin and Elizabeth dining at the Peninsula Hotel. Martin's dalliance with the woman named Yvonne was common knowledge in the Colony where gossip still flourished despite the evacuation of most European women; and I knew that Elizabeth was involved with Noel Gudgeon. My Commanding Officer, Lieutenant Colonel Monkey Stewart had been informed and in my appointment as Adjutant, his personal staff officer, I was entrusted with such matters. Noel had been a friend ever since we had entered Sandhurst together. I did not hesitate to ask about him. 'How is Noel, Liz?'

She was looking tired and sad but when I mentioned Noel she smiled and seemed much happier. 'He's fine, Tony, wonderful, speaks Malay fluently, likes his Malay soldiers. He's Adjutant of the Malay Regiment Depot at Port Dickson.'

'Is he? I'm the Adjutant here. It's great working for a CO like Monkey but I've been abroad for over six years now and I may be sent home. Noel has been abroad almost as long. Is there any talk of him being sent back?'

'I don't think so but he longs to go home to Westmorland and the fells. You wouldn't recognise Singapore now, Tony. It's full of troops. The Australians are super, huge bronzed diggers. They came like a breath of fresh air into stuffy old Singapore . . .' She went on talking about Singapore, Raffles, Tanglin. Clearly her thoughts were there—and with Noel.

Martin and Elizabeth were poles apart but they continued to go about together. At the sedate United Services Club where the Middlesex Regimental Band played sweet 'Palm Court' Sunday music, Martin introduced Yvonne to Elizabeth—a gauche act.

Shortly afterwards they separated. Martin lived in the Mess. Daily, Elizabeth received cables from Noel, imploring her to be strong, to return; and batches of passionate love letters, pouring out his heart, beseeching her to return. She would have gone at once but she had Mark's future to consider; she would never be parted from him, the dear little boy who had been so good during these satanic upheavals, and whom she loved beyond all else.

Colonel Monkey spoke to Elizabeth. An immensely human man, he was kind and sympathetic as she told him of her love for Noel and how her adolescent love for Martin had faded. He knew Martin's side of the drama and was sorry for him; he had little chance to establish his marriage, for between the end of Colonel Newnham's restrictions and the evacuation of families, they were together for only three months and had been apart for fourteen months. Martin was a fine young officer, a company commander; Monkey did not wish to see a divorce in the Regiment between brother officers.

'In wartime,' he said, 'marriages often break up. We live in an unreal world, faced with death, civilians and soldiers alike. Impetuous passionate affairs occur with people who would not dream of doing so in peace. Go straight home to England, Liz, let time settle the matter. Who knows who will be killed, who will survive?'

But her adoration for Noel was not a casual wartime affair, as Monkey implied; it was so strong that her prolonged stay in Hong Kong was driving Noel almost insane with anxiety. He became depressed, frantic with the thought that he might lose Elizabeth for ever. Forceful in character, he could be fanatically determined to achieve his desire, quite insensible to any advice. In long intimate letters and telegrams, some with as many as a hundred words, he begged her repeatedly to be 'strong', 'stand firm', 'forsake all'. The bombardment of letters and telegrams made it increasingly impossible to resist his demand to return to Singapore; and indirectly it gave Martin little chance to patch up the marriage, even if he wished to.

Nevertheless, Elizabeth proposed to accept Monkey's advice and go straight to England, but Noel said he could not wait for her until the end of the war if she went there. He seemed to have a fatalistic premonition that he would not survive the war which made him absolutely determined to be with Elizabeth as long as he possibly could. He sent her the passage money for a ship called *Kutsang* and became quite frenzied when she did not sail in it. When eventually Martin demanded a divorce and cut off Elizabeth and Mark from all financial support, Noel was overjoyed and sent more money for her to embark in the SS *Cremer* with Mark and Amah.

An exasperated Elizabeth sailed out of Hong Kong harbour with a long-suffering Amah and poor little Mark, a pawn in this terrible struggle. Sadly she watched her old family home on the Peak, where she had been so happy with John and at the Peak School, fade away into typhoon-clad clouds and, as on that day of the evacuation, she sailed again into a typhoon. This time she was glad to leave. The ridiculous conditions she lived in under Newnham's regime, the frightening evacuation, the degrading last months with Yvonne in the shadows, had destroyed any desire to see Hong Kong ever again. She hated the place—an indefensible pathetic little colony.

10

Malaya
Love and War

She had returned. She sat in the front seat with him, the patient amah and wide-eyed Mark in the back, as they sped through the island, across the causeway into Johore and onwards. Together once more, they were supremely happy; she was home again in this green wonderland, speeding beside enormous primeval forests, long straight lines of rubber trees, undulating rows of pineapples. Familiar place names were music to her: Ayer Hitam, Labis, Segamat—where they lunched with close friends, Paddy and Rikky O'Flynn, FMS Police—Gemas, Seremban and finally Port Dickson, at most of which Mark's little enamel potty had appeared.

Overlooking delightful beaches, their home was Harper's Bungalow, the property of a trading company, Harper Gilfillan, fully furnished and with a Malayan staff to look after them.

Gentle sea breezes flowed into the bungalow; the placid warmth helped to make them relaxed and happy. Mark, a year old on Elizabeth's twenty-third birthday, thrived in the salubrious climate, growing rapidly, destined to become a large man.

Just as they had never hidden their relationship, they lived quite openly in Harper's Bungalow. Noel told his Malay Regiment commanding officer and his parents in the Vicarage at Appleby that he would marry Elizabeth; and she told her parents in London. They joined in the life of the Regiment and were accepted, despite the conservative upbringing of the officers and their wives. Perhaps the war had mellowed them.

Elizabeth watched Noel playing rugger for Negri Sembilan against Selangor at Seremban, where five years previously Noel and I had played for the Army against a State team led by the ferocious Hugo Hughes, now a spectator with Elizabeth. After the match, Elizabeth and Noel dined and danced in the

Sungei Ujong Club; and when he played at Kuala Lumpur, they joined parties in the renowned 'Spotted Dog', the Selangor Club.

They lived on borrowed time and made every minute of it last as long as possible. Together they walked miles on enthralling sandy beaches, drank milk from coconuts to quench their thirst, climbed a long hill and steep steps to Cape Rachado Lighthouse, swam naked in the warm sea on enchanted moonlit nights. Theirs was a seraphic paradise of passion and love and beauty, a honeymoon in the twilight of civilisation when the lamps were about to go out all over the Pacific.

Noel and Elizabeth realised with great sadness that their idyll must come to an end. They decided for safety and their future that Elizabeth should return to England, as she had assured Monkey in Hong Kong. This paradise could not last for ever. The critical situation with Japan made most people aware, in spite of what has since been written about Malaya, that their time was limited in this lovely green land.

After a last wonderfully happy day with Noel, Elizabeth, Mark and Amah caught the night mail from Seremban to Singapore. George Wort, a Malay Regiment friend, met them and took them to the house at Pasir Panjang Hill. With George's help, Elizabeth set about looking for a ship, but before this could be arranged the war with Japan started. Singapore was bombed and landings were made in north Malaya. Hong Kong was attacked also— and at last America was in the war.

Elizabeth watched with horror the bombs falling, but they certainly settled her mind that she had to go, as Noel agreed in endless telephone calls. When he came on leave to say goodbye, they knew they were right in their decision, although the sadness of parting was awful, neither knowing what lay ahead for either of them. Elizabeth was anxious also about Martin now that Hong Kong was fighting a losing battle. Both the men she loved were engulfed in a terrifying war with a deadly and savage enemy who would show no mercy.

Finally, she sailed in a troopship, a terrible departure with distraught families around her, but glad that Noel was not there to break down her outward calm and composure. She had never felt so awful. She was leaving this beautiful shattered land and Noel—to what? Saying goodbye to Amah alone had reduced her to tears. Elizabeth's world was crumbling and falling apart. It was horrific.

At dusk the ship crept out of Singapore, from a wounded city enveloped in the smoke of burning buildings. Elizabeth recorded her last hours in Malayan waters:

> At 10.30 I went across to the side by Malaya to keep a last vigil with
> Noel. I saw Cape Rachado—our Lighthouse, our Light to each other

in the utter darkness of the future and Mount Ophir. For one hour I stood and watched Port Dickson go by. It was intensely sad to think of Noel there, of all the love we had and of the dreadfully empty and uncertain future. The worst part was that he didn't even know it was me going past. I felt queer to be so near and unknown. Goodnight and goodbye, Noel, my darling. Take care of yourself and God bless you. I love you.

Elizabeth and Mark sailed onwards from Noel and Malaya. At Durban the South Africans were wonderfully kind to the pathetic refugee passengers, giving them practical help with winter clothing. Letters and cables from Noel greeted Elizabeth. Although he seemed apprehensive, he was confident that all would come right in the end.

I try not to think of you slowly sailing further and further away from me, but darling, this is all part of what we have got to go through before we can be together again. I felt sure that you were sailing past our Cape Rachado and Port Dickson. I woke up in the middle of the night and felt you were very near to me. I am so glad though to have got you away. This country is no place to be in now and it would be a terrible source of worry to me if you were here. It'll be all right after a few defeats. The native population is very jittery but they trust us. Cookie is expert at the race to the air raid shelters, beaten by a head only by Mrs Cookie. The other day he took the washing line full in his chest—lucky for him it wasn't lower down!

Moving on to Port Elizabeth and Cape Town, a lovely city, she embarked in the *Arundel Castle*, on board which were 150 RAAF pilots, all Queenslanders, bound for England to fly Lancaster bombers. Splendid young men, happy and friendly, they took the refugee families under their wings, caring for the children, cheering distraught mothers, helping them to face the appalling news of defeats in the Far East. Regrettably, many of these brave young Australians were killed on active service in bombing raids over Europe.

A fast ship, the *Arundel Castle* travelled alone, unescorted, through seas infested with hostile submarines, zigzagging to avoid torpedoes. Elizabeth and Mark became used to not undressing at night and sleeping in jerseys and trousers, with a small bag packed ready to take with them to the lifeboats.

A moment of great drama occurred when a raft was sighted with a man on it waving frantically. The passengers expected the ship to stop—instead, the great liner turned in its own length and headed straight for the protection of the huge harbour at Freetown, West Africa. Destroyers of the Royal Navy temporarily escorted the ship through the cruel seas of this part of the Atlantic, littered with mournful evidence of sunken ships—chairs, tables, lifebuoys floating among the tragic debris. All passengers kept watch, warned that any ship sighted must be suspect. The discomfort and intense cold of watch keeping was accepted willingly, even as the liner passed the Azores, and sailed close to Iceland before entering harbour at Gourock, Scotland.

After years of living in luxurious tropical warmth, the frigid damp climate of England and its dreariness, a complete lack of sunshine and colour, depressed Elizabeth. Singapore had fallen, she felt her life had ended; moreover, her parents' welcome in London was as frigid as the weather—but waiting for her were letters from Noel. His letters came like drops of blood from an open wound which would never heal . . .

> You are my inspiration in everything, always I see your sweet little face before me, advising me, smiling at me, cheering me up, giving me the strength which is so necessary these days and which I need so much. I am a pretty stubborn and warlike creature, but it is a terrible thing that in this year of grace 1942 almost the whole world should be fighting—for what? Presumably what it is busy destroying—food, buildings, life and happiness. Human beings are despicable, they have kept you and me apart. I feel like a drug addict whose whole being is crying out for you, your gentleness and understanding. You brought me such utter happiness that I wonder whether you are a mere human being at all.

Soon after Elizabeth's arrival in England, Noel's sister wrote to her and Noel's mother travelled south to meet her. They were both kind to Elizabeth, understanding the strong love Noel had for her; and Elizabeth admired them for their brave behaviour.

Noel's letters in brown army envelopes bearing stamps showing the King's head on a green Malayan field, the last of such stamps ever issued, continued to arrive in batches, taking months on the long journey, but many were lost in the mail. Elizabeth had written and cabled him from South Africa; he did not receive them, but nonetheless, he wrote almost every day, his way of talking to her, the only means of easing his pain. These letters he wrote while he was being bombed, from railway trucks, road ditches, in the jungle, from slit trenches under shell fire. In this one the fighting had reached his—and Elizabeth's—beloved Port Dickson:

> This is now a defended area and we are expecting a Jap landing any moment. The gunners are shooting at a junk out at sea, a great spectacle. Cookie has disappeared. I have volunteered for a special

job in the jungles. Evacuees are streaming south on all roads. All families have gone from here [the wives and children of Malay soldiers were evacuated to a Malay Astana in Singapore]. We left PD and reached Seremban to get the third last train, so we only just got out of PD in time. It took 25 hours to reach Gemas. It was all rather different to the last time I went by rail, when you met me that morning in Singapore. I was so proud to see you, my darling, standing there on the platform, so tall, slim and wonderful looking, just as I had always hoped I would find a girl waiting for me one day.

The mail train ahead was bombed, a direct hit, a nasty mess, 20 people were killed. The main road immediately behind us was machine gunned. At the time we were stuck in a station with a broken down engine. I got a spare engine, but ran short of coal, found a bomb-damaged coaling plant, coaled the engine with ten of my soldiers—shovelled for all I was worth. The train drivers came from the East Surreys, Leicesters and Australians.

From Singapore his letters begin to show despondency, the futility of the struggle:

Here we have had several raids but little damage. A bomb dropped in front of your house at Pasir Panjang. The fact that angers me most is that the Japs are now in places which I hold sacred to you and us: the Station Hotel at KL is a ruin, so is the Majestic, so is the 'Dog' and OUR Harper's bungalow is probably occupied and most of those places up country where a short time ago we were together and so happy have passed out of our hands.

Our war is going just about as badly as it could. We need a real fighting general to tell the Japs to stuff themselves. In another few days we will be a beleaguered island. The news is bad and will be worse in a few days. We are in for a grim time for the next month or two, but feel it's all 'Allah punya suka.' I am frightened in air raids, frightened of being under fire and of dying, but confident I do my little bit quite as well as anyone else. People who don't feel frightened have something wrong with them. Normal healthy people know fear but it is a question of being able to control it and I can do that. When I think of the happiness we have known together everything fades into the background—the horrors, the misery of war, the suffering, the cruelty and the injustice—one thing remains: our love for each other. I can never thank you enough, my heart's darling, for all you have been to me, done to me, and mean to me.

Darling, write to me, tell me about England, the green fields, oak trees and the cold dank smell of winter. I long to see it all again. One view I especially want to see is Crossfell and the Pennines from the top of Whinfell. I don't think you would understand that, but there is something about the fells in Cumberland and Westmorland which absolutely gets me. I suppose I am horribly homesick for home and you really.

Elizabeth received one more letter from Noel, written during the fighting at Pasir Panjang. He seemed to know the end was close; the letter is typical of a man's feeling in the climax of battle:

By the time you get this letter, darling, both of us will know a good deal more about what is happening out here than we do now. Life is very disturbed. The one remaining prop left to me, my darling, is you. It is hardly a time for writing long letters even if there is so much I want to say to you and it is a time of strain and tension however much of an optimist one is.

I have been in some very close air raids. I had a curious feeling when I realised I was face to face with death. First I prayed exceedingly hard that the little blighters would go away. I was bloody frightened. I think, darling, that if I hadn't met you, life would be of small account and I wouldn't mind very much whether I caught a packet now or later. But now that I have so much to live for, I don't want to die and I feel confident that I won't. Fate has been very good to us and I don't think it will fail us now.

It takes time to get adapted to the fact that we are besieged and being attacked and that I may be dead tomorrow. I look back on my life and ask myself the big question: Have I made anything of my life and am I ready to die? I think I can answer both these by saying that having won your love and trust and having known you I have done something and that if I am called on to die I am ready. Sorry to be so morbid, but I am very short of sleep. I do so depend on your love and long for your letters. In any difficult times that lie ahead your memory and what has been between us acts as a beacon to me. I will never let you down and I will try and be worthy of you and our families in what lies ahead. My love for you grows ever more strong as we go through these tribulations before we meet again. I think of your loveliness, wanting you, your tenderness, longing to experience your gentleness and looking back on what has been between us. Thank you for your love. I love you. It's all in the hands of God: 'Allah punya suka.'

On Saturday morning, 31 January 1942, with a brave display of glamour, the Commanding Officer and pipers of the Argyll and Sutherland Highlanders, the last men of a defeated army, crossed the causeway between Johore and Singapore. The causeway was then breached. Singapore island became a beleaguered citadel with a splendid moat to defend it. The green wonderland of the Malay peninsula and the gentle, dignified Malays, cherished by Elizabeth and Noel, were abandoned to the brutal domination of bloodthirsty Japanese martial hordes, bestial inhuman creatures that recognised no civilised codes of war.

During the final battle Noel fought in the southern sector of the naked island with his beloved soldiers of the Malay Regiment, trying desperately to hold the Pasir Panjang ridge with a heroic and stubborn defence. In the last days of fighting, Noel was defending the battalion headquarters when mortar bombs blew off an arm of his friend George Wort and severed a leg of his former rugby opponent Hugo Hughes, but Noel was not wounded.

At the capitulation on Sunday 15 February 1942, Chinese New Year, the Year of the Horse, the British and Malay officers were imprisoned temporarily in Gillman Barracks—incongruously the same barracks that Noel and I had occupied when we first arrived in Singapore in April 1936. Poor Noel had completed a full circle. The Malay officers were taken away and executed by the Japanese because they refused to renounce their loyalty to the British, dauntlessly keeping faith with their Regimental motto, *'Ta at-Stia'* (Loyal and True).

With thousands of other prisoners-of-war, Noel marched along the long east coast road to Changi, to Selerang Barracks, the original home of the Gordon Highlanders, whom Noel and I had known so well in the blessed carefree days of peace. Like other prisoners Noel suffered from the effects of the prolonged bombardments and bombings, the shock of defeat and from a ghastly humiliation and depression. Many thousands of those who entered the gates of those barracks were destined to die from starvation and mistreatment.

Noel was now cut off completely from the outside world; he had no means of communicating with Elizabeth, no means of easing the perpetual pain of missing her by talking to her in his letters as he had ever since she had been evacuated from Singapore. The Japanese guards would not permit letters to be sent out of the camp or prisoners to receive letters. They introduced a card on which a prisoner was restricted to a few words only. Generally, these cards were not despatched, and letters or a similar type of card sent to prisoners were not delivered. This was one of the methods the Japanese used to deliberately hurt the prisoners and, of course their parents,

(5/56u) Wt. 44492. Dx564. 750M. Pds. 3. B. & S. Ltd. 51-6175.

NAVAL MESSAGE.

S. 1320b.

Revised December, 1935.

For use in Signal Department only

Originators Instructions: Degree of Priority, Intercept Group, etc.

Codress/Plaindress

No. of Groups:

TO:

FROM:

Write Across

System | P L Code or Cypher | Time of Receipt / Despatch | Operator | P.O.O.W. | Date

Changi P. of W. Camp.
18 July 1942

My Darling Little Elizabeth,

I won't waste time and paper writing about things which George can tell you about if he ever gets away; but I am writing th.. [illegible] that [I] may be repatriated one of these days [illegible] for [illegible] [illegible] to have raised us up a bit, don't it, but thank God something [illegible] prompted me to get you away from here when I did. [illegible]

I feel in a very difficult position now because I don't even know that you ever reached home (you may be at the bottom of the sea [illegible]), nor do I know what effect my [illegible] love letter home in which I said I was prepared to give them up for you if necessary caused, nor whether you really think and hope the same as you used to when you were here with me.

Certainly you and I have had plenty of time to think everything over and to decide whether we really do love each other or whether it was just a passing phase. Need I tell you, my darling, that I do love you more if possible than before and that I have not changed an atom in my determination to go through anything for you. I was lucky enough to be able to save two small snaps of you which I carry about in the [illegible] case you gave me and they are the only tangible objects I have to remind me of you, but on the other hand there are so many intangible ones and you are so real in my thoughts that to be quite frank I am rarely bother to look at your photos as they are not necessary to remind me what you look like.

You can't visualise, darling, what a state one gets into mentally in a prison camp especially after the ugly chapter which the Malayan campaign was and, in order to quieten my peace of mind in after years and to regain my self-respect I [illegible] to escape if I possibly can. I fear it may be some time before we meet again but our sufferings are no worse than those of countless others and I am prepared to put up with them if you are [illegible] for your sake.

Whatever I do I think only of your arms my darling, your love and your feelings and I look ahead to our reunion unmindful of what lies in between now and then. I wish I could do more for you [illegible] nor am I quite certain what is happening [illegible] for any I am normally paid

Noel's last letter to Elizabeth.

---

wives or sweethearts. Only one card was ever received from Noel, addressed to his parents, which was not received until July 1943.

CAPT HNC GUDGEON
20 JUNE 1942

DEAR ALL
I AM A PRISONER BUT WAS UNWOUNDED
LOVE TO YOU ALL. I THINK ABOUT YOU A LOT
PLEASE TELL ELIZABETH I AM WELL
AND THINKING OF HER

LOVE
NOEL

Noel was sent to Siam, to a 'holiday camp', lied the Japanese, and worked as a slave on the Burma railway. For months he bravely withstood the terrible ordeal of starvation, beatings, frightful treatment and the ravages of tropical diseases. During these awful months of constant pain and the excessive demands on physical endurance and suffering, Noel retained a silver cigarette case in which he kept two photographs of Elizabeth. She had given him the case. He loved the pictures of her, taken on a happy picnic in Johore. The case and photographs served as a lasting link with Elizabeth and gave him hope to try and survive the dreadful nightmare. Even when he was very ill, when he had sold every other possession for food, he still clung to the case. He could not release his bond with Elizabeth.

He died on 15 June 1943 at Takanon South, Kilometre 218 on the Siam-Burma railway, aged twenty-eight. His friends sold the case for food—and even in death Noel saved his mates. When they returned to England they gave his parents money for the case, together with his pen—the pen with which he had written his letters to Elizabeth.

One last letter written at Changi was handed to Elizabeth by George Wort. Noel thought that the severely wounded prisoners might be repatriated and gave this letter to George to take with him. The Japanese did not repatriate the wounded, so Elizabeth did not receive the letter until late 1945. Noel wrote the letter on a Naval Message form, overwriting the game of 'battleships' which prisoners had played on the second sheet, the only writing material he could find. Noel's letter is probably the only letter to come out of that terrible Japanese prison camp.

11

Hong Kong
Die-Hards

The Duty Officer woke me. It was 5.30 a.m., Monday 8 December 1941. 'Message from Fortress,' he said. 'We are at war with Japan.'

It was not unexpected, almost a relief in fact. For years Hong Kong had been surrounded by the Japanese Army and Navy. The 38th Imperial Japanese Army Division, with a supplement of artillery and tanks, had been waiting for months just north of the frontier over the Sham Chun River to attack the little Crown Colony. Battle-hardened, with four years of active service in China, its troops had been trained particularly for the assault on Hong Kong. I had watched their preparations and came to accept invasion as inevitable. But I was reminded of the words of one of my soldiers when war with Germany was declared: 'It won't be no bloody picnic.'

The Commanding Officer of the 1st Battalion The Middlesex Regiment, Lieutenant Colonel H.W.M. Stewart DSO OBE MC, who slept in the Hong Kong Club just across the Queen's Road from Murray Barracks, was not in the least surprised when I telephoned him. He simply said he would come straight over to the barracks.

I transmitted the ominous message to the Company Commanders who were deployed in battle positions in command shelters. Their men manned medium machine guns mounted in concrete pillboxes which were scattered round the shores of Hong Kong island, except for the eastern part of the north shore. They were all fully trained and ready to resist an amphibious landing.

From the verandah of the Battalion Orderly Room Colonel Monkey Stewart and I watched the destroyers *Thanet* and *Scout* steam away.

'There goes our navy,' Monkey said. 'They are going to Singapore. We have only *Thracian*, a gunboat and MTBs left. Rather different from the days when the whole China Fleet was here.'

Suddenly, at 8.00 a.m., from out of the blue sky above the Kowloon Hills, thirty-six bombers escorted by fighters swooped down on Kai Tak airfield. Puffs of smoke from anti-aircraft shells followed but did not deter them. The airfield was damaged severely and all aircraft on it were destroyed.

'That's the end of those old Wildebeest torpedo-bombers and the Walrus amphibians,' Monkey declared. 'We'll have to face up to a lot of bombing. All the Japs have to do is to hop over from airfields near Canton or Formosa or from aircraft carriers. We have nothing to stop them. Anyway, Tony, it's time we moved to Leighton Hill.'

Leighton Hill was situated between Causeway Bay (home of the noonday gun), Wanchai (a flourishing red light district) and Happy Valley Racecourse (with stables packed with horses). The hill provided excellent views across the harbour to Kowloon and the mountains running eastward to Devil's Peak. On the island we could see the industrialised north-eastern foreshore, the rugged brown slopes of Mount Butler and Jardine's Lookout, Wong Nei Chong Valley and Gap, and the fir covered Mount Nicholson. I had selected the hill and its solidly built European houses for the battalion battle headquarters some two years ago, since when we had manned it on numerous training exercises. Only 800 yards from the waterfront, the hill was an obvious site for a command post. The Japanese must have thought so as well, for it was bombed as soon as we occupied it and later heavily shelled by artillery on the mainland.

As Adjutant of the battalion I set off with the RSM, Bob Challis, to visit the companies, requisitioning a brand-new Ford V-8 sedan for a luxurious drive round the island. We stopped with A Company in the south-west and at Major Marsh's C Company at Repulse Bay, where we were refreshed with San Miguel beer. Beaches covered by medium machine guns had been blocked with obstacles, barbed wire and mines weeks previously and ammunition, oil, petrol and food had been dumped in quantity near each Company. The Middlesex men, the Die-Hards, were well prepared, highly trained and, like most Londoners, cheerful and resourceful.

The Volunteers, excellent natural soldiers, well acquainted with the topography of the island, offered us ambrosial port at Captain 'Bots' Botelho's No 6 AA Company and hospital brandy at Lieutenant Colonel Lindsay Ride's Field Ambulance.

A manifest sense of bravado was apparent among the Volunteers and the Middlesex. The Japanese were 'a lesser breed without the Law'.

'We'll see off the little yellow bastards all right.' It was an astounding optimism in view of the victorious campaign waged by the Japanese Army in China since July 1937.

Next we met the newly arrived Winnipeg Grenadiers and the Royal Rifles of Canada. Both battalions were untrained, some men just recruits. They were bewildered by the mountainous ground, the twisting narrow roads and the winding footpaths. However, they were friendly and generous with Canadian Rye.

Captain Martin Weedon commanded B Company which covered the Stanley peninsula and beaches on either side. I stayed with him over a whisky. Now twenty-six, a handsome, robust man in the prime of life, Martin was determined to resist fiercely:

'We'll stand fast. The Nips won't get Stanley.'*

Finally, on the east coast, Captain West's D Company gave us a toast for the road to help us navigate the tortuous roads. When I reached Leighton Hill I ran gleefully up the path to the Command Post and reported to Colonel Monkey.

'Morale is very high, Colonel!'

'So are you!' retorted Monkey, not at all pleased. 'You had no right to requisition a car, no right to use so much petrol. We shall need every drop to withstand a long siege.'

The mention of a long siege sobered me. I was sure the Chinese National Army and the Allied Fleets would relieve us before long. Monkey had just heard that the American fleet at Pearl Harbour had been mauled severely. Later came the awesome news that the battleships *Prince of Wales* and *Repulse* had been sunk off the east coast of Malaya on 10 December. The Japanese navy now had complete control of the China Sea. There was no hope of relief from the sea.

On the mainland, the Japanese 38th Division crossed the Sham Chun River on a broad front and fought its way into the New Territories. One Company of the 2/14 Punjab Regiment, with armoured cars and demolition teams of the Volunteers, delayed the advance but by Tuesday evening the Japanese were facing the thinly held Gindrinker's Line.

A plan to defend the line which my Regiment had prepared so laboriously in early 1938 had been abandoned later. Over the years the weapon pits had fallen in, the barbed wire had rusted or been stolen by the Chinese and the concrete pillboxes and shelters with connecting tunnels had deteriorated.

However, when two Canadian battalions arrived to reinforce us in mid-November 1941, Major General C.M. Maltby MC, the recently joined GOC China Command, decided to man the line again. The 2nd Battalion The Royal Scots held the left or western end of the line, including the Shing

---

* The enemy did not capture the peninsula. B and D Companies held out until ordered to surrender.

Mun Redoubt, an important position which dominated our other defended localities. The 2/14 Punjabis were in the centre and the 5/7 Rajputs on the right.

Numerous gaps in the eleven-mile-long line were uncovered by fire. The ground was mountainous, broken with deep ravines and covered in scrub— ideal for an attacker. Air Chief Marshal Sir Robert Brooke-Popham, C-in-C Far East, considered that at least two divisions would be required to hold the line securely. Its defence was a hopeless task for three battalions. However General Maltby, underestimating completely the strength and ability of the Japanese forces, expected to hold the line permanently to protect Kai Tak airport and to launch offensive operations from the Gindrinker's Line.

The previous GOC, Major General Grasett, had said that an addition of two battalions would make Hong Kong strong enough to withstand an attack for a prolonged period. He handed over to Maltby on 20 July 1941. The failure of these General Officers to appreciate the situation accurately is appalling.

During the night of Tuesday/Wednesday, 9/10 December, the Japanese daringly penetrated barbed wire fences and attacked the Shing Mun Redoubt, held by an under-strength Royal Scots platoon which engaged the enemy in fierce close-quarter fighting for an hour until it was overwhelmed. Then at 7.30 a.m., from the dominating position of the Redoubt and under cover of an artillery barrage, the Japanese attacked Royal Scot companies holding the line towards Golden Hill. The staunch defence of the Jocks and a ferocious bayonet charge, led by Captain David Pinkerton, repulsed the attack. I can imagine David, a tough rugger player, charging in with the bayonet as he did into a scrum. Initially, many of us innocent of deadly battle fought it like a football game.

The position was untenable. General Maltby ordered a withdrawal to the island of all troops on the mainland. Second Lieutenant Jim Ford, who held the highest point of Golden Hill, was left, with only seven men remaining out of his platoon of twenty-six, to cover the withdrawal for one hour.

Later in the fighting on the island I met Jim, a recent Edinburgh University graduate, who said that that was the longest hour he had ever known, alone on an almost bare hill, protected from constant mortar fire only by slits scraped in the rocky ground and seeing his men killed one by one. The Royal Scots casualties in the mainland fighting were severe, including five officers killed, two of them company commanders. Although saddened by the loss of fine men, they retained their traditional Scottish resilience, courage and resolution.

The 5/7 Rajputs, the last battalion to leave the mainland, retired through Devil's Peak, fighting a rearguard action which inflicted several casualties on the Japanese. By Saturday morning, 13 December, the siege of the island of Hong Kong had begun: a beleaguered citadel cut off from the civilised world, standing entirely alone. At short range from the mainland, Japanese artillery bombarded the island's north shore, skilfully destroying concrete pillboxes, using secret British maps which had been stolen by spies and which showed every defensive position.

The bombardment, including aerial bombing, continued ceaselessly for the next thirteen days. Our artillery counter-bombarded, adding to the tumult. Middlesex machine gunners fired hundreds of thousands of rounds at any movement on the Kowloon side in the Star Ferry terminal, Tsim Sha Tsui Police station, YMCA and Peninsula Hotel using Mark 8Z ammunition which travelled further than ordinary .303 bullets. The machine gun fire increased the ear-shattering noise but strengthened morale. We were hitting back.

Leighton Hill was more heavily bombed and shelled than usual on the 16th. RSM Challis was wounded. Monkey ordered me to move the battle headquarters to Ventris Road alongside the racecourse. However, the racehorses, terrified by the bombardment, broke loose. An idiot reported that Japanese cavalry had landed. In the panic someone shot a horse, which caused a stampede. The commotion angered the Colonel so we moved back to Leighton Hill, much to my delight for I had stocked it with food and liquid to withstand a prolonged siege.

The bombardment kept on, day and night. On Thursday, 18 December 1941, it was even worse, a deafening roar filled with piercing screams of shells and crashing explosions. Most of it was directed at Leighton Hill and eastwards along the shore to Lye Mun. Lawns in front of the houses in which the headquarters was sited were pitted with shell holes, and house roofs and top floors were smashed to pieces.

In the evening, sheltering from the satanic blast in the sand-bagged Command Post, wearing greatcoats and steel helmets, I remembered it was Monkey's wedding anniversary so I opened the champagne, calling in the signal officer, the intelligence officer and Major 'Robot' Hedgecoe, the second-in-command.

A furious battle was raging outside; the thunder of shellfire was increased now by the clatter of rifle and machine gun fire. It was obvious that a landing was imminent. But for a few precious moments we were oblivious to the noise and strife—the delicious champagne smothered it. Monkey was happy, his usual charming self but, suddenly recalling the enormity of the task ahead, he recited dramatically King Henry's prayer before Agincourt:

> O God of battles! steel my soldiers' hearts;
> Possess them not with fear.

And finally he said, 'Don't open any more bottles, Tony. Keep them for Christmas.'

I did not see the bottles again. The Japanese drank them. That was the last relaxed moment we had together, the last time we were able to behave as normal people, a kind of Last Supper. From then onwards the ceaseless bombardment continued; we lived in a mad nightmare of attacks, counter-attacks and endless days of horror but, under Monkey's command, with hearts of steel.

Intermittent rain and black smoke from burning oil tanks darkened the night but shell bursts, tracer bullets and searchlights produced the effect of a fireworks display. The Japanese landed at San Wan, Taikoo and North Point on the front held by the 5/7 Rajputs. It was nonsensical that around the island every possible landing place was covered by pillboxes, wire and mines and manned by the Middlesex Regiment, armed with Vickers medium machine guns, except for this stretch on the north-east shore which was left unmanned until the Rajputs were withdrawn from the mainland. The Indians took several casualties fighting on the mainland, had little time to prepare defences and did not have Vickers guns. The Japanese had been on our frontier since October 1938. Surely it was obvious the invasion would come from the mainland, the traditional Japanese method of attack adopted at Port Arthur in 1905 and Tsingtao in 1914, and that the landing would be attempted on the north shore of the island, not by hazardous amphibious assaults on the southern beaches.

A signalman handed me a telephone. It was Colonel Newnham from Fortress Headquarters with a request that we assist the defenders at North Point. I ordered Z Company, which was holding defensive positions round Leighton Hill, to send a platoon. They shot off in a hurry in trucks and were shot up almost immediately by Japanese troops, which had just landed, but a few forced their way through to the Point and defended it bravely from there.

Colonel Monkey directed me to find out what was happening on our north flank, to make contact with the Royal Scots and to discover if Japanese had landed on Kellet Island. I grabbed a rifle and three men and wandered apprehensively through empty streets. The Chinese inhabitants, terrified by the bombardment, were hiding in the cellars or crammed into the few air-raid shelters. At a street junction a challenge rang out, a strong Scottish voice:

'Halt!' And after a pause, 'Who goes there?'

I was startled. 'Me, Tony Hewitt!' Another voice came out of the blackness. 'You bloody fool, you're meant to give the password!' It was Jim

Ford, the hero of Golden Hill. His reinforced platoon was holding this part of Wanchai.

I went on to Causeway Bay, near the noonday gun. There were no Japs on Kellet Island. As we crossed Hennessy Road, a shot was fired at us from a doorway. I crept up to the open door and slung in a grenade which was answered after the explosion by a burst from a sub-machine gun. We chucked in another grenade. There was no response. We would walk into a trap if we entered so I continued with the patrol. If they were Japanese they would have attacked us, so they must have been Wang Ching-wei followers, Chinese traitors of the National Peace and Regeneration Army led by Wang Ching-wei, head of the Japanese sponsored 'puppet' government based in Nanking. They were a 'Fifth Column' working behind our lines, carrying out sabotage and assisting the Japanese.

At Leighton Hill at about 3.00 a.m. I saw a Verey light from Mount Butler answered from Jardine's Lookout. 'Oh God,' I said to myself, 'Surely the Japs haven't got that far.' But they had, infiltrating halfway across the island on the first night of the landings.

The whole weight of the Japanese landings fell on the 5/7 Rajputs; their officers were killed and leaderless sepoys drifted onto Leighton Hill which, with Chinese Cemetery Ridge, formed a bastion that stopped a Japanese advance into the city.

Virtually in the front line, the Command Post was perpetual bedlam. Middlesex machine gunners just in front of the CP were firing long sustained bursts. Enemy bombs and shells exploded around us by the minute. Japanese were reported to be everywhere; messages poured in appealing for support. I answered three telephones at the same time. I informed the Colonel, relayed his orders, called for artillery supporting fire, sent situation reports to Fortress HQ, marked the operations map, wrote the war diary. It was a relief when a shell shot straight through the CP and burst in the next room, cutting the cables temporarily.

In the respite, I watched a company of the Royal Scots make an attempt to rescue West Brigade HQ at Wong Nei Chong Gap, advancing in spite of heavy enemy fire from Jardine's Lookout. The few who actually reached the Gap were killed. All the company officers were killed or wounded and out of the seventy-six who went into the attack, fifteen were left.

The slaughter continued. All over the eastern half of the island the defenders furiously resisted the invaders with abundant acts of supreme individual courage. Pillboxes, uselessly lining the southern shores, were quickly vacated by Middlesex men as they joined in the general fighting. However, Fortress HQ was in concrete shelters twenty feet underground. Control of the battle from there led to piecemeal attacks without concern for the location of the enemy or the arduous terrain, against which even superb heroism could not compete.

One afternoon on Friday 19th, a force of Punjabis at Leighton Hill was ordered to counter-attack, under an artillery barrage from eight field guns, to relieve remnants of the Rajputs holding out in Tai Hang village, in a valley about a thousand yards to the east. Our guns failed to open fire. There was no barrage or smoke screen. Heedlessly at 'H hour' at the sound of whistles blown by company commanders, the sepoys rose obediently from their slit trenches and advanced. Exposed nakedly to deadly machine gun and mortar fire, the gallant Indians were cut to pieces.

At the same time three companies of the Royal Scots were ordered to advance up the Wong Nei Chong Road and take Jardine's Lookout, the Gap and West Brigade HQ. Again, the expected artillery support did not occur. They began to suffer severe casualties until their Colonel delayed the attack till nightfall. In ferocious close-quarter fighting the Scots led by David Pinkerton took the Gap Police Station but were driven off before they could reachWest Brigade HQ, where the Brigade Commander, Lawson, a Canadian, was killed. Pinkerton was wounded and carried out by Jim Ford, whose elder brother Douglas* rallied the few survivors and established defensive positions at Mount Nicholson.

The Japanese now advanced to Repulse Bay, where a Middlesex platoon, under Second Lieutenant Peter Grounds, attacked some Japanese who were beating up captured Canadian soldiers outside the hotel garage, drove the enemy out and released the prisoners; but Peter was killed leading the charge. His gallantry was typical of many young Middlesex platoon commanders, most of whom were killed or wounded.

A Middlesex pillbox in Causeway Bay was partly demolished by shell fire. Japanese infantry crept into houses on both sides of the street. The pillbox commander, a young officer, requested permission to abandon the pillbox and fight back to the next position near Leighton Hill. Colonel Stewart ordered him to stay and fight to the last man and round. I listened on the telephone still connected with the pillbox, and heard our machine guns firing incessantly, followed by explosions, obviously enemy grenades thrown down ventilating channels. Then silence—all were dead. It horrified me: the awful loss of a brave officer, only twenty years old, and his courageous crew. Was it necessary?

The killing increased. The Japanese gained ground, drove half the garrison eastwards towards Stanley, encircled Leighton Hill in the west by the capture of Mount Nicholson and by a lodgement on Mount Cameron. Major Henry

---

* Douglas Ford was tortured and executed by the Japanese while a prisoner of war. He was awarded the George Cross for conspicuous gallantry.

Marsh's C Company resisted an enemy advance towards Aberdeen, assisted by a naval detachment and part of A Company, the remainder of which reinforced Z Company at Leighton Hill. Captain Martin Weedon's B Company and Captain West's D Company fought near Stanley under Brigadier Wallis, the East Brigade Commander. The entire Middlesex battalion was now in contact with the enemy.

The sheer weight and ferocity of the attacks showed that the enemy was determined to smash the Leighton Hill stronghold, which blockaded the direct route straight to Fortress Headquarters, only 1½ miles from the Hill. If they broke through, the Japanese General could capture in person the British General and the Governor, the Commander-in-Chief; a finish reminiscent of medieval battles often related in Japanese history. A glorious finale to the conflict for Japan was being thwarted by Colonel Stewart and the defenders of the Hill.

Leighton Hill, therefore, came under intensive artillery and mortar fire and dive-bombing. Colonel Monkey was determined that the hill would not fall. Even if it meant keeping the Command Post in the front line, he stayed on day after day, hoping his presence would preserve the resolve of Z Company, the heroic defenders. However, Wang Ching-wei followers and Japanese infantry had infiltrated behind the hill into Wanchai, killing ambulance crews, despatch riders and the local Chinese inhabitants. Some of the buried civilian telephone cables, which provided our communication, were cut. Casualty evacuation was impracticable. At last Monkey decided to withdraw the Command Post. He ordered Z Company Commander, Captain Christopher Man, to stay and fight it out to the last man and the last round.

The Battle Headquarters set off in groups, Monkey and Robot leading. Firing rifles and throwing grenades they fought their way through Japanese and Wang Ching-wei sniper bullets, grenades and light mortar bombs to set up the post at Dodwell's Garage in Hennessy Road, west of Mount Parish. I manned the CP on the Hill until I made communication with the garage.

I left the Hill with two riflemen, well equipped with grenades and ammunition. Terrified Chinese inhabitants were crowded into house cellars or air-raid shelters, a mass of trembling, helpless humanity. God knows what happened to them when the Japanese entered in strength. Already the streets were littered with dead Chinese bodies, mostly from aerial bombing. Stepping over grotesque shapes of dead people, we were forced at first to cross streets at right angles to our direction which made us easy targets. We jumped into houses to avoid snipers' bullets, forcing our way through to the next street. Twice houses were occupied by Wang Ching-wei people but by quick and dexterous chucking of grenades we escaped injury.

Later on the way we reached Wanchai Road, from the eastern end of which a small Japanese field gun was firing indiscriminately down the road. These wicked little guns were easily dragged about by the soldiers and their shells had often just missed me on the hill; I hated them. With our three rifles, we opened fire on the gunners, caught them by surprise and hit the whole crew.

After weeks of bombardment, especially the intensity of the last week, with no sleep at all, I had become battle-drunk, like a boxer punch-drunk. I was battle-happy; I did things automatically; I felt no pain; I did not eat; I did not care if I was killed or wounded. My two intrepid companions, long service regular soldiers, were battle-drunk also. Now all we wanted was to kill Japs and Ching-weis, as many as we could. We had a glorious fire fight all through the wretched slums of Wanchai, slaying our detestable enemies until we ran out of grenades and ammunition.

Victoriously, I found the garage. Monkey thought I had been killed and although relieved to see me his greeting in this tense situation was abrasive:

'Where the hell have you been?'

'Sir!' I replied, nothing more. Mortar bombs and shells were dropping around the position and, even though I was battle-happy, discipline prevented me from saying what I might have said:

'On a bloody picnic in Wanchai—with Susie Wong!'

And I had been on a picnic, a shooting one, a killing one and I had enjoyed every minute and felt great for it.

Although most of us were probably battle-drunk, Robot Hedgecoe, the second-in-command, a splendid, staunch and brave man, was undoubtedly the sanest. Quickly he organised the defence of the HQ, sited machine gun posts and fields of fire and placed the CP in an office where telephones were still operative. Aided by Ching-wei, the Japs soon bombarded the garage with bombs and shell fire, the explosions of which covered us with broken glass from a plate-glass roof above. Grimly we carried on, wearing thick greatcoats and steel helmets for protection. Dauntlessly ignoring the bombardment, the Governor, Sir Mark Young, arrived to read a message from Churchill. These words I have always remembered:

> There must be no thought of surrender . . . the enemy should be compelled to expend the utmost life and equipment . . . a prolonged resistance can win the lasting honour which we are sure will be your due.*

Mount Cameron, the 1,000 feet massif above Wanchai, which gave access into roads leading to the Peak and City, was seized by Japs. The Royal Scots

---

* Churchill, *2nd World War*, Volume III, p. 563.

fearlessly resisted the savage onrush and held the 'Thin Red Line' in keeping with the traditions of the First of Foot.

Hourly the situation grew worse. Z Company took an awful battering. Japs surrounded Leighton Hill and infiltrated into Wanchai streets. Casualties reduced the Company's strength to less than thirty, many of whom were wounded. It was pointless to defend the Hill longer. Colonel Stewart ordered Captain Chris Man to fight back through Wanchai. Meanwhile Battalion HQ, heavily harassed by fire from Japs and Ching-wei, moved to the Naval Dockyard.

Somehow we kept in contact by telephone with Brigadier Wallis at Stanley. The incompletely trained Royal Rifles of Canada had lost eighteen officers killed or wounded and the commanding officer was convinced that they could do no more. Accordingly, the Royal Rifles were withdrawn into Stanley Fort on the southernmost point of the island and remained out-of-battle for thirty-six hours. Composite companies under Middlesex and Volunteer officers were formed to hold the line in Stanley village. Captains Weedon and West fought valiantly with the depleted force but West was killed and Martin was wounded leading a counterattack.

All through Christmas Eve at the Naval Dockyard the terrible bombardment went on, smashing our ear drums, destroying our normal sensations. There was no respite, no rest, no sleep. We knew we could not last out forever but our spirit was strong, our morale high (but very dry!). Colonel Monkey Stewart was resolved to fight to the end.

The few Royal Scots officers who had survived so far were really battle-happy. They were joined willingly by every man who could stand up and fire a weapon, irrespective of wounds—Jocks, Cockneys, sailors, airmen, Tommies, sepoys, civilians—as they prepared for a final glorious, suicidal attack against the Japanese. 'We'll take as many of the yellow swine as we can with us, before they get us.' These Scots officers, angered by the brutal killing of their men, gave the Japs no mercy. They flung themselves into battle yet again, almost as if they wished to emulate Julian Grenfell's epic words:

> And he is dead who will not fight
> And who dies fighting has increase.

On Christmas afternoon I moved the HQ into Murray Barracks. Back into the Battalion Orderly Room, where Monkey and I had been at the start of the war, eighteen days previously. It seemed more like eighteen years in true measurement of time.

At 3.00 p.m. General Maltby telephoned and asked how long the defensive line in Wanchai could hold. Monkey replied:

'If the present intensity is continued, not more than an hour.'

At 3.23 p.m. Maltby ordered Monkey to go to the Japanese headquarters, stop the fighting and surrender. I heard every word of the conversation; it made me sick. Monkey, his face drawn and grey from exhaustion, went very white. He was the last person in the world who would ever have surrendered voluntarily. I collected a pole and attached a white bedsheet to it. Monkey would not let me go with him but took the white flag and walked silently through the barrack gates into the Queen's Road—and the stark satanic fury of the battle. I was sure he would be killed.

Hours later, the firing ceased. The silence was unreal, unnatural, frightening and eerie. Monkey returned, utterly exhausted. I fetched him a mug of tea. He did not speak for a long time; he had been humiliated by the Japanese, roughly treated, with jeers and abuse. Eventually he said:

'When the Japs come here, after we have laid down our arms and are defenceless, they will massacre us. You are very young and fit. There is no obligation for you to stay. Find a boat and get away.'

I searched the waterfront for a craft I could sail away—across the harbour to the New Territories or through Lyemun to Mirs Bay or south-west to Macau. The shelling and bombing had left no craft undamaged. I wanted to escape but I was not in the mood for it. I was suffering from extreme exhaustion, sleeplessness and shock from the bombardment; and I was beginning to feel the euphoria of having survived now that bullets, shells and bombs had stopped flying at me.

Into Murray Barrack, which had been looted by Chinese during the battle, crept the Middlesex survivors who had fought in the western half of the island. Many were angry that a surrender had been made: 'We had plenty of ammunition, we could have fought on,' they complained. 'We would rather have been killed than be prisoners of these bloody coolies.'

At Stanley, Brigadier Wallis at first refused to accept the surrender and only did so on receipt of a written authority signed by Colonel Stewart on behalf of General Maltby. Martin Weedon, who had distinguished himself in holding the line at Stanley, was evacuated to the British Military Hospital at Bowen Road. He was awarded the Military Cross for his gallantry.

Brigadier Wallis praised the Regiment. 'No praise can be too great for the fighting spirit, tactical control and fine discipline of the 1st Battalion The Middlesex Regiment . . . they held their positions in the Stanley area with great bravery. Great credit is due to Lieutenant Colonel Stewart for their achievements.'

On that forlorn Christmas night, the King's and Regimental Colours were buried in the grounds of Flagstaff House. These Colours, which had been presented by HRH The Prince of Wales, the Colonel-in-Chief, shortly before the Battalion embarked on its overseas tour in 1931, carried the Battle

Honours gained by the Regiment since its formation in 1757 in every campaign that the British Army had fought. With the Colours went a record of our regimental history, of the battles for which many thousands of brave men had laid down their lives.

The Regiment had fought with distinction everywhere on Hong Kong Island and maintained the tradition of the 57th of Foot, the Die-hards, at the Battle of Albuhera on 16 May 1811 in the Peninsular War. The words that Napier, the historian, used in praise of the fighting at Albuhera apply without any change to the Regiment at the Battle of Hong Kong in 1941:

> . . . and then was seen with what a strength and majesty the British soldier fights.

On the first day in captivity, Boxing Day, Friday 26 December 1941, Colonel Stewart commanded me to send a letter to all ranks of the Battalion. Here is the letter:

To All Ranks

I am directed by the Commanding Officer to inform you that he wishes all ranks to know how proud he is of your magnificent behaviour in the short period of hostilities which unfortunately ended in the surrender of the Crown Colony of Hong Kong. The garrison was up against a division and a half of the enemy. We had no Air Force and no Navy and, regrettable as it sounds, this was unavoidable.

The gallantry, devotion to duty, and the loyalty displayed by all under the most harassing and nerve racking conditions has not only earned the praise of H.E. The Governor and the General Officer Commanding, but the entire civilian population of Hong Kong, who now realise what this battalion has done. Individual acts of gallantry have been performed but the Commanding Officer finds it difficult to single out any particular soldier as one and all did their utmost to deserve his praise.

The 'sticking power' shown by all is traceable to the high standard of discipline which Colonel Stewart has insisted upon ever since he was honoured with the command of the 1st Battalion. He knows that all ranks, after due consideration, will realise this.

Lastly, while in captivity he looks to all ranks to uphold this fine tradition of unflinching obedience to all orders. The time will one day come when we shall reach what we most wish, namely, our homes wherever they may be. Time will hang heavy but patience must be exercised.

The Regiment has nothing to be ashamed of. Fortune has not shined on us just lately but remember that all things work together for the good.

His thanks are due to you all,

Hong Kong	A. G. Hewitt
28.12.1941	Capt & Adjt 1MX

POSTSCRIPT: The buried Colours were not found after the war and were probably eaten by ants. They were not discovered by the Japanese. New Colours were presented to a reformed 1st Battalion in Austria in 1953 They included 'HONG KONG' among the Battle Honours awarded for the Second World War. As the only officer on the Presentation Parade who fought at Hong Kong I received the new Regimental Colour and laid it on the Drums for consecration by the Chaplain. Those two words, 'Hong Kong', enshrined for perpetuity on the silk cloth of the Colour, established finally that we had won the Lasting Honour which was our due.

BATTLE FOR HONG KONG CASUALTIES

In Japanese prisoner of war camps the battle casualties were calculated and were submitted to the War Office in November 1945 in Major General Maltby's Despatch. The tables below show the approximate casualties.

A SUMMARY OF APPROXIMATE CASUALTIES.

Officers

Unit or Formation	Killed or Died of Wounds	Missing	Wounded	Total Strength
H.Q. China Command	2	2	3	33
H.Q. R.A.	-	1	-	6
8 Coast Regt. R.A.	-	-	3	19
12 Coast Regt. R.A.	1	1	1	16
5 A.A. Regt. R.A.	-	8	1	23
I Hong Kong Regt. H.K.S.R.A.	3	7	3	24
965 Def. Bty. R.A.	-	-	1	3
22 Field Coy. R.E.	-	1	-	7
40 Field Coy. R.E.	2	-	-	7
R.E. Services	-	1	1	18
2 Royal Scots	12	4	11	35
I Middlesex Regt.	10	2	4	36
Canadian Staff	2	4	3	14
Winnipeg Grenadiers	6	8	12	42
Royal Rifles of Canada	6	8	4	41

Continued overleaf

Unit or Formation	Killed or Died of Wounds	Missing	Wounded	Total Strength
5/7 Rajput Regt.	6	4	7	17
2/14 Punjab Regt.	3	-	5	15
Royal Corps of Signals	1	-	-	7
R.A.O.C.	3	2	1	15
R.A.S.C.	2	-	3	24
R.A.V.C.	-	-	-	2
R.A.M.C.	2	1	-	28
Royal Army Dental Corps	-	-	-	4
R.A.P.C.	-	-	-	5
Hong Kong Mule Corps	-	-	1	3
Indian Medical Services	-	1	-	5
H.K.V.D.C.	13	6	13	89
	74	61	77	538
Total battle casualties	212			39.5 per cent

British Other Ranks.

Unit or Formation	Killed or Died of Wounds	Missing	Wounded	Total Strength
8 Coast Regt. R.A.	19	2	23	285
12 Coast Regt. R.A.	15	2	24	200
5 A.A. Regt. R.A.	16	11	10	31
I Hong Kong Regt. H.K.S.R.A.	2	2	10	30
965 Def. Bty. R.A.	2	4	8	58
22 Field Coy. R.E.	8	20	9	213
40 Field Coy. R.E.	2	7	1	220
R.E. Services	2	5	1	51
2 Royal Scots	96	45	188	734
I Middlesex Regt.	94	25	110	728
Canadian Staff	6	10	5	78
Winnipeg Grenadiers	28	222	60	869
Royal Rifles of Canada	42	157	160	963
Royal Corps of Signals	16	5	11	177
R.A.O.C.	13	26	4	117
R.A.S.C.	23	10	11	183
R.A.V .C.	2	-	-	3
R.A.M.C.	13	3	3	146
Royal Army Dental Corps	-	-	-	6
R.A.P.C.	-	-	2	25
Military Provost Staff Corps	-	1	-	3
Corps of Military Police	-	-	-	1
Army Education Corps	-	-	-	8
H.K.V.D.C.	196	139	135	1 296
	595	696	778	6 645
Total battle casualties	2 069			31 per cent

Indian Other Ranks

Unit or Formation	Killed or Died of wounds	Missing	Wounded	Total Strength
8 Coast Regt. R.A.	-	1	4	233
12 Coast Regt. R.A.	3	-	3	187
5 A.A. Regt. R.A.	24	80	15	332
I Hong Kong Regt. H.K.S.R.A.	144	45	103	830
965 Def. Bty. R.A.	2	-	4	80
5/7 Rajput Regt.	150	109	186	875
2/14 Punjab Regt.	52	69	156	932
R.I.A.S.C.	-	-	1	13
Hong Kong Mule Corps	1	5	5	250
I.M.D. and I.H.C.	-	2	-	55
	376	311	477	3 893

| Total battle casualties | 1 164 | | 30 per cent |

NOTES .

1. All figures are approximate as accurate information can only be obtained when the Casualty Bureau has all facts and figures.
2. The wounded does not include lightly, or returned for duty, wounded. The total wounded shown is 1,332 but A.D.M.S. states that 2,000 wounded men passed through our hospitals alone, and many of the wounded of the 5/7 Rajput Regt. fell into Japanese hands Ind have not been recorded.

The final figures will probably be approximately:-

	Killed or Died of Wounds	Missing	Wounded
Imperial Officers	74	61	)
Imperial Other Ranks	595	696	)
Indian Other Ranks	376	311	)
	1 045	1 068	2 300

3. It has been impossible to collect any reliable data regarding the casualties suffered by the 450 locally enlisted Chinese.
4. Regarding Japanese casualties, a local paper reported a Memorial Service held at Kai Tak Aerodrome to 1 995 Japanese who fell in the attack on Hong Kong. That figure is certain to be an under rather than an over statement. A Japanese Medical Major told me early in January 1942, when I was appealing for assistance for my sick and wounded, that he had 9 000 wounded on his hands in Kowloon and on the Island.

Taking the wounded figure to be correct, and remembering that many must have been drowned on the assault on the Island, the averages of the last war should give about 3 000 and *not* 1 995 killed.

The Japanese admitted in broadcasts and in conversation to me that they had suffered severe casualties. True figures will never be known, but from the above a fair estimate of three thousand killed along with nine thousand wounded can be made. Many of the latter died of their wounds, for funeral pyres near their hospitals were observed regularly for some months.

12

China

Escape

Two pigeons flying high,
Chinese vessels sailing by,
Weeping willows hanging o'er,
Bridge with three men, if not four.

It became a mythical bridge to freedom, that willow pattern plate bridge. As a passage to China, the highway to liberty over the bridge was perilous; it could be travelled only by taking a one-way ticket to eternity. It was a sure route to decapitation but, rather than stay in a prison camp and die from beatings, starvation or disease, it was a risk worth taking. At least my spirit would torment my executioners.

Who were the three men, if not four, to tread that hump-backed bridge? I led, Douglas Scriven was next, Eddy Crossley third and Jim Ford could have been fourth, but he suffered from a battle wound and was unfit. The risk of death was too great to invite a person to escape, and the place of the fourth man was not filled until we came to a scene resembling a willow pattern plate—but that was very much later.

Shamshuipo prisoner-of-war camp was situated on reclaimed land about three miles from Kowloon. Square in shape, two sides faced Chinese slums, one side a typhoon anchorage and the other the sea. It was surrounded by barbed wire fence except at a slipway and a jetty called Bamboo Pier in the south-west corner. Sentries were posted on the land side; the seaward side was covered by machine guns firing on fixed lines.

Within the camp stood rows of wooden huts and along the sea wall there were two long rows of four-storeyed concrete apartments called Jubilee Buildings, into which the officer prisoners were herded. The buildings were close to Bamboo Pier. I shared a room with nine men, all dreaming of food.

The staple diet was rice, the only food we received. It was mere sweepings—broken grains, husk and gravel, yellow and smelling of sulphur and sheltering maggots and weevils. We hungered, craving for food.

I had lived in Shamshuipo camp for over four years and knew the country north of the camp in intimate detail. Just above, from west to east, stretched the Kowloon hills, sparsely covered in scrub and pine, but forbidding in stark ruggedness. Beyond the hills lay the pleasant terrain of the New Territories, of high mountains, terraced valleys, walled villages, pretty inlets and bays. Then the frontier with China, marked by the Sham Chun River, about twenty-five miles from Shamshuipo.

I knew my way across country through the New Territories to the Sham Chun River. Beyond the river lay a belt 100 or more miles wide of Japanese-occupied territory, about which I knew little. I supposed that provided I could keep walking I must eventually reach Free China. It would not be a picnic by any means, but if I hid from Japanese, robbers and bandits, I might get through. Anyway, it was a chance; provided I could break out of the prison camp.

I made plans with my companions. Douglas Scriven was a doctor in the Indian Medical Service, a small man who wore a monocle, often cynical but likeable. His assets were his resolve to escape and his fluency in Cantonese. Eddy Crossley, in the Royal New Zealand Air Force, was always ready to 'have a go' at anything. His asset for escape was his physical strength and determination.

I found an officer with an excellent map of the country north of the frontier and copied it onto tracing paper. Eddy found a Crown Lands and Surveys Office map of the New Territories and I turned up a school atlas of China, showing clearly the provinces, cities and large rivers. I pointed out to Eddy and Douglas the East River, up which we would have to go deep into China, and the provinces through which we would have to travel if we were to reach Chungking, the wartime capital on the Yangtze River: Kwangtung, Kiangsi, Hunan, Kwangsi, Kweichow, Szechwan. It was as exciting as wading through a travel brochure but the distances appalled us.

Eddy built up a store of bully beef, sardines and condensed milk, Douglas prepared a first-aid kit and I acquired a compass. Daily we trained, marching round the camp, trying to become as fit as possible for a long march. At night we watched the movements of the sentries and their behaviour.

It was an absorbing way of existing in a prison camp. I forgot the disgrace of defeat, the humiliation of being a prisoner and my hunger; even being told by the Japanese that by becoming a prisoner we had abdicated honour, virtue, dignity and the right to stay alive. The Japanese were absolutely unpredictable, a mixture of naivety, hysteria, and the sadism which led to fearful beatings of prisoners for no perceivable reason.

I decided to escape as soon as the moon was full, but as the moon grew in size I became remorseful at the prospect of leaving my battalion—it had been my family for almost seven years; I knew nearly every man. When I saw the remnants of the battalion on Muster Parade my heart went out to them; they stood so splendidly, proud and resolute, defiant of their jailors. They had fought magnificently in the battle, these courageous and valiant London warriors, these true Die-Hards. I hated leaving them. However, just after the surrender Colonel Monkey had suggested I should escape and instinctively I knew I must go. Now Monkey gave me his formal permission and said: 'There is one chance in a hundred of getting through but it will be marvellous if you do.'

Then General Maltby sent for me. He listened to my plans to escape, then handed me two letters for the British Embassy in Chungking and authorised the Command Paymaster to give me $800. It was a fantastic gift and one of the factors that saved our lives. We had money, food, a compass and maps and were bursting to go.

In the early hours of a cold, moonlit February night, in eerie silence, we sat hidden in the wet and smelly slipway at Bamboo Pier, waiting for a sampan to arrive. It was to bring food to a group of Volunteers sitting with us. The sentries from the north-west corner had been firing machine gun bursts along the barbed wire fence but now silence prevailed, broken only by the sound of the sea lapping against the pier.

Suddenly, there came another sound, a splash. Looking over the wall, I saw a small sampan, a man amidships, a coolie propelling it. The Volunteers pulled it in and grabbed the food. In a flash Douglas jumped in, planting $300 into the astonished man's hand. Eddy leapt in, I joined the mad rush; we were away.

I was tremendously excited to have broken out of that gruesome camp. It gave me an euphoric feeling of splendid carelessness. The Chinese man, terrified at having prisoners in his boat, shrieked and yelled and the coolie began shouting, demanding more money. Attracted by the loud voices, Japanese sentries immediately opened fire at us, forcing the coolie to grab the single oar, paddle like mad and race the sampan close to the anchorage breakwater, with cover from rifle and machine gun bullets.

Because we had been seen we would be followed relentlessly, but there was no time to worry for the sampan soon ran aground. Jumping ashore, I chased up the beach straight into a Chinese who yelled, 'Stop thief, stop thief!' The three of us dashed across a road, up a footpath and fir-lined tracks into the hills. Firing broke out behind us; a Japanese patrol was following, shooting into shadows, and we climbed much faster.

Dawn broke and caught us struggling over the crest of Golden Hill, 1 000 feet above the sea. Running fast downhill we hid in thick undergrowth near Smuggler's Ridge as a bugle from Shamshuipo called reveille. I wondered if I would ever hear a British bugle call again.

Not long afterwards a Japanese patrol of about fifteen men led by a warrant officer with a huge sword came slowly along a pathway close to us. Their appearance terrified us; we lay still, hardly daring to breathe. They passed on but then 'more bloody Nips', as Eddy called them, came past in charge of Chinese coolies and returned later. We were in a dangerous position but dared not move in daylight.

At night, before the moon rose, we set off, became lost in the difficult rugged terrain, and were forced to follow the Tai Po Road. I led the way along the verge, using shadows as cover until I climbed a spur. Only a few yards in front of me stood a Japanese sentry, the unsheathed bayonet on his rifle flashing in the moonlight. I stayed still, my heart beating wildly, until he turned away. Terrified, I crept quietly back to Eddy and Douglas.

'There's a Jap sentry over there,' I whispered hoarsely. 'Come this way.'

Quickly we scrambled through the undergrowth, Eddy and Douglas became entangled in a barbed wire fence, we waded the Shing Mun River, followed the course of a stream, climbed a large wooded hill and settled in a horse-shoe shaped Chinese grave.

In daylight I woke up with a shock.

'Christ,' I said, 'That's a Japanese bugle call!'

'It's a Japanese bugle call, all right,' confirmed Eddy, looking over the side of the grave, 'And there's a Jap army post below us.' We moved stealthily away but were seen by Chinese villagers. Three youths from the village demanded money to show us the way, to which we submitted quickly to get away from the Japanese post. They left us near Grassy Hill and soon afterwards a Chinese man caught up with us, saying that Japanese were following. We hid on a salient on the hillside in deep undergrowth. He said his name was Wong, that he was a communist guerrilla and would find a junk to sail us to Mirs Bay. It seemed a heaven-sent opportunity to get through the Japanese to freedom. Wong extracted $100 from us, came back again in the night and collected another $70 and a watch. We waited for him to return again.

About three o'clock on that damp and cold morning seven men rushed over the brow of a hill shouting in Cantonese that they were Japanese people and attacked us. Douglas hit one a crippling blow with his fist; Eddy, with a tremendous blow from a stick, smashed at another man wielding a huge chopper; while a third flew at me aiming an axe at my head. I dodged the axe, knocked him flat with a full right hook on his jaw and jumped on the fallen body, beating his brains out on a rock. It was all very familiar to me— it had happened before in a recurring nightmare in which I had fallen into a void and died. In this current fight some robbers rained chopper blows on my head and right hand but I continued to strangle the man on the ground, who let out a hoarse horrible scream before he died. Rolling over on my back, I drew up my knees and gave another attacker a shattering kick with both feet into his stomach, the force of which drove me backwards off the crest of the hill, so that I plunged head first down a steep cliff. I did not care, I was alive, I had defeated the nightmare, exorcised an evil spirit.

Meanwhile, Eddy beat the robbers away with fearful blows from his stick. With yells and shouts of abuse they picked up the body and ran off up the mountain. We had won the Battle of Grassy Hill, as Eddy called it. He had saved our lives.

We crept away and hid in bulrushes in a stream. Douglas cleaned my head wounds and made a splint for my right hand which had been nearly severed from the base of the thumb. All day we hid in damp bulrushes listening to people searching the undergrowth for us. In the evening we broke cover and immediately yelling Chinese men chased us downhill like wild animals.

Evading the hunters, racing over a humpbacked bridge spanning a river, we were suddenly stopped and invited into a Hakka village by children— heavenly little creatures like big dolls. We entered, unsure whether we were walking into a trap. The villagers were friendly, washed the blood off my face and hands, fed us with delicious Chinese food, laughed at Douglas' monocle. Finally the children took us out through a beautiful moon-shaped gateway, little ones poking fingers into our legs to find if we were real, braver ones holding our hands. A guide led us to a path to follow.

A patrol of sixty Japanese soldiers had searched the valleys for us during the day, the brave Hakka villagers told us. The gang that attacked us had captured some foreigners the previous day and dragged them for a reward to the Japanese who had beheaded them in Tai Po Market. When I met Jim Ford after the war, he said that three decapitated heads had been thrown into the camp by the guards. He rushed along to see, thinking, 'There goes old Tony—and there but for the grace of God I might have gone too!' The heads were those of three Canadian soldiers.

I listened to bugle calls and raucous shouts of Japanese soldiers nearby in Tai Po and tried to forget the beheadings by absorbing the great beauty of the moon rising over Tolo Harbour. The moon was my lamplight to freedom, I rejoiced in its resplendent power, the enormous beauty it brought with it.

That night, as I led the way, trekking over highlands, the magnificent scenery lay stretched out before me like a landscape painting—the gleaming waters of Tolo Harbour, vivid mountains, shaded obscure valleys. The beauty inspired me, but I tired of finding the crooked way, climbing hills and stumbling down them on rough pathways of rocks, stones and pebbles, wading streams and rivers, always searching the next few yards ahead for any sign of attack. It became an enervating struggle against nerves and vitality. I became careless, walked straight through a village instead of finding a way round it, and crossed a main road just before the headlights of a car swept round a corner.

I led my two trusting companions between two villages near Cloudy Hill. The villagers chased us; Eddy pushed me against a tree and turned to face a howling mob of peasants, as a stag turns to fight in the last extremity of the chase. He beat them back with fearful blows from a swinging pack until we were overwhelmed and dragged into the village, where Douglas shamed them for their lack of traditional hospitality to strangers. They let us go but followed to rob us. We fought back, using our army clasp knives, but they beat us with long poles, robbed us of most of our possessions and drove us away like pariah dogs.

We crawled into a haystack, sore, tired, hungry and cold. Douglas rebound my bandages. We were not desolate, we had survived the Battle of Cloudy Hill. The words of Paul came to me: 'And now abideth faith, hope, charity, these three; but the greatest of these is charity.' We had an abundance of faith, we had never abandoned hope, and we had charity, or love, in the comradeship that now existed between us.

In a dawn full of hope I led onwards through Birds Pass, and hid in a Chinese grave overlooking a main road frequented by Japanese trucks, and the Hunters Arms, now occupied by the Kempeitai, the secret police. I knew it all so well; Sun Wai camp, where I often lived; Kwan Tei racecourse, where I fell off a mule, and Laffans Plain, over which lay our route to freedom. The area was called Fanling, after the town nearby. Elizabeth had had a contented childhood here with her father, and a few happy months with Martin. I wondered if she was still in Singapore and how Noel was fighting with his gallant Malay soldiers. I had heard no news of Malaya since I was captured on Christmas Day.

Leaving the grave before dark, we attracted the attention of Japanese sentries supervising coolies repairing a road bridge. We stood terrified on the verge of the main road in full view as a truck with Japanese soldiers swept past, and we advanced into the plain without being shot! Someone was looking after us.

Through a starlit night we strode quickly over the Plain, sure that a patrol was chasing us or waiting for us on a road our side of the Sham Chun River. Creeping up to the track we stopped and listened, reached the river—much wider than I expected—and then as the tropical moon rose over the mountains in the east, we were over the river and in China. In a euphoric state we shook hands, 'We've bloody made it to China!'

As the moon set and the sun rose, I climbed to the crest of a hill to observe the way to go and descended to search for a place to hide in the scrub when four Chinese, armed with knives and bayonets, jumped on us and pushed us into a creek. One of them ran off, ominously towards Lo Wu, a Japanese army base.

Suddenly, a large Jamaican-Chinese man came from behind the robbers and surprised them. He asked what was happening, and said he knew Douglas and me. I remembered him; he owned a radio shop in Kowloon. He harangued the robbers, told us to be ready to run and then shouted, 'Now, follow me!' We raced away in a glorious cavalcade, leaving the astonished robbers standing.

His name was Percy Davis. He said he would hand us over to a band of brigands who would lead us through to the Chinese National Army. I did not relish the prospect of being handed over to brigands but the fugitive, the hunted man, suffers from a humiliation and despair that becomes all-devouring; anything was better than being hunted or chased again.

We came to a lake enclosed by green-clad mountains, encircled by willow trees. An old stone bridge spanned a river, beyond which stood an ancient pagoda, five storeys high. Willow trees hung over the slowly flowing river as if beckoning a sampan drifting idly on the waves. The scene reminded me of a willow pattern plate and the rhyme about it.

There was the bridge—and we were the three men—and now Percy was the fourth. The willow pattern bridge became a mythical hump-backed bridge, symbolic of our struggle, and which eventually must be crossed to discover freedom.

'Over there across the water,' Percy pointed, 'are seventeen brigands waiting for you. Captain Hewitt, lead the way over the old bridge.' I crossed and found the brigands to be friendly. They led us past the graceful old pagoda, guarding travellers from water devils, with a shrine for Kwun Yam, the Goddess of Mercy, to bless me on my way.

With the merry brigands as escort we sped in daylight over pleasant countryside normally unfrequented by Japanese occupying forces; and in the brief twilight and starlit night we ascended the Wu Tung mountains. Although we had been walking for days and nights with little sleep or food, the excitement carried us up 2 000 feet to the crest. In youth the limbs have a marvellous, supple resilience, with immense power of recovery from fatigue.

We halted under an old lychee tree close to a village where a wedding ceremony was taking place, filling the air with sounds of merriment, gongs beating, crackers exploding and with the fragrant smell of incense. The village patriarch appeared, a venerable old man, who praised us for escaping from a Japanese prison camp, predicting that it was our *fungshui* or destiny to reach freedom safely. It is not uncommon in China for old patriarchs to be prophets. The dear old man, practising the traditional custom of hospitality to travellers, then handed Douglas a roll of bank notes, $60.

Percy explained that the Japanese had built a line of block houses interspersed with pickets. The only way through them was by a steep ravine, seldom used. He said. 'The Japs will know that three escaped prisoners are in this country and they will be searching for you. We must get you through tonight, in the dark, before the moon rises; the longer you stay in this country the more likely you are to be caught.'

We understood also, that if we were taken these brave brigands, the wedding ceremony villagers, that delectable old man, all would be slaughtered.

We few, we happy few, descended the twisting crooked mountain track in pitch darkness with our band of brothers, raced jog-trotting over narrow paddy bunds and after five miles arrived at the ravine.

At first the scouts reported that the Japanese were at the summit but then discovered that they had just moved on, leaving a fire burning. Climbing an almost perpendicular pathless incline we scaled a cliff at the top, found a gap in the barbed wire fence, leaped over dying embers of the fire, slit trenches, more wire and we were through, all seventeen of us, just as the moon rose, racing along like a stampede of brumbies. We were through the Japanese lines!

We jogged on, all night. At dawn we were many miles north of the romantic little wedding village. They should be safe now. While we hid in bushes, the brigands brought food from a village—wicker baskets full of hot rice and vegetables. Our voices disturbed a crow pheasant, a cuckoo with dark brown plumage and light brown wings, which fluttered away into the wooded hillside.

At midday, still jogging, we came close to the railway, along which hundreds of refugees from Hong Kong struggled. Armed men stood at a bend. As soon as the brigands saw them they dashed into nearby sugar cane fields. Percy yelled at us to take cover and we jumped into a ditch just as the armed men opened fire with Mauser pistols and rifles. Soon they were on us, pointing rifles with fixed bayonets at us, marching us off with our hands raised. They were the Communist Red Army, they said. Percy demanded to see their officer, Comrade Lee, who surprised me by his unmilitary appearance. He was a scholar rather than a soldier. He knew Percy and welcomed us, saying he would take us to his base and eventually to Free China. We shook hands with Percy—little compensation for what he had done for us, but he understood how grateful we were. Just as he was leaving he gave Douglas some money, 'To help you find your *fungshui*,' and walked away, his huge frame sloping along, not in the rhythmic trot of the Chinese but in the supple stride of a West Indian.

At the Communist Camp, hidden in a labyrinth of small hills, valleys, defiles and gullies, a boy sentry dwarfed with a rifle and bayonet greeted us and a Malayan Chinese took us to a small hut. It seemed I had been marching forever, for days and nights on end with little food. Dead beat, we lay down on the straw and went out like a light.

In the morning, Chan, the Malayan, brought us rice, vegetables and fried ducks' eggs, which we ate ravenously. I thanked Chan in Malay and we became firm friends.

Comrade Lee asked us to help train his men. Douglas taught first aid and took care of all the sick and wounded. Eddy told them how to camouflage the camp. With the help of Chan I gave lessons on weapon handling and minor tactics and enjoyed meeting the boy and girl recruits and the seasoned guerrillas. They came from the peasantry, with a tough and hard background, able to accept extreme hardship. All had a deadly fanatical hatred for the Japanese. They enjoyed shouting communistic slogans and singing patriotic songs, and believed they were fighting for their homes, their land, their country.

Our onward journey was delayed until the Commander, Comrade Wong, returned from skirmishes with the Japanese. We were the guests of honour at a special dinner held to mark the return of Wong, a splendid soldier in smart uniform. Wong opened the dinner with a toast:

'To our dear international friends!'

Douglas replied: 'To the brave *yau kik toi!*'

The food was served, with knives and forks laid out for all to use. Wong and the others looked decidedly uncomfortable until Douglas asked if it was permitted to use chopsticks. With instant applause everyone grabbed chopsticks.

Wong proposed: 'To English people!'

I replied: 'To the Communistic people of China!'

After another speech Wong, now a little flushed, toasted: 'To the English King!'

Douglas answered at once: 'To Chairman Mao!'

Each toast was accompanied by a *kan-pei*, emptying a glass of rice wine. Comrade Lee explained to Eddy, 'You must drink in one gulp, otherwise you get headache.'

We had headaches all right as we set off the next day with Chan, the Malayan Chinese, and four guerrilla escorts. Chan now became the fourth man on the willow pattern bridge. In freezing weather we marched half the night and all next day and into the dark until we came to the solid walls of a village looming up against the stars. Guards threw open huge gates and welcomed us:

'*Goong-hay fat-choy*.' It was Chinese New Year, the Year of the Horse!

With guerrillas, peasants and their children, in a village recently half-destroyed by the Japanese, we celebrated the New Year with raw rice wine and patriotic songs and ate all the food. In the morning we stood by an animistic shrine at the foot of an old banyan tree. The children, tiny creatures in padded clothing, ran to offer us each a small dumpling. I gave my donor a hug to help overcome the horror of being close to a foreigner; and I swallowed the dumpling, making a wish that this New Year, the Year of the Horse, might end the suffering in China and in the world. It was 15 February 1942, the day Singapore fell. The New Year brought terrible suffering to the prisoners of war, those whom I had left in Hong Kong and thousands in Singapore, whom the Japanese treated abominably.

The guerrillas were formed up for the march by Chan. I had a *lai wong*, an understanding, with Chan; we spoke to each other as equals, there was no colour bar between us, we were just two soldiers of slightly different pigmentation. Happily we marched onwards for four days, successfully evading an ambush by bandits on the way, but the Red Army soldiers left us when we came close to the Chinese National Army. With emotion I said goodbye and watched them trotting away, rifles slung, rolled blankets on their backs, figures gradually diminishing into the vastness of China.

We were alone again, still striving to cross the metaphoric bridge to freedom. Ahead, a pass, just a cleft in two hills, represented the boundary between communists and Kuomintang. It was a frontier dividing ideologies, separating the people, tearing apart the old civilisation, the Celestial Kingdom, by a political catalyst.

Two Chinese soldiers greeted us with a salute and led us to the headquarters and to the commanding officer who entertained us royally as guests of the nation, praising us for escaping from the Japanese and for making them lose face.

A medical orderly dressed the clean gaping wound on my hand, which Douglas had attended so carefully, and applied a black ointment. Thereafter the wound became infected and painful.

Next day we arrived in the badly damaged city of Waichow, accompanied by a voluble army escort. We proceeded like conquering heroes through rubble-strewn streets full of citizens, conscripts and refugees. A Military Governor congratulated us for escaping and placed us in the charge of a Chinese priest, Father Ma, at the Italian Catholic Mission. Dressed in a long brown gown and leather sandals, he had a round fat face full of humour and compassion. He greeted us with warmth and immediately became the fourth man on our mythical bridge, in place of Chan. The Father entertained us to a lavish dinner, for which we paid with the Governor's money. Finally the three of us slept on the hospital verandah in a large wooden bed under a thin blanket, for which we were grateful.

At first light I met a sister walking elegantly through the gardens and followed her to the Mission Chapel. Father Ma said, 'Anthony, we welcome you to Mass.' I knelt at a tiny wooden pew and thanked God for my deliverance from the Japanese and other dangers. Little nuns sang and chanted beautifully to an old organ played by an elderly nun. I returned refreshed to my two companions.

In the shadow of a giant pagoda Eddy and I collected a sack of rice from a feudal Mandarin type of official: 'petty bourgeois', my communist friends would have called him. The sack, our rations for the journey, was deposited in a flat-bottomed river barge in which we were to travel up the East River.

After another evening meal with Father Ma, we squatted down for the night in the overcrowded barge. There was not enough room to lie flat, flies and bugs abounded, but we had a supply of rice wine and were grateful that we did not have to march again.

Our fellow passengers were refugees, fleeing the Japanese, clinging to their few possessions wrapped in pathetic bundles. China had suffered so much foreign and civil war and revolution that these tenacious people accepted the turmoil stoically; only their delightful children, little round faces, deep brown eyes, straight black hair, were bewildered and frightened.

With university students, two of them attractive girls, we sang the Eton Boating Song and swung together up the pretty East River. My hand was highly infected, swollen and painful; as Douglas dressed it I fainted but was saved from falling off the barge by Eddy. I was so pleased to have escaped from that barbaric prison camp that whatever happened to me could never be as awful, but I worried about atrocities being perpetrated on defenceless prisoners in Hong Kong.

At night the barge tied up at towns and paid for protection from pirates who were in union with the thieving townspeople. Even a beautiful wide stretch of water where stood the Temple of the Goddess of Mercy, Kwun Yam, was not immune from attacks. Sure enough, in the late evening, as the motor boat towing the barge was struggling to reach the protection of a village, pirates attacked the barge but were driven off.

After seven days in the barge we arrived at the town of Hoyun, where a ceremony took place, traditionally fifteen days after New Year. From a temple came a dragon, glittering and writhing. Men held it aloft on poles as it swayed and reared in a dragon dance through the streets. The explosion of crackers and banging of gongs added to the excitement, exhilarating the people who hoped the dragon would keep them free from disease and bring good fortune. The children were either thrilled by the dragon's antics or awestruck, in tears, even screaming.

With the university students and a family from the barge we hired a sampan to take us the next four days up the river. The boatman, his wife and four daughters poled the boat along the shallow river. The sampan was clean; we travelled in comfort, guarding it at night from bandits and pirates with arms provided by the owner.

At the river head, Long Chun, a Military Governor, placed us on top of salt sacks in a Dodge truck. A crazy driver drove the truck like a drunken cyclone up mountains and down valleys, leaving us in the care of a delightful Irish priest, Father O'Brian, who fed us liberally with brandy until after midnight.

Climbing more mountains, descending into more valleys, we followed a part of the route that Mao Tse-tung and that great soldier, Chu Teh, took when the Red Army burst out of the Kuomintang blockade on 16 October 1934 to begin the famous Long March. I could still see derelict fortifications, forts and entrenchments where seven years previously the battle had taken place. I thought of the dreadful slaughter, the cruelty, the flowing of blood and the agony of the wounded. The valleys were full of ghosts, of spirits whose owners had been cut off in the prime of life, who would have little chance of ever reaching paradise.

Earlier, when sailing up the East River, a pretty Chinese girl had told me that when I die my spirit will go to the 'Home of Ten Thousand Ages'. It could stay there many years depending on my behaviour and the comfort I received from gifts from my children and relatives—money wrapped in red paper, food and presents placed on shrines or in front of Buddhas. A good spirit might travel to the 'Western Heaven', above great mountains that contain China in the west. Lucky spirits might change and travel in different form into the 'Blue Light of Ultimate Reality'.

It distressed me that so many millions of young men killed in battle would have little chance of progressing beyond the 'Home of Ten Thousand Ages' because they were unmarried and childless, with no one to place gifts before Buddhas. This was why so many spirits roamed these sinister valleys in anguish.

Three long days in the back of the truck knocked hell out of my injured hand. It made poor Eddy turn green. 'My word, mate, it's bloody crook.' I needed shelter, rest. This town was bomb-damaged; there was no room at the inn. Douglas harangued the innkeeper, insisting strongly for a room until the reluctant man showed us to a cubicle with one large bed. Throughout our long odyssey we had slept huddled together in Chinese graves, on flea-infested straw, in bug-ridden wooden beds, on boat decks—we were used to lying three in a bed.

The cubicle delighted me; it had porcelain pillows on which an enterprising artist had painted a soporific scene of two green and brown loving ducks under a flowering magnolia tree, a delicately coloured porcelain potty in the shape of a duck, a red lacquered barrel as a thunderbox, a wash basin and candlelight—and a packet of anti-bug powder. Such luxury.

Douglas said: 'We'll arrive at Kukong, the wartime capital of Kwangtung, tomorrow night and you, Tony, must go straight into hospital to try and save your hand. That will break us apart. Let's have a final party tonight, a sort of "last supper" and make the most of it.'

At the restaurant Douglas pondered over suggestions from the owner and advice from customers, and ordered a sumptuous meal of many splendid dishes. The rice wine, poured from teapots as was customary, glowed with a rich smoothness on the palate. We were happy.

The bridge with three men, the mystic willow pattern hump-backed bridge, had served its esoteric purpose; the three men were stepping off it to go their separate ways, dissolving a remarkable comradeship.

The break out from the prison camp, the escape through Japanese lines, the amiable Chinese people, Communists and Nationalists alike, had made it all a fabulously exciting and marvellous adventure, unique in that it could never be repeated.

The adventure had given me a glorious feeling of freedom, free from the inhibitions that had confined my life, shackled by stringent rules and discipline at school, Military College, the Regular Army, a stifling form of oppression. I had been liberated, emancipated, free to do and act as I wished. When I arrived in Kukong I was sure to find a British official who would issue orders; I would return to authority and bureaucracy. I dreaded the end of this amazing, dream-like adventure.

The strong truck swirled round blind corners, smashed over the corrugated road and drove into the valley of the great North River, the Peh Kiang. It stopped at a large monastery, its red lacquer gates guarded by enormous griffin-like figures. The *Lao Yeh* (Venerable Father), with wrinkled shaved head and in a saffron robe, showed me an old camphor tree which had been dead for many years but had just blossomed. Legend said this was a sign that China would become great and united again. Seven years later, in 1949, the Chinese mainland became one country, the People's Republic.

In the evening the truck arrived in Kukong. I said goodbye to my Chinese travelling companions and gave the lovely girl who had taught me about the Western Heaven a little farewell kiss, not wishing to offend her sense of propriety.

Colonel Lindsay Ride, an Australian, Dean of the Faculty of Medicine at the University of Hong Kong, Commander of the Hong Kong Field Ambulance, who had escaped from Shamshuipo prison camp two weeks before us, welcomed us in a typically warm Australian manner. 'Congratulations, well done, well done indeed, all three of you!' Then, to me, shaking my left hand, 'Good on you, Tony; good on you!' He was now commanding the British Army Aid Group, designated to help prisoners to escape from Japanese camps and to set up an intelligence organisation.

Douglas took me to the Methodist Mission Hospital to Dr Moore, a graduate of Dublin University, an excellent surgeon and a devoted missionary. I was placed in a private ward, into a bed with a mattress and clean sheets; and sweet little Chinese nurses to look after me. It was sheer bliss. An attractive English Matron, Constance Green, prepared my hand for the operation. Dr Moore and Dr Gordon King, an Australian from Hong Kong, cleverly and successfully joined up the severed tendon. The hand had been cut open seven weeks previously; it had swollen to the size of a football and I had septicaemia, which had made the operation more difficult. There was no penicillin in those days; sulphonamide drugs cured me.

Eddy came to say goodbye before leaving for Chungking and India, smart in his newly-cleaned RNZAF uniform. He had saved my life at the Battle of Grassy Hill; I knew I was going to miss him greatly. Douglas was sent south to Waichow to set up the BAAG. I remained in the hospital for five weeks. An Anglican missionary took down the complete story of the escape and typed it on rice paper; and wrote a letter to my parents which was copied in England and distributed widely.

A Chinese tailor made me a cotton suit, rather like pyjamas, with no badges of rank, very suitable in the warm April weather for walking in the hospital garden, full of English spring flowers, or trekking through orchards and over the river to other missionaries with Constance, whose company I enjoyed. The river was full of song, the Peh Kiang Boat Song.

Sadly I had to continue my journey, my lonely vigil. Constance came with me in a sampan across the river to the railway station and waved goodbye as the monstrous train dragged me away.

The train roared northwards all night and deposited me at Hengyang, in Hunan, where I stayed a night with an American missionary. Travelling south-westwards I left the train to visit a British and Australian military mission, 204 Commando, which was teaching the Chinese commando tactics. Next day I arrived in lovely Kweilin in Kwangsi province, a city nestling in an astonishing landscape of extraordinary limestone mountains jutting sheer out of the earth as if beckoning the heavens. The River Li wandered through the rocks adding to the strange beauty of the place.

It took three weeks to obtain a seat on an aeroplane to Chungking. The Japanese gave me a final farewell salute by bombing Kweilin airfield just before I boarded the Junkers aircraft for Chungking, where I reported to the British Military Attache and remained a few days in the British Embassy. A US Army DC3 flew me to Kunming and, in the company of some pilots who had flown in General Doolittle's raid on Tokyo, the plane bounced over the Hump into Assam and onwards to Calcutta.

From the airport I went to the Great Eastern Hotel. The Parsee reception clerk was not impressed with my Chinese pyjama suit.

'Have you any baggage?'

'Yes.' I held up my little Red Cross bag containing all my worldly possessions. He refused to give me a room, but luckily I met Freddie Guest, of my Regiment, who had evaded capture in Hong Kong. He had a spare bed in his room. Next day I transferred my custom to the Grand Hotel where a kind Hindu clerk welcomed me.

I found my way to Fort William to report my presence in India. No one took any notice of me, not even the MPs at the gate. I did not wish to go straight back into the army after months of freedom and adventure, but I needed money. Then I saw a notice: FIELD CASHIER. A benign Bengali *babu*, with whom I quickly made friends by addressing him in Hindustani, gave me 1 000 rupees. I ran out of the Fort in glee and enjoyed myself in Calcutta.

When I was broke I reported formally to the Fort and was posted to a battalion on the Assam border, in contact with the Japanese. I was most certainly not going to that battalion, so I ignored the order, took a train to Delhi, booked in at Maidens Hotel, and stayed in bed while my pyjama suit was being washed, starched and ironed. In the evening I dined with Ivan

Lyon, of the Gordon Highlanders, a friend from No 5 Company at Sandhurst and in Singapore. He had evaded capture in Malaya, sailed to Sumatra and then to Ceylon. (In 1943 Ivan took a fishing boat, the *Krait* from Australia to Singapore and destroyed shipping in the harbour, but on a subsequent daring raid on Singapore in 1944 he was killed by the Japanese.)

The next day, smartly attired as a respectable Chinese gentleman, I reported to the Military Secretary, an amiable and amused Major General.

I was posted to the 1st Bn. The Lancashire Fusiliers in Cawnpore, where the Colonel took me to dinner in the Club and told me that I would be commanding a detachment of his battalion at Ranikhet in the hills, and that I would be promoted to the rank of Major. General Wavell, the Commander-in-Chief India, sent a letter congratulating me 'on the skill and determination that you displayed in effecting your escape from Japanese hands.'

Everything seemed to be going well for me. As I marched out of Wheeler Barracks at the head of the detachment I was proud; thrilled to be in command of these splendid Fusiliers, happy to be in the army again. After all, I had been born to this life in this land of Kipling's soldiers.

I sped along the straight roads of the Plains, past Lucknow and its famous Residency, besieged in the Mutiny for eighty-seven days, the Union Jack that was never lowered flying bravely in the wind. The colourful life on the Grand Trunk Road brought memories of my childhood; it had not changed, any more than it had from the days of Kim and his Lama searching for the River of Life. Still there were the holy men, fakirs, beggars, pedlars, bullock carts meandering across the road; *gharris* pulled by half-starved horses; carts, mules, donkeys, highly decorated elephants. There were old forts and palaces, temples and mosques, mango and banyan trees, women in gaily coloured saris. And as the army truck sped onwards, I happily returned the *salaams* and waves of old pensioned soldiers wearing campaign medals and the handsome people in the fields as if I was telling them I was glad to be back in my land.

The convoy of trucks halted for the night at a military camp site and I slept on the parched earth under an enormous moon, my friend and guide in China. Hills appeared out of the plain and the truck climbed through pleasant wooded country; at 3 000 feet strawberries were for sale, apricots and peaches at 4 000 and at 7 000 feet I arrived at Ranikhet, a hill station on the foothills of the Himalaya.

My adventure in China had come to an end.

13

The Raj

The Hills and the Plains

Giant mountains, white and beautiful, shrouded by strips of cirrus cloud, shone in glorious splendour. They were like Chinese scrolls of the 'Western Heaven', a celestial paradise where spirits reside in blissful comfort and from where deserving souls may fade into the 'Blue Light of Ultimate Reality'.

During my long journey through China the 'Western Heaven' became my mythical goal, so when at last I gazed upon these mighty mountains towering into space towards Tibet, I experienced a sublime feeling of happiness and my heart sang with joy, the joy of being free, free from the Japanese. Moreover, I had arrived at my esoteric 'Blue Light of Ultimate Reality'.

My odyssey in China ended, I now stood on a forested ridge at an Indian hill-station and stared in wonder at cone-shaped Nanda Devi, one of the highest mountains in the British Empire,* standing majestically in shining glory ahead of other magnificent Himalayan giants. Subsidiary ranges, covered by fir trees, rose and fell in diminishing succession from Nanda Devi's stately slopes to my lowly ridge, a mere 7 000 feet high, yet it felt as if the massive mountains were right on top of me.

Deep valleys between these ranges resounded with a roar of raging streams, their steep banks ablaze with sweet-smelling wild rhododendron and juniper, a captivating fragrance which added to my gladness that I was back in India, the country of my birth, a land of Kipling's soldiers, where I was now deemed to resume my military profession.

The extrinsic beauty of mountains is deceptive; their enormous power may well inspire pleasure but it can create disasters and kill people by avalanches, landslides or violent storms. In fact, mountain behaviour is almost

---

* 25 645 feet or 7 818 metres.

as frail as that of nations, which engage in monstrous warfare. At this time in 1942 the world's most powerful nations were struggling against each other in ferocious deadly contest. In India, Germanic hordes approached from the distant west while Nipponic swarms threatened from the east. The Japanese were already close enough to be an immediate danger. I had witnessed their brutality and the terror they brought to conquered lands, destroying all before them. I prayed they would not outrage this mountain paradise.

The hill-station at Ranikhet, built precariously on a slim ridge of the Himalayan foothills, belonged to this paradise, but it could only be a momentary paradise for me. Before long the detachment of soldiers which I commanded would be ordered to return to the dusty heat-ridden Ganges Plains and ultimately to the Burma battlefields. However, for the present I was here with the Army enjoying the cool high-country climate and training in internal security duties, a sound knowledge of which was vital before we descended to the Plains, the scene of frequent riots; for our current role was to preserve law and order—a duty we disliked intensely, far removed from the kind of soldiering which we had elected to serve.

As a child growing up in India I often saw Indians rioting, mostly communal riots, Hindus and Sikhs fighting Moslems; or sometimes Sikhs, armed with *kirpans*, sharp thin swords, attacking Moslems or Hindus. They were an everyday occurrence, a way of life which, in spite of the carnage they caused, brought excitement into the drab lives of the people.

Communal strife and bloodshed had continued for centuries. Hinduism was established in India thousands of years before Christ by Aryan hordes descending from the north-west to subjugate the ancient Dravidian inhabitants. To perpetuate the enslavement of the dark-skinned Dravidians, the Hindus evolved a caste system, called *varda* meaning 'colour', a diabolic system similar to apartheid, in which the dark races were condemned by birth to the lowest social scale, that of the Untouchables.

Much later the faith of the Prophet came to India with the warriors of Genghis Khan and Tamerlane storming out of the Khyber Pass to impair the Hindus' domination of the great plain of the Ganges. For centuries Moslem Mogul emperors ruled northern India and most of the sub-continent, a lavish yet pitiless rule, spreading the message of Allah and the Koran. During this Mogul regime millions of low caste Hindus converted to the faith of Mohammed to escape their misery, but were treated by Hindus as Untouchables, thus provoking violent antagonism between the peoples.

A martial Hindu renaissance spread across India in the eighteenth century when the Mogul Empire collapsed, causing a wave of fraternal bloodshed. Later the British attempted to force peace upon the warring peoples, but failed—the suspicion and distrust was too inbred between Hindu and Moslem.

The two great faiths are entirely different in doctrine; Hindus worship God in any form they wish, animals, ancestors, natural forces, God being a kind of cosmic spirit; while Moslems worship one god, Allah, the Merciful. A Moslem worships in a mosque, a solemn bare place, prostrating himself on the floor facing Mecca. As a child I listened often to an Imam calling the Faithful to prayer and to the chanting in unison of verses from the Koran, a mesmeric lament. I never entered a mosque, but I frequently strolled in and out of Hindu temples, almost as if temples were market places; and I gazed in inquisitiveness at idols in every shape or form, goddesses with snakes coiling from their heads, elephants with angels' wings conversing to the clouds, fiery-tongued six-armed gods.

Hindus would not eat with Moslems, prohibited Moslems from their kitchens; a high caste Brahmin would go crazy if touched by a Moslem. From my childhood I recalled vendors' cries of 'Hindu *pani*', 'Mussulman *pani*', and wondered whatever could be the difference between the two types of water.

Provocations that caused animosity were many. Some Hindus gained superior education and better employment; apart from the upper classes, who were landlords and soldiers, the Moslem masses were the petty craftsmen, labourers and peasants. The worship of cows, that meandered everywhere eating whatever they wished, enraged the Moslem as being utterly repugnant; the sight of cows being driven to the slaughter-house by Moslems could inevitably cause a riot. With many other matters that provoked enmity there was little scope for any mutual accord between Moslem and Hindu; the religion of one was an anathema to the other.

It was in this environment of communal strife that the British Army lived in India, but it was called out in aid of the civil power only when the situation escalated beyond the capability of the Indian Police. Communal rioters, who knew the British soldiers were impartial and intervened only to stop the sickening fratricide and savage fighting, seldom opposed the soldiers and even seemed amused at the patronising attitude of Army officers. These officers, invariably sons of families of impeccable breeding, mostly educated at one of England's major public schools, frequently behaved as if they were still prefects at those same schools and treated the 'natives' like naughty schoolboys as they quelled the trouble and restored law and order.

In anti-Government riots the situation was vastly different. The Army faced abuse and violence from riotous mobs who raged in fury at the soldiers and were intent on killing them. The soldier was there simply to dispel the riot and was offended by the abuse, astonished that the many benefits Britain had brought to India were not appreciated. In the last resort the Army could suppress a riot only by opening fire with live ammunition, not blank cartridges or rubber bullets, aimed directly at the rioters, generally at ringleaders, and not over the heads of the riotous crowd, because stray bullets could hit innocent people unconnected with the troubles.

In Ranikhet we practised internal security drills by placing a platoon against a simulated riot mob to train each man to carry out his task automatically during the stress and strain of a riot. The practices were noisy affairs, giving much scope for acting and tomfoolery by soldier 'rioters', and were watched with amusement by the natives; a *char-wallah* appearing miraculously out of nowhere immediately the drills were completed with char and wads for the victorious warriors and dejected actors.

Peace reigned in the mountain town, but storm clouds covered the distant peaks, as if trying to hide from the drills of licentious soldiery. To escape from this military scene, I asked the *syce* for a horse and rode out through pine forests along soft pathways covered with pine needles, absorbing the priceless beauty of the mountainous landscape.

As I came to small villages, the occupants salaamed and made *namasti*, joining hands in front of the chest, palms together. I talked with them, friendly natives content with the nearby presence of British troops whom they could rely upon to protect them from the terror of communal feuds. It was problematic why we should practise riot drills when these people were so peaceful. The true India was the rural community, the impoverished villagers, who were more concerned with the daily struggle for survival in this harsh climate and over-populated sub-continent, than with Independence. There would be no impartial forces to defend them after Independence.

In fading twilight I cantered back to the oil-lamp lit streets of the military settlement. The whole garrison was out on a spree, swinging along the tree-lined Mall. Eager young soldiers walked out with attractive girls who clung to strong masculine arms, and sedate warrant officers and sergeants, immaculate in starched khaki uniform, marched with wives or sweethearts. Everyone was making for the Institute, a sort of club, or for moving-picture houses, Chinese cafes or the Rink Dance Hall, the most popular of all places. With the hill-station full of women sheltering from the blistering heat of the Plains, female dancing partners were plentiful, so at the Rink gallant Lancastrian men took this opportunity to show off stylish skills learnt on the floors of palais-de-dance halls at Blackpool or Southport. Hob-nailed ammunition boots presented no problem—squatting always at the Rink entrance a smiling Moslem shoe-wallah sold soft leather dancing shoes for a few anna only.

In the Ranikhet Club the scene was more formal than the Rink Dance Hall; here ladies wore long evening dresses, civilian men black dinner jackets, Army officers drab wartime uniforms. Club members sank into leather armchairs in the reading room, gazing nostalgically at the *Illustrated London News* or *Tatler* or joined others in the drawing room, its armchairs and sofas covered with rose-patterned chintz, its walls hung with heads of tiger or deer. They ate in the dining room at tables lit by shaded candle lamps. Pathan servants in flaring turbans moved swiftly and silently about the solemn surroundings, attending the members. The environment was similar to clubs I had known in my childhood and brought back vivid memories. In a corner of the flowered garden children played, just as I had played in my parents' club garden with other European children, mostly spoilt by the indulgence of the native servants. Like them, I was seldom far from my Madrassi *ayah*, whom I adored, a gentle and sweet-natured woman, dressed always in beautifully coloured sari and blouse, wearing a shiny nose ring and large ankle bangles. I remembered her delicate soft hands and her quiet voice, calling me 'Baba Sahib' even when I was quite old, and how I spoke to her only in Hindustani, a strict rule enforced by parents to prevent children speaking English with the sing-song accent of the country-born.

Cries of *'Koi Hai'* summoned bearers in long white gowns secured by cummerbunds in gaudy club colours, who brought numerous 'chota-pegs', small whisky and sodas. After dinner people danced on the out-of-doors floor, romantic in the cool night air under a great Indian moon in sight of immense snow covered mountains. Most officers were atrocious dancers, some very sloppy, scarcely moving an inch in a slow fox trot, clinging desperately to wretched partners. It was fashionable, in fact, not to be a good dancer; if you were seen too frequently on the dance floor you could be described as a 'poodle-fakir', a womaniser!

'Mind they don't call you poodle-fakir,' Tommy, a brother officer, teased, as I returned to his table. 'You're never off the floor.'

'Nonsense, Tommy. I don't care if I'm called poodle-fakir, or for that matter any other kind of fakir!'

I liked the company of women, having discovered them to be fascinating creatures, intellectually superior to many of my gallant comrades. Only recently I had witnessed the fall of Hong Kong and the complete destruction of our way of life in that Colony; I had been incarcerated in a literal 'valley of the shadow of death' in a prison camp. Worse disasters could happen, but in the meanwhile I was determined to enjoy myself.

'Don't worry, Tony, you're a bloody awful dancer, you could never be a poodle-fakir,' laughed Tommy.

'We should be pleased to have even a chance of being poodle-fakirs with the situation in the world as it is now. It's pretty grim.'

It was July 1942. The Germans had launched a general offensive into Russia in June and Sebastopol had surrendered, German and Italian armies had driven Australian, British, Indian and South African forces across the North African desert and had reached El Alamein; Japanese troops had captured Burma and Guadalcanal and were advancing into New Guinea; terrible losses had been suffered by the Allies at sea and in the air. It was an horrific situation and ironic that people sheltering in hill stations seemed outwardly unconcerned by these events, but in truth all had suffered already in various ways from the war, and many would suffer even more, several to be killed or maimed in combat.

The dancing over, the revellers rolled home. Thomas Atkins led the way along moonlit pathways, needlessly carrying a hurricane lamp.

'Over there,' he pointed, 'are the married quarters. Out of bounds to the likes of us, because the husbands are away. No chance of getting in—look at the pickets.'

Groups of Regimental and Military policemen stood at intervals close to the buildings.

'It's twenty-eight days detention for the rank and file if they get caught, but most plead "not guilty", that they were dragged in against their wishes! Even if that's a truthful defence, we all know that "single men in barricks don't grow into plaster saints".'

The detachment marched away from the little colony crouched on its forested ridge to the measured beat of 'The British Grenadiers', played vigorously by the Band and Drums, the Fusiliers swinging along with the swank and bravado of truly professional soldiers. Tearful young wives and sweethearts wished them goodbye; Indians, impressed by the striking smartness of the troops, waved and shouted, *'Shabash, shabash!'* (well done, well done); and excited children followed them as far as possible, trying to keep pace with the big black boots, swinging tiny arms in time with those of the proud warriors. The white towers and ridges of the Himalayas soared into a pale sky and then dissolved as the detachment drew away, its tour of duty in the hills ended.

They were marching downhill to the plains, singing lustily as they descended, 'Bless 'em all', a song ridiculing sergeants and WO1s, 'for they're sons of guns', fortifying themselves for the tortuous route that lay before them. The crooked earthen track dropped steeply a thousand feet or more in twisting bends then rose to the next precipitous ridge a few miles distant, but only some hundred feet lower, and repeated its exhausting passage in dwindling rise and fall to the flat ground of the plains.

Led by me, we marched all day, with halts in deep valleys beside sparkling rivers of ice-cold waters. As we climbed ridges fallow-deer pranced away through pine forests in terror at the crunch of boots; monkeys shrieked in defiance as we strode downwards through jungles; inhabitants of neat white cottages surrounded by terraced fields salaamed us. At night sentries were posted round a camp site, field rations were cooked by camp fires and the men slept on the hard dry earth with their rifles chained to their wrists. At dawn we woke to the shrill call of a bugle blowing the long reveille and then marched into the relentless heat of the plains, to the railhead and a long dusty troop-train waiting for us.

At night the groaning train rumbled through the flat land until it stopped at dawn for the huge engine to draw water at an isolated halt in a desolate, lifeless landscape of brown sunburnt earth stretching levelly to the horizon. Here the troops took hot shaving water from the engine and smartened up in preparation for our arrival at Cawnpore. When enough steam was raised, the engine puffed away and the old train rolled and rocked along. It soon reached a long rusty iron bridge spanning Mother Ganges, the river filled with semi-burnt floating corpses, debris from impoverished Hindu funeral pyres. As it reached Cawnpore, pungent odours of this monstrous city filled our carriages. There was an overpowering faecal stench, a foetid smell of half a million people and sacred cows, elephants, camels, horses, mules, donkeys, cats, dogs, monkeys, fumes from factories and motor vehicles and smoke from fires cooking aromatic Indian food.

My detachment from the hills now rejoined the remainder of the 1st Battalion The Lancashire Fusiliers in Wheeler Barracks, named after a General savagely murdered in the Indian Mutiny of 1857, not far from the grisly well into which the mutilated bodies of European women and children had been dumped in that same Mutiny. It was hardly a salubrious environment.

The troops settled into huge barrack blocks, sited in echelon in the hope that the prevailing wind flowed through each building unimpaired by a neighbouring one. Built in Victorian times, these blocks were erected in the strange belief that a constant breeze blew away the cholera germs. In fact, only a light wisp ever entered the long gaunt rooms each containing fifty men, cooled only by cloth fans suspended from the ceiling and pulled by *punkah-wallahs*. In extremely hot and uncomfortable conditions a soldier's life in Wheeler Barracks was not a happy lot.

However, the discomfort of barrack room life was eased considerably by camp followers employed to look after the soldier, such as the *nappy*, who shaved men in bed before reveille; the *chokra*, who pressed uniforms; the *dhobi*, who washed clothes; the *char-wallah*, who brought the pre-reveille mug of tea and who, with other vendors of milk, eggs, ham and sweets was always close to the troops, even on the highest mountain; the *bhisti*, Kipling's Gunga Din, who carried water; and then the friendly *mehtar*, or sweeper, cleaner of latrines, a man of untouchable caste, who adored the soldiers, the only people with whom he could converse.

In sharp contrast to a barrack room, I lived in a rambling old pre-Mutiny bungalow, an enormous edifice in its own grounds. My bearer greeted me 'Salaam Sahib', as did the *syce, mali, dhobi, punkah-wallah* and *mehtar*. The bearer's wife in purdah and her children stood in the shade of the servants' quarters and waved to welcome me. A large household attended to me, lacking only a cook, for I fed in Mess.

The bearer brought me a pile of letters heaped on a tray, letters from my parents, Colonel Maurice Browne, the Colonel of the Middlesex Regiment, from relatives of men who had been killed or imprisoned in Hong Kong— and one from Elizabeth.

She told me of her evacuation from Singapore, the heart-breaking parting with Noel, her journey to England. It was wonderful to learn that she had not been imprisoned by the Japanese. She wrote that Martin's mother was very worried about Martin. Did I know how he was wounded?

In that hectic battle for Hong Kong, we had fought in small units in desperate skirmishes, unaware of what was happening on other fronts. After the surrender Martin was admitted into the Military Hospital and I did not see him again. In the prison I heard a story about him, but soldiers' accounts were generally apocryphal. However, I wrote to Elizabeth:

> The Japs were trapped in a small house . . . so Martin climbed on the roof of the house and dropped grenades down the chimney. When the Japs started coming out he picked them off with his pistol, but another Jap fired a small-calibre machine pistol at him and got four shots into his back.

I finished the letter with these words:

> England must be lovely now in June. India is intolerable. I am back in Cawnpore and it is 122°F [50°C] in the shade. We long for the rains to break. I am quite lonely in India with my Regiment and all I had once lived for captured by the Japanese. I would love to hear from you.

Cawnpore's connections with the Indian Mutiny in 1857 recalled memories of the bungalow in which I was born in Dharwar in Southern India.

A British officer was murdered in that bungalow during the Mutiny and his mutilated body buried in the lawn in front of the house. A sunken cross

Martin and Elizabeth.

Elizabeth Bell

*Elizabeth Hayley Bell has an-
nounced her engagement to Martin
Pryce Weedon, The Middlesex
Regt. (Duke of Cambridge's Own).
She is the daughter of Lt.-Col. F.
Hayley Bell, D.S.O., Headquarters,
Malaya Command, and Mrs. Bell*

Elizabeth in the dress with brown buttons.

Elizabeth and Noel.

Harper's Bungalow where Elizabeth and Noel spent their happiest times.

Noel Gudgeon.

Colour Party 1st Battalion The Middlesex Regiment, Duke of Cambridge's Own
His Majesty the King's birthday parade, 9 June 1938

(left to right from rear) Sergeant J. Ramsey, Drum Major G. Jeffree, Sergeant H. Ramsden, Lieutenant T. W. Chattey, Colour Sergeant R. Bayles, Lieutenant A. G. Hewitt

These colours were buried on Christmas night at Flagstaff House, Hong Kong. The photograph was taken at Nanking Barracks, Shamshuipo, which became a Japanese prisoner-of-war camp. On the left is Jubilee Building, from which I made my escape to Bamboo Pier, which is near the hut in the far left-hand corner. In the background are the Kowloon Hills which I climbed at the start of my long journey to freedom.

Coronation parade for His Majesty King George VI, 12 May 1937: The Middlesex Regiment on Singapore Padang. Tony (third from left) carrying the King's colour.

appeared over his grave and no matter how often the hollows were filled with earth, the cross sank again. My mother often saw the officer's ghost striding along the verandah in a blood-stained uniform.

When my father left India, as a Chaplain to the Forces, for the War in August 1914, my mother and three sisters remained alone in the house and my mother felt that the officer's ghost, whom she called 'a brave soldier of the Queen Empress', was always nearby to protect her, a protection needed for five long years. It was not the Indians, mainly Marathas, gentle and peaceful folk, that she feared, but the wild animals, tiger, elephant, leopard, from the vast jungles of Mysore, which often roamed the cantonments. She remained serene from fear in her staunch belief that the macabre phenomenon of the murdered officer's ghost shielded her.

During those lonely years, my father served in Mesopotamia, then France, where he was gassed in the trenches, Egypt, Palestine with Allenby and did not return until 1919.

I was born in September 1914, with the birthmark of a cross on my left arm. So the ghost made an imprint on me as well.

The heat in Cawnpore that July afternoon was intense, over-bearing. All India was asleep—all except a sweating uniformed messenger bicycling hurriedly up the dusty drive to my bungalow. Dismounting at white-washed steps under a porch, he rang his bell persistently. The bearer, his sleep so rudely disturbed, raced through the house, shouting:

'Sahib is sleeping. Stop the noise!'

'I am bringing message from Colonel Sahib.'

The message said, 'Political situation deteriorating. Battalion flag march 1600 hours.'

The whole battalion, 800 strong, formed up on Wheeler Barracks parade ground dressed in ceremonial drill order. As we marched into the city, a troop of Indian Police Lancers, large handsome men in full dress with blue and white turbans, mounted on bay horses, led the long column, followed by half of the battalion, then the Corps of Drums, the Colonel, myself and the other half of the battalion.

Thousands of jeering Indians lined the wide streets, some on roof-tops of three-storey buildings, others hanging out of windows, many wearing white Congress Party caps, all shouting, 'Quit India! Quit India!' and yelling abuse. A deafening roar swept through the hot streets, rising to a crescendo as the column passed by, and from all angles a barrage of missiles descended upon us.

Stoically we ran the gauntlet, oblivious to the tumult. We continued with the march, rifles with fixed bayonets at the slope, swinging to the steady beat of the Drums with the bravado and swank typical of a fine Regular Army Battalion. We were splendid soldiers of the King Emperor, here to 'Show the Flag', to impress our presence on his subjects, to calm the unrest. Dressed ceremonially, not in steel helmets and webbing equipment, without ammunition, we marched proudly and nobly on a mission of peace.

Our noble peaceful mission did not seem to be appreciated. As we advanced further into the city, the thunderous roar increased together with continuous volleys of missiles; bricks and stones tore into us, knocked off topees, bruised and cut us. Suddenly right in front of me a brick smashed straight through the skin of a side drum. The drummer shouted, 'Look at me f…ing drum!' In a second the Colonel was with him: 'Take no notice, take no notice, Drummer, just go through the motions!' Reluctantly the Drummer continued his march, beating a skinless drum, with rigid poise and utter forbearance.

All the way, all the time, it was bricks, stones and other objects and a ceaseless repetition of *'Jai Hind. Jai Hind'*. The troops were expressing their opinions—not that they could be heard above the tumult, but marching in the ranks I could still gather some choice basic Lancastrian English. It gladdened my heart.

The RSM, who marched to the rear of the Colonel, turned his head slightly and snapped at my Company Sergeant Major, 'Keep the language down.' The CSM looked back at the stalwart ranks behind him and shouted, 'There's too much f…ing language! Watch it.' The troops saw the humour in the command at once, laughed and stopped the bad language.

'It'll be about 125° in these enclosed streets,' Tommy said to me. 'It's an excellent recipe for heat stroke. I hope no one falls out, these Hindu bastards would tear him to bits in seconds. Have you noticed there are no Moslems in these crowds?—they're always more friendly—but there're plenty of Sikhs, armed with *kirpans*. We're defenceless, no ammo, only bayonets and rifle butts. We wouldn't last long against this mob if it turned into a fight.'

I hated this ridiculous march, the Hindus and Sikhs, the dust, smell and heat but I knew no one would fall out. These Fusiliers were staunch, solid, dogged men, brought up in Spartan conditions in Lancashire coal mines and factories, steadfast in adversity. A man knocked out by heat-stroke or a brick would be carried along by his mates as they marched in the ranks.

At last we were stepping over the railway level crossing, the crowds dissolved, we were back in Wheeler Barracks and quickly dismissed to attend to our cuts and bruises and stained uniforms. The 'flag march' was over.

It was 1 August. The Lancashire Fusiliers celebrated the Battle of Minden, 1759. Drums, clothed in black, marched through barracks in remembrance of those who were killed, Officers drank a toast to the fallen with the WOs and Sergeants; at dinner officers ate a rose dipped in champagne, to remember the gallant men who plucked roses in the Minden fields as they advanced into battle to defeat the French.

It was a day to recall Regimental history, of a famous Regiment that had captured the Heights of Abraham at Quebec under General Wolfe in 1759, had been awarded six Victoria Crosses before breakfast at the Landing at Helles at Gallipoli in 1915, and had fought in almost every war and campaign since its formation in 1688.

For weeks the political situation had been volatile, compounded by Gandhi's slogan 'Quit India', and his proposal that the British should relinquish power in India immediately and 'leave India to God or even anarchy'. He preached that if the British retired, the Japanese would have no reason to attack India. It was a preposterous idea.

At midnight on 8 August 1942 at a Congress Party meeting in Bombay, Gandhi demanded 'freedom immediately' and urged his followers to 'do or die', to 'free India or die in the attempt'.

Forewarned by intelligence sources, the Lancashire Fusiliers deployed before dawn to internal security posts—power stations, roads and railway bridges, railway stations and police stations. I took B Company, 140 men, to the Central Police Station in the city of Cawnpore.

Before dawn Gandhi and the entire leadership of the Congress Party were arrested and placed in jail. As the blazing sun burst over the horizon, news of Gandhi's arrest caused an enormous explosion of violence throughout India and particularly in the United Provinces. From inside the police station we soon heard the noise of crowds gathering, developing into a massive roar of anger. They were not far away—already missiles were landing on the station roof.

Valiant Indian policemen, tall thin-legged men, patrolled the streets throughout the morning, breaking up unlawful assemblies, dispersing dangerous mobs. Police casualties were evacuated to the station, brave policemen fearfully wounded.

It was an alarming situation, made worse by not taking part, by having to sit and wait until our aid was requested. The soldiers may have felt as apprehensive as I did, but they did not show it; they talked continuously, chain-smoked evil-smelling cigarettes, drank endless cups of tea and laughed at everything. They showed an inspiring, indomitable spirit in the face of danger.

In the afternoon the senior European police officer told me that about 150 000 people had assembled in the main street, intent on destroying the police station. 'It's a very ugly situation,' he said despairingly, 'I don't think we can hold them much longer. You had better be ready.'

I paraded the Company behind the station, three platoons formed into squares, the leading platoon, number 4, commanded by Nobby. Dressed in steel helmets and battle equipment, carrying rifles at the high-port, we looked far more ferocious than we did during that burlesque flag march of a few days ago as now we marched steadily into the main street and up to the brave Indian policemen struggling to hold back the raging mob by beating the people with long *lathis*.

A blast, almost a wave, of heat, dust and ear-piercing noise hit us as we emerged, the roar of the angry crowd reverberated against shaking buildings on each side of the street. An astonishing barrage of missiles descended on us. Through the missile-rain I could just see the immense crowd, thousands upon thousands of brown faces packed closely together, white caps, white clothing, arms waving about, arms throwing things, everyone yelling at the top of their voices.

It was simply terrifying. The shattering noise waves made me shudder and shake, I felt I had been hit in the stomach, I could not think, I had to force my rag-doll legs along as we marched towards the mob and I kept saying to myself, 'Tony, you must do it, you must keep cool, you must not show you are frightened.' It was a ghastly moment, made worse because I could see that all of us were suffering from the shock, feeling the same terror.

Fortuitously, the crowd registered some shock as soon as they saw us; from past experience they knew that the only course the military could take to disperse them was to open fire—to fire directly at them to kill; and perhaps we looked fiercer and braver than we felt. The noise decreased a little but the sinister forward movement of the crowd persisted. It seemed that nothing could stop this huge human tidal wave, that in a few seconds we should all be crushed to death.

The police could no longer withstand this terrible avalanche of struggling brown bodies and began to break up and withdraw hastily into our ranks. A dejected European police officer, bleeding profusely from head-wounds, rushed to the Magistrate, a pale-faced shivering Indian strongly held and supported by two robust Fusiliers, and implored him to hand over immediately the civil power to the military.

Almost simultaneously Nobby and I raced up to the Magistrate. My numbness, the fear and terror, suddenly disappeared in this moment of instant danger and I knew that immediate action must be taken to relieve this highly critical situation. The same reaction had obviously happened within Nobby, there beside me looking remarkably cool and controlled. We needed at once the signed piece of paper from the Magistrate authorising the transfer of power to the military.

'Get the chit from him at once!' I yelled at Nobby. I now stayed close by within this leading platoon, feeling strangely calm and collected, in complete personal control in amazing contrast to how I had felt a few seconds earlier.

Nobby, acting as he had been trained in Ranikhet, took the paper from the magistrate. Grabbing a megaphone and shouting loudly through it so that his men could hear, he ordered:

'PLATOON—ten rounds—load!'

The action of the cartridge clips being forced into magazines drew the crowd's attention and the volume of noise and the missile barrage diminished slightly. The most noisy and violent Indians were now in the rear ranks of the crowd.

'FRONT RANK—kneeling position—*move!*'

The movement again attracted the people's attention, reducing the momentum of the human steam-roller. They knew that those standing could fire over the heads of the ones kneeling, which could produce a deathly volley of fire against them.

'BUGLERS—blow the fire call!'

The buglers blew the loud resounding call: 'There's a fire, there's a fire, there's a fire', the only appropriate call they knew for a riot. The 'Charge' would have been quite wrong.

'DISPERSE or I FIRE!'

The yelling and shouting died down slightly, except for those in the rear who might escape the bullets. But one man, in Congress cap, white blouse and dirty dhoti, who had climbed a lamp post, was raving and frothing at the mouth, screaming and shouting:

'KILL the British—rush them—run over them—kill them—KILL the BRITISH!'

Nobby moved slowly to a Fusilier standing in the second rank. Ten thousand eyes were upon him and the noise abated faintly as they waited to see what he would do. Despite the tension, despite the fact that if he acted rashly or too slowly or made a mistake, this enormous crowd of 150 000 violent people could overrun him, crush and kill all the British troops in seconds, outwardly Nobby appeared to be perfectly calm and collected, moving with care and deliberation. I admired him for his personal discipline; it was a superb exhibition.

Nobby tapped the Fusilier on his shoulder and said. 'Point your rifle at that bastard up the lamp post, just point, do not fire. OK? AIM!'

The soldier adopted the aiming position, rifle butt on his right shoulder, pointing straight at the man up the post. The man saw immediately what was coming and leaped down in a flash, accompanied by jeers from the crowd, crying out that he was like a monkey, *'Bundah ke hucher.'*

Quickly Nobby shouted again through the megaphone:

'DISPERSE, DISPERSE QUICKLY, or I'LL FIRE.'

Nobby ordered the front and rear ranks into the aiming position while the buglers blew the fire call again and again, blowing their hearts out. Mercifully the crowd began slowly to withdraw and as the movement became more definite, a police officer with a large fresh squad of riot police dashed past, shouting to Nobby:

'OK, OK, well done, *shabash*, I'll take over,' and raced into the street, driving the mob away.

Nobby relinquished his authority to the now smiling Magistrate, who congratulated him on his superb sense of mob psychology. Later, when I congratulated Nobby, he replied, 'I never want to be in a riot again. It's dreadful, far worse than any battle!'

14

India

Tony

Before the Great War, my father was an Army Chaplain in Poona. His family and household are shown in a photograph portraying my father in a clerical dog-collar, his hand holding a cane chair recently vacated by his youngest daughter, who ran away just as everyone posed for the shot; my mother and governess, in tight-waisted long cotton dresses, both looking startled and trying hard to ignore the errant child; two worried little girls in party frocks, anxiously expecting a rabbit to pop out of the black camera box; and nine dutiful servants.

Emblazoned in the picture is a dignified bearer and second bearer, a prominent army orderly, a friendly *mali* and *dhobi*, an old *khanasama* and his *chokra*, a smart carriage and horse with a proud *syce* in charge of the reins, and in the background the *dewan*, an aloof retired soldier.

Absent from the photograph is the devoted *ayah*, too modest to attend; the *chokidar*, inevitably asleep; the likeable *bhisti*, drawing water; the sweeper, whose untouchable caste prohibited him from being photographed with men of higher caste; and finally, me, not yet more than a sensuous twinkle in my father's eye.

After the Great War I lived a carefree happy existence in Ahmednagar in the Deccan, sixty miles north-east of Poona, in a land where everybody seemed to be a friend, ever ready to protect me from any danger. There was always someone to help, to rush to the scene of trouble. When screams and yells arose from the *gussal-khana*, the bathroom, the sweeper and the *dewan* would dash about with long sticks. My mother would say, 'It's just another snake. They love the cool wet mud floors of the *gussal-khana*.' Everyone would race to see the fun, to find the *dewan* holding triumphantly an enormous dead cobra, announcing proudly and obviously, 'Snake, memsahib, *burra* snake.'

I followed the *dewan* to watch him throw the snake over the compound fence onto the *maidan*, public land. The vultures would quickly devour the dead reptile, he told me, as he returned to his sentry box and shelter at the main gate. He was a handsome retired soldier, his faded uniform decorated with campaign medal ribbons, my particular friend. He was brave, killed snakes and scorpions, drove away mad dogs and kept the beggars out of the compound. He fed me with delicious Indian sweets, strictly forbidden by my mother, but sweeter because they were illicit. He often told me tales of the Indian Army, stories of frontier battles, but today he listened to me telling him how a ghost had implanted a cross on me: 'Look *Dewan*, there is the cross on my left arm; the ghost put it there!'

'*Acchha chota* sahib, the ghost is gracious. He will look after you. One day you will be officer sahib.'

I did so want to be an officer sahib one day. I would join the Durham Light Infantry, in barracks on the Ridge. Their fast marching and quick arms drill enthralled me, but more so the Regimental silver when it was laid on the dinner table for guest nights. Running round the table was a railway line of silver rails on which ran a silver engine pulling silver carriages holding decanters of port, sherry and madeira. The kind Mess Sergeant would allow me to push the train round the table, once only—every Thursday afternoon, which day was a holiday for the army in India. Other silver pieces on the table commemorated famous battles in the Peninsula, Crimea and South Africa. I would certainly join the Regiment—but they were relieved by The Argyll and Sutherland Highlanders, and I lost my heart to the kilt and bagpipes and was determined to become a Highland officer sahib.

The *syce* was another friend. He led up my pony, carefully groomed, and I mounted quickly, thanking my pleasant ally. My sisters, already mounted, shouted at me to follow and we all cantered through the gateway and then broke into a mad gallop across the flat open *maidan*. We were free, we could ride wherever we would in this sun-drenched country of deep blue cloudless skies, across the rolling plains, past ruins of old forts, gaudy temples and glittering palaces, through sugarcane fields, jumping fences and ditches, riding with hearts full of joy with the thrill of it all. At villages, neat clusters of houses built around a well and a huge banyan tree, we would stop and dismount and talk to the friendly people, who would offer us sugarcane or corn roasted on the cob. We kept well clear of the sinister temples but we explored widely the huge Maratha fort (besieged by Sir Arthur Wellesley, later the Duke of Wellington, in a Maratha war), a place of great excitement, full of snakes, hyenas, baboons and other monkeys, jackals and weird *sadhus*. Daily we repeated exciting wild rides across the open country in different directions, learning the meaning of freedom and adventure.

My idyllic life in Ahmednagar varied in style when my father was stationed in the immense city of Bombay. The so-called chaplain's bungalow was a monstrous two-storey house, built in stone to last a thousand years, drawn by an architect who must have been an alcoholic or opium addict to have produced anything so ugly and ill-proportioned, a mixture of towers, gables and turrets. Close by stood the garrison church, built in the same hideous stone, a monstrosity capable of housing two battalions.

Every Sunday the residents turned out to watch and cheer the smart troops spotlessly turned out, rifles and fixed bayonets, the band and drums leading, as they marched to church. Quickly the men filed into church, clutching rifles, sheathed bayonets and topees and ammunition, placing their rifles in slots cut into the pews, the rifle butt conveniently close to a hob-nailed boot. The splendidly disciplined British soldiers sang the hymns and psalms fervently and responded vigorously to the prayer book, filling the officiating clergyman's heart with joy, but sadly all the psalms and hymns were sung to soldiers' words only, to obscene yet funny words, certainly sacrilegious. During the service my father pretended not to notice, but he knew the words and often laughed about them with us. He loved the British Tommy and knew a great deal about him, and knew also that if his sermons were ever too long he would soon know by the noise of boots tapping rifle butts, increasing in tempo until he stopped.

Ever since the Indian Mutiny the troops had taken their rifles and bayonets and twenty rounds of ammunition per man with them into church. The Mutiny broke out at Meerut, forty miles south of Delhi, on Sunday 10 May 1857, as the British were going to church without arms. My father was generally reticent on what exactly happened, declining to admit a family connection with the Meerut garrison commander, General Hewitt, who was condemned for his inactivity and had been described as being 'nearly seventy, a stout and easy-going man, "liked by all and respected by some."'

The Congress Party's 'Quit India' campaign intended to disrupt the war effort and cut the main lines of communication between Bombay and Burma, but the rebellion was aborted in August 1942 when Gandhi and the leaders were imprisoned. Little internal unrest followed except communal disturbances, mainly disputes between Congress Hindus and Jinnah's Moslem League concerning the partition of India.

I became an itinerant lecturer, a sort of Army guest speaker, and I rode about India quite peacefully for months in hot, dirty, overcrowded trains with the majority of the passengers clinging precariously to carriage roofs, trains pulled by huge engines, dragons emitting great puffs of steam and smoke. Living in close proximity to thousands of Indians, diversified in race and colour from pale Pathans in the north-west to black Tamils in the south-east, I grew painfully accustomed to clambering over hundreds of bodies asleep on railway station platforms, to the constant cries of vendors and beggars, the strong nauseating smells. Then there was the frenetic scramble for a space in the train, which frequently resulted in my gallant bearer fighting off the mobs, sitting on the doorstep of my compartment and kicking away the intruders.

The purpose of my travels was to deliver propaganda lectures to British troops about the barbaric behaviour of the Japanese during their conquest of Hong Kong in December 1941. I told them about Japanese atrocities, the killing of the wounded and prisoners during the eighteen-day Battle for Hong Kong, the killing of wounded soldiers lying in hospital beds, the killing of hospital doctors and rape of nurses at St. Stephen's Hospital at Stanley, and the brutal treatment of prisoners, including starvation in prisoner-of-war camps. As I was one of the very few men who had been incarcerated in a Japanese prisoner-of-war camp, my authentic experiences were expected to raise hatred against the Japanese and make British troops fiercer.

I could never forget the barbarity of the Japanese and the heinous crimes they committed against the men of my Regiment, the 1st Battalion The Middlesex Regiment, in Hong Kong, but I disliked my role in delivering these propaganda lectures. I felt it was a mistake to attempt to de-humanise the British soldier—it might even incite him to carry out atrocities against the Japanese. The British fought and killed cleanly, without viciousness, as a matter of duty and discipline and for the honour of the Regiment.

After one of my lectures to the 14th Indian Division in the Arakan in Burma, a Sergeant Major said to me, 'One thing we've learnt today is never to be taken prisoner. We'll fight harder for that reason!' So perhaps my efforts did some good.

Relieved at last from this duty, I became an Instructor at an Officers' Training School at Belgaum in Southern India, close to Dharwar where I was born, and the old pre-Mutiny bungalow with the sunken grave in the garden and the ghost of the murdered English officer. This is an attractive part of India, green and thickly forested, high up in the Sahyadri Mountains; and it was here in Belgaum that I felt I had returned to my home.

Here Elizabeth wrote to me, congratulating me on the award of the Military Cross, and saying that she worried about Noel. I replied:

> I am so sorry, Elizabeth, that you have had such a worrying time. It
> must be awful for you. Please do not think that I have ever criticised
> or judged you for what happened. At the time I did not really know
> very much about what was happening—it was after all a purely

private affair. Later, when I learnt more I was terribly sorry for both of you, and I certainly do not blame you, Elizabeth. I hope you have a happy time as a Wren. You ought to look very dashing in your uniform. Please write to me, Elizabeth.

Rumours reached me that the Lancashire Fusiliers were about to go into Burma, so I gained permission to rejoin them in Cawnpore. General Wavell, the Commander-in-Chief in India, came to bid us farewell. Of solid frame and with one eye only, artistic by temperament, honest and forthright, a gallant soldier of renown and a fine leader of men, he immediately won the affection and adoration of the Battalion. The spontaneous cheers that followed his talk wishing us good fortune in battle resounded throughout and beyond the cantonment, every Fusilier, 'Minden Boy' yelling his heart out.

Unfortunately our departure was delayed and we remained kicking our heels into the dirt and dust of the Ganges Plain. I applied for leave.

The Calcutta Mail roared through the black night, belching red hot sparks from its mighty engine, clanking to a stop at Delhi where I transferred to the Bombay Express, which charged furiously over the rich pastures of the Punjab, waiting patiently at Ambala for the Sahib-*log* passengers to eat lunch in the station restaurant, stopping briefly at Amritsar, home of the Sikh's Golden Temple and of General Dyer, whose appalling suppression of a riot (13 April 1919) permanently wounded British and Indian relations.

At Lahore, the enormous walled city on the Ravi River where Kim once supposedly sat astride Zam-Zammah, dinner was served, and then the majestic Express continued its thunderous journey through a starlit night until I crept out with relief at dawn at Rawalpindi, now 800 miles from where I started in Cawnpore.

A roguish bearded Sikh sold me seats for myself and bearer to ride 175 miles to Kashmir in his aged American Plymouth taxi-cab. Soon we were climbing the foothills to Murree, fir forested and cool at 7 000 feet, renowned for its whisky, a few tots of which blew off the top of your head. Speeding like a drunken cyclone, the Plymouth descended crooked twisting earthen roads into the valley of the River Jelum, rushing blindly round corners, horn blazing. Often petrol stoppages and burst tyres delayed our wild progress and we halted for lunch and tea at Dak Bungalows, State resthouses. Gliding through the inspiring beauty of the valley of Kashmir on a road lined with poplar and silver birch within sight of giant snow-capped mountains, climbing again to 7 000 feet, the taxi deposited me at last at a Dak Bungalow where I thankfully stayed the night.

As daylight came a golden oriole sang cheerfully in a tree, a little song to welcome me to Kashmir, and coolies leading small dapple-coated ponies contested loudly with shouts and yells for my custom to carry me and my baggage up the mountain, a climb of 2 000 feet in four miles. I declined a ride on a pony—the wretched animal looked half-starved—but I hired it to appease the impoverished owner. A strong Kashmiri coolie, with calf muscles bulging in large knots, carried my baggage on his shoulders from a strap bound around his forehead which relieved some of the weight.

At the top of the mountain pass I looked down on Gulmarg, a green sugar bowl filled with quaint wooden houses, hotels, clubs and golf courses and surrounded by pine forests and giant mountains, the closest 14 000 feet high almost on top of the settlement. It was supremely beautiful, cold, fresh and lovely.

The days were filled with fun—golf, parties, dancing. Like the hill-station Ranikhet, this place was crammed full of women, sheltering from India's sunny clime, and I made many friends; if Tommy Atkins had been with me he would have again accused me of being a poodle-fakir. Hiring an intrepid hill pony I rode many miles through the surrounding hills on narrow pathways between pine trees, sometimes alone, often on picnic parties with attractive girls. I climbed the 14 000 foot mountain and was fascinated by the hundreds of wild flowers that sprang up as the snow receded. On other days and nights I trekked in the mountains, fishing in the cold clear streams, cooking fresh trout on charcoal fires.

One evening, in the Gulmarg antiquated moving-picture house, I watched, utterly enthralled, Noel Coward's remarkable film *In Which We Serve*, completely unaware that John Mills, the little cockney Able Seaman called 'Shorty Blake', would one day become my brother-in-law, or that Noel Coward would be a guest at my wedding reception in London.

Descending from Gulmarg's enchanting paradise, I stayed on the Dal lake near Srinagar in a houseboat. Cocktail parties began in the morning in houseboats closely moored, champagne flowed all day as occupants visited other boat-parties, diving frequently into the cool green water to sober up. Kashmiri gondolas, named 'Cheek to Cheek', 'Love Boat' or like title, comfortably appointed with deep sensuous cushions, glided through canals and lakes and took me to the Club at Nagin Bagh to dance, and then to beautiful Shalimar, where streams ran through wild flowers and dripped gently from waterfalls into still waters concealed by huge lotus flowers. Of course, pale hands were there—it was pure fantasy, a dream, utterly unlike the real India of heat, dust, smells, disease and appalling poverty to which I now had to return.

Green treetops rose and fell in waves over the huge landscape like a rolling emerald carpet of great beauty. Scarlet splashes of flame trees and coloured leaves broke the verdant green of the jungle so newly revived by the monsoon; birds returned to relish the rich harvest such as long-legged white storks and sweet golden brown ruffs, both migrating from North Europe, and noisy lesser cuckoos from North China; and everywhere there was movement by animals of all kinds, deer and antelope, leopard and tiger.

In the far distance, ornate red towers of Orchna Palace rose majestically out of the lush forest. They reminded me of the viridescent temple towers that appear surprisingly out of a forest at Angkor Wat in Cambodia, which I had visited before the War. The resemblance enthralled me because of the sinister appearance of Orchha Palace, lonely and half hidden in the deep jungle. It was in fact the preserve of an Indian State, ruled by an autocratic Maharanee violently opposed to the Indian Government and any trespass of her small State.

I had no need to trespass: my business was in Orchha Camp placed close to the raging Betwa River, a muddy camp of hundreds of bivouacs and a few Indian pattern tents, where I now served with the Lancashire Fusiliers transformed into Chindits of the 77th Independent Infantry Brigade Commanded by Mike Calvert. He had been a friend in pre-war Hong Kong, dangerously impetuous, tirelessly energetic, remarkably strong physically and a fine and courageous leader who had successfully led a Chindit column well into Burma on the first Chindit expedition of long range penetration.

Our superior commander was Orde Wingate, well known for his exploits in Palestine, Ethiopia and Burma. Aged about forty, he astonished us by his appearance in creased ill-fitting uniform, an out-of-date Wolseley helmet and untended beard. He carried an alarm clock instead of a watch and a fly-whisk instead of a cane. Often he stood about naked in front of his bivouac, brushing his body hair with a horse brush and scratching himself with a curry-comb, seldom washing in water; nor was he averse to giving out orders while still completely naked. His behaviour made him generally disliked; if he joined a group of officers sitting round a fire in the evening many would drift away, unable to accept his egotistic eccentric manner and rudeness. His dogmatic, bigoted opinions often involving the Old Testament in which he was deeply concerned, almost to the extent that he seemed to be a reincarnated David. He was ruthlessly ambitious, intolerant and arrogant. Mike Calvert and Bernard Ferguson, another courageous distinguished column leader in the first expedition and commander of another brigade (later Governor-General of New Zealand), stood up well to Wingate, but lesser souls withered in his devastating blast.

Of Wingate, Winston Churchill wrote:

> He is a man of genius and audacity, and has rightly been discerned by
> all as a figure quite above the ordinary level. The expression 'the

Clive of Burma' has already gained currency . . . his force and achievements stand out.

The Gateway of India, a huge monument of yellow basalt commemorating the landing in India of Their Imperial Majesties George V and Queen Mary on 2 December 1911, stands in stately splendour on a little promontory by the shores of the Bay of Bombay. Thereafter, as long as India remained a part of the vast British Empire, Viceroys and Governors entered India ceremoniously through the vaulting Gateway of India, and bade farewell to India by passing out of the same regal archway in the opposite direction.

These occasions were heralded with spectacular pageantry, red carpets, shattering gun salutes, glittering guards of honour, cavalry in dazzling uniforms mounted on magnificent horses, resplendent carriages and mounted escorts. Alongside nearby at a pier a large beflagged ocean liner was tied up in which the honoured personage had either arrived or was about to depart.

No such ceremonial honour was bestowed on me when I left India. The closest I came to the Gateway of India was at the docks not far from that haughty archway, where a big American ship bound for Australia lay waiting restlessly with steam up for me to embark. Soldiers with over six continuous years of service overseas were being sent to theatres of war in temperate climates and, as I had been in the tropics for more than eight years, I was one of the first to go under this edict.

I was leaving an India full of delightful childhood memories, but an India now in the twilight of the Empire torn by demands for independence and communal strife for partition. It saddened me to leave so many friends departures and postings to new countries and battalions were a part of Army life but did not help the aloneness I felt, moving always onwards as a single stranger. Nevertheless, having recently lived for months in hot, claustrophobic, verdant jungles and having just travelled across the vast sub-continent for days and nights, my immediate reaction to departure was of joy at boarding a large clean American troopship.

As the troopship sailed, the Gateway faded into the dusk, but it still brought memories of when, many years previously, I walked with my mother through the Gateway before embarking on a passenger vessel bound for England—and boarding school for me, aged ten. We were seen off with ceremony by our household servants, who placed sweet-smelling flowered garlands over us and wept in deep distress. I was tearful at leaving India, a country of happiness and friendly people, blue skies and sunshine, horses and brave soldiers. I dreaded the thought of going to a boarding school in a country quite foreign to me.

15

London

Rendezvous

In the dawn, a crazed artist splashed paints against the heavens and the whole sky burst into gaudy coloured streaks as if saluting a giant liner ploughing its way through the Indian Ocean. It carried prisoners of war, lonely, homesick men singing sentimental songs. Their jailors treated them with humanity and did not believe that prisoners of war abdicate honour, virtue, dignity and the right to stay alive, as did the Japanese. As head jailor, I sympathised with the prisoners, aware of the humiliation they suffered. I was OC troops, in command of two hundred British soldiers who guarded two thousand Italian POWs. The Italians painted the interior of the ship, played deck games, enjoyed American food, lay about in the sun and sang with guitars pleasing Italian songs. They were contented until the ship approached Australia, when they became agitated and demanded to stay on board and go on to the United States, where every man had a relative. Vociferously they pleaded not to be disembarked in Australia.

'We know the Australians; they captured us in the Desert,' they said. 'Australian soldiers are very tough, strong men and were rude and rough to us. In Australia we will be harshly treated. Please do not send us to Australia.'

It was a comical, absurd request. Obviously, they saw this as a chance to remain in the USA after the war and join the large Italian population there. I explained that they were needed on the land that Australian farmers had left to fight Italians and Germans and told them how lucky they were that the Geneva Convention, Red Cross and civilised custom between European nations protected them. For such an impertinent request the Japanese would shoot prisoners of war, or beat them severely, maiming them for life. The Italians did not believe me. 'But the Japanese are nice people,' they said.

When the ship berthed at Woolloomooloo in Sydney I did feel a little for the Italians at the sight of the Australian soldiers waiting on the dock, enormous, powerful men in battle order with rifles and fixed bayonets. No wonder the Australian soldier was renowned worldwide for his fighting ability if those were typical diggers. In double time all the 'wops' and 'dagoes', as the Italians were now addressed, were hustled off the ship, some casting disparaging glances at me.

Built round the shores of a splendid harbour, Sydney was a really marvellous city, full of friendly vivacious people, gregarious and hospitable. I was taken everywhere, to 'our bridge', to sparkling Bondi Beach, its wide sands littered with gorgeous sunburnt female bodies and to the famous Sydney Cricket Ground. I was entertained in grand houses at Point Piper and Vaucluse with extensive views of the harbour, and in the Officers' Mess at Victoria Barracks, where a General welcomed me and where I was presented with an Australian battledress, greatcoat and woollen underclothes, for I had no warm clothes to wear on my arrival in Europe.

I discovered the Hotel Australia, the 'Pub', more like a club where everybody met. In the basement bar crammed full of soldiers a huge private greeted me, 'I'll shout you a drink,' and the diggers surrounded me and did not permit me to buy a drink, 'One for the Pommy Major,' they kept repeating. Later it became, 'One for me Pommy mate.' They had fought in the Desert, some in New Guinea. They had joined the army voluntarily; they came from wealthy families, the land, professions, all walks of life. As it grew closer to six o'clock, they poured strong Australian beer down their throats in increasingly rapid succession until astonishingly the bar closed, bang on six. But nightclubs existed, Prince's, Romano's and Carl Thomas. I rolled home to Woolloomooloo by the light of a silvery moon.

I liked the Aussies, their frankness and friendliness. This fine nation was making a tremendous war effort, remarkable for its small population I regretted leaving them as I sailed away for the Panama Canal and New York.

It was winter and cold in New York; I was glad of my Australian clothes. An attractive girl from an Officers' Welfare Committee at the Grand Central Station took me all round New York: the Empire State Building, Broadway and to superb shops, where I bought a suitcase and filled it with silk stockings, panties, nighties, scent and cosmetics hoping, I suppose, that I would find eager young arms to receive them in war-starved England. I spent three weeks in New York and then embarked with my loot, cases of cigarettes and boxes of tinned food, in the *Andes*, a large liner bound for England.

On board were the hardened long service British regular soldiers, veterans of the North West frontier and Burma battlefields, who had been with me from Bombay, and a few thousand newly enlisted American troops, part of the force being built for the invasion of Europe. To the British regulars, the American men and especially the officers appeared to be appallingly soft and green, needing months of hard training and discipline. The regulars teased them with apocryphal horror stories of battles and fights and robbed them shamelessly at the gambling game of Crown and Anchor. The Americans were glad to disembark.

The *Andes* entered the Mersey and berthed at Liverpool Docks. I had arrived in dear old England after an absence of eight years. In this bombed city, dreary in fog and damp cold, England, 'this sceptred isle', did not seem like a 'demi-paradise' or a 'blessed plot', but it was so in truth and had withstood the terrific onslaught of Germany.

Armed with ration cards and clothing coupons, strange to me, I travelled south, to the Middlesex Regimental Depot at Mill Hill to see the Colonel of the Regiment, Maurice Browne, a great friend of my father; and then to my home in Kent where I received a momentous welcome.

Odysseus' journey home to Ithaca took ten years and he finally found Penelope. My odyssey, travelling around the world by sea and land, took eight years. I was home, but a stranger in England with no Penelope.

I was alone, missing my way of life in the East. Mrs Tidbury, wife of the Colonel in Singapore days, invited me to speak at a meeting in London to relatives of men imprisoned in Hong Kong. I accepted gladly, hoping to meet old friends, perhaps Elizabeth.

She *was* there, sitting in the front row. My heart literally beat with joy. She looked wonderful, attractive in her uniform, a Jenny Wren. As soon as the meeting closed I jumped off the platform and embraced her, thrilled to see her again. It was now January 1944, almost four years since I had last seen her, and she renewed memories of happy times in Singapore and Hong Kong, a way of life that had ceased with this grim war, a forgotten era in the twilight of the British Empire.

Together we walked into the foggy gloom of blacked-out London. In Shaftesbury Avenue at Daly's hamburger bar I ordered tasteless wartime food, not really caring what I ate or drank, I was so happy to be with her. I felt I had rejoined one of a family, my lonely vigil since the fall of Hong Kong had ended.

We talked of ourselves, our lives in Malaya and China—'distant footsteps echo through the Corridors of Time'—and about the present; how Elizabeth was proud to be serving in the Royal Navy, the WRNS, and liked her uniform. It suited her tall figure so well. She laughed at quaint experiences in the Wrens, the distinctive laugh full of fun that I remembered so well; but beneath her gaiety I detected that she had suffered greatly.

'You've had a hard lime, haven't you, Liz?'

'Yes, awful, Tony.'

'Have you heard any news of Noel?'

'Not a word, except that he is a POW. I think about him a great deal and pray for his safety but I have ghastly fears that all is not well with him.' She paused, looking wistful. 'He seems very close to me all the time.'

She explained that last year she had been given leave from the WRNS and had taken Mark to Cornwall.

'I thought of resigning from the Navy and staying with Mark but I had a definite sensation I should not do so—that I must remain in the Navy. It was so strong emotionally it seemed that someone was actually telling me what to do. I often wonder if it *was* Noel and if he *is* dead. Do you think that is a silly idea?'

I did not reply. From my experience in a Japanese prison camp, I knew it would be miraculous if many survived years of ill-treatment, starvation and disease. To comfort her I took her hand. She had lovely hands but I noticed she still bit her fingernails.

She went on. 'That was an incredible night when Noel's message came to me. In the early hours of the morning a flying boat crashed on the beach close to my cottage. The survivors struggled ashore carrying their dead mates and laid them gently on the cold sand. I could not think of anything to say to them, it was too awful. Those pathetic bodies lying in crumpled heaps made me feel certain that Noel was dead. I don't know why but all I wanted to do was to cry for him.'

The flying boat was a Sunderland manned by an Australian crew. It was attacked by eight Junker-88 fighters. The Australians shot down four of the fighters but the flying boat was crippled, many of the crew were killed or wounded and it only just reached a beach in Cornwall.*

Tears were in her eyes. 'I'm behaving like a child now, aren't I?' She laughed, ashamed. 'Do you remember how alike our childhood was, Tony? We discovered that when we first met in Singapore in 1936. You said we were orphans of the Empire, because we were separated from our parents who were always in China or India while we were sent to boarding schools in England. I was unhappy and lonely.'

I remembered too well those wretched years in England away from my family, in sharp contrast to blissful early childhood days in India, similar indeed to Elizabeth's in China. It was wonderful to find someone who understood so well what it was like to be one of Kipling's 'Outcast children of the East'. Thinking of children reminded me of her child:

'How is Mark?'

---

* Flight-Lieutenant Colin Walker, 10 Squadron, RAAF, was the captain of the Sunderland.

'Terrific, very advanced for his age. Yesterday he said, "I'm going to kiss you." I asked why. "Because I know how!" Another experience for me!'

'Thank you for your letter from India about Martin. His mother is grateful for it but we have not heard anything more.'

'It was a terrible battle, fought against insurmountable odds. Hong Kong was indefensible.' I paused for a while, recalling the horror of the fighting. 'After all those disasters in the East it's marvellous to be in England with this feeling of impending victory around.'

'Yes, it is and London is fantastic.' She sipped the tasteless coffee and was obviously used to it. Passing by were men and women in various uniforms, not only British, but European and American, vigorous people all set on victory.

'Wartime London is the most marvellous place; I'm so glad I'm here. It's an exciting day to day existence, Tony, you never know what will happen next. You are completely fatalistic. The Londoners are marvellous people. There's a great sense of comradeship; everyone helps each other.'

It was new to me; I had been out of England for eight years. I was shocked when I saw the terrible damage caused by the German bombing, especially in the East End, and I was astonished that people could survive in the ruins but I was beginning to understand Elizabeth's enthusiasm for London and its people. There was a palpable degree of equality among the English; class consciousness had vanished and with it an inherent dislike of foreigners. Those who had found refuge in Britain such as the Norwegians, Poles, Dutch and French were accepted and admired for their courage, and the Americans were a symbol of the new optimism.

'I love this brave city and its people,' Elizabeth said, 'Especially the Cockneys who are tremendous; they keep their sense of humour even in the worst conditions. The Yanks are great, they brought colour and fun into England when she was becoming drab, tired of war, weary of set-backs—and they have lovely uniforms.' She laughed at me in my dull Australian battledress.

'How did you like Australia, Tony?'

'I went to Sydney, only. That's the most lovely city, superb harbour. I like the Australians very much.'

'So do I. There was a draft of RAAF pilots in the ship on my way home from Cape Town, wonderful men. I met one of them later who sent me a telegram from his airfield: "WALTZING MATILDA RITZ 1700 FRIDAY"!'

It was time for Elizabeth to return to her ship. We strolled along dimly lit streets, Charing Cross Road to Leicester Square and towards the Underground at Piccadilly Circus. People walked carefully, avoiding each other skilfully, and vehicles with shaded lights rolled sedately round the

Circus. When I had known Piccadilly Circus in Sandhurst days in peacetime I had wondered how Eros, perched on a stone pedestal in the centre, could stand the deafening noise of the people and the roaring traffic and why he did not fly away on his golden wings to mother Aphrodite. Now in war he had gone—to some celestial paradise, I hoped. The pedestal was boarded up. How incongruous that the Germans with their destructive bombs had released him from his agonising stance, freed him from rude staring mortal eyes. I had been dreaming of my youth and time now gone, but they say, 'The Past is the Future grown old; the Present is the Past still young.'

It was January and cold so I gave Elizabeth my greatcoat. The Jenny Wren in an army coat—and an Australian one at that—looked remarkable and rather sweet but I hoped we would not meet a Naval Police Patrol.

Soon we were underground. Platforms in the station were crammed full of people who were either homeless or sheltering from air raids. Whole families were down there with mattresses, camp chairs, food and drink. Some played cards, read newspapers, engaged themselves and passengers in cheerful banter; others were asleep sprawled across the platform so that we had to step over them to reach the train. Many of these Londoners must have slept down here night after night ever since the bombing of London had started in August 1940. Stoically and cheerfully they accepted their fate.

In a crowded train we sang war songs, sentimental and patriotic, with men and women in uniform irrespective of sex, race or rank, all mates in this momentous struggle—we belonged to a warrior fraternity.

At Stanmore we jumped out. There was no air raid that night but searchlights sustained a relentless watch raking the skies with savage claw-like strips of light. London in the war was indeed a wonderful city; it was rewarding to be here. At last we came to the gates of HMS Pembroke. Elizabeth invited me to meet her here at the Wrennery in a few days' time.

I kissed her goodnight and watched her walk away, a Jenny Wren now, but the same girl I had first met eight years ago in Singapore, the girl who had lived in China as a child . . .

Hundreds of girls in blue WRNS uniform converged from camouflaged huts and hurried towards the ship's gate, smoothing down jackets and adjusting sailor caps, saluting the streaming White Ensign at the Quarter Deck, clutching leave passes to present to the Gate Picket. They had just finished a watch and they were going ashore from HMS Pembroke, a stone frigate moored rigidly in the heart of Middlesex.

The noise of shrill voices increased to a crescendo as Wrens burst out of the Wrennery, a mass of attractive young women, buoyant and excited at being ashore. Liz waved frantically, worried I might miss her in this sea of

Wren beauty and walk off with a blooming blonde, and she was with me in a flash, grabbing my arm.

'Come on, soldier, we'll catch the tube.'

'Where are we going?'

'I'll show you the sights of London. Tonight we'll make it Quags, shall we?'

Elizabeth had in tow a stranger to London, a sort of colonial country bumpkin, who knew nothing of the nightlife in London's West End. I had left England in 1935 as an impoverished second-lieutenant who could not afford to go to nightclubs but as I 'sweated it out' in the outposts of Empire I felt that I was missing a lot of fun that contemporary men were having in London. In wartime, prices in these places were restricted and I could afford them on the pay of a Major. I wanted to make up for what I had missed and I needed someone to take me round.

The foreboding wail of air-raid sirens shrieked as we ran along paved streets to Quaglino's where a stalwart commissionaire pushed us down steps into a smoke-filled restaurant full of gallant men in uniform, recently returned from the battlefields, dining and dancing with girlfriends. Suddenly a bomb screeched towards us. Instantly, all the brave soldiers flung themselves under tables for cover, but wives or sweethearts remained where they sat or stood, nonchalantly unperturbed. The bomb exploded, with a boom and blast that shook the building. 'Near miss,' someone cried, with relief. The soldiery scrambled sheepishly to their feet, brushing dust off bemedalled tunics.

Liz was highly amused. 'I don't think much of you men,' she laughed. 'The other day we were on parade for Divisions, three hundred Wrens standing on the open quarter deck, when there was an air-raid and a bomb hurtled towards us. Not a soul moved, the Wren officer went on reading a prayer. Then the bomb exploded, very close. Still nobody moved. The Officer said 'God Save The King!' We replied 'Amen!' as if nothing unusual had happened! Pretty good for girls, don't you think?'

The music started again, the dance band playing the haunting tune of 'Lili Marlene' with which the Desert warriors, reminded of their recent victory over Rommel, joined in fervently, their valour suddenly restored.

During that night at Quaglino's Elizabeth told me about her life in England since her return from Singapore. Convinced that she must take part in the war effort as well as support Mark and herself, she joined the WRNS, arranging to be stationed close to London where Mark was cared for by her mother. She relished her life in the Navy, knowing she was really in the war, helping to win it by breaking German codes* in company with girls proud to be serving their

---

* Elizabeth worked with the Ultra Secret organisation breaking German codes on the Enigma bombe. She claimed proudly that she won the war!

country. She did not reach any dizzy rank—there was little promotion for code breakers or, later, three-ton lorry drivers—but she did whatever she was asked to do, lived her life to the full and enjoyed it.

Quaglino's was not unlike other glossy Mayfair hotels, restaurants or clubs, where we often dined and danced whenever Liz was off watch. We came to know them well: the regal Ritz; the fashionable Mayfair; the Berkeley where some guests seemed to accept the Berkeleian philosophy which denied an objective existence to the material world, especially in the early hours; the historic Savoy in the Strand, bombed and disfigured but retaining its impeccable service; the flashy Ciros; the aristocratic 400; the small, jazzy, lovable Bagatelle. In each a common spirit prevailed of people happy yet utterly fatalistic about their future and their survival in the war, just living for the day, just for the moment.

We were served tiny quantities of food, all that was permitted by rationing regulations, and were healthier for it; we paid excessively for spirits and wines, but we danced enraptured to superb bands led by renowned leaders like Glenn Miller, Jack Hilton and Harry James, who elevated simple tunes into classics, the memory of which remained forever. These bands swung and crooned quicksteps, foxtrots and waltzes throughout the night to tunes such as 'A Nightingale Sang in Berkeley Square', 'As Time Goes by', 'I'll Be Seeing You'. In these exciting and lively places Liz and I forgot the traumas that had overtaken us or lay ahead; momentarily we lived under the spell of Ambrose or Carol Gibbons—or Vera Lynn singing 'Yours'. At times we walked about London: Green Park and St. James's Park, where air-raid shelters and trenches and anti-aircraft batteries provided a sense of security; past the gaunt edifice of Buckingham Palace, its smashed windows boarded up, a naked palace without guardsmen clad in bearskins and scarlet tunics. Remembering always the gallantry of diminutive Nelson, we crossed Trafalgar Square to St. Martin in the Fields and found immediate sanctuary in the Crypt and I knew I was in love with her, a love that could not be admitted by either of us.

We moved openly about the West End, often meeting members of my Regiment who may have disapproved but were ever kind. Colonel Maurice Browne saw us crossing Piccadilly Circus and sent for me the next day. He looked quite fierce. 'Officers do not walk about holding hands with Wrens ! There was only one response, the army refuge. 'Sir!' I saluted, about-turned and marched out. There was nothing else for me to say. I had been admonished, my abrupt departure was not impertinent; I could have never been so to that beloved man.

I was posted to an Infantry Division training in the North of England where the distance from London and difficulties of travel in the few overcrowded trains should have served to separate us. Placards at every railway station asked: 'Is your journey really necessary?' But the tyranny of distance failed to prevent Liz from seeing me whenever she could acquire a leave pass. With a Wren friend or two she hitch-hiked in lorries up the Great North Road. In those days a higher moral code made it perfectly safe for young women to hitch-hike throughout the country—it never occurred to Liz that she might be molested; women in uniform were respected.

For a few hours only we met in cold and grimy pubs stinking of beer, full of raucous soldiery in the public bar, but found a little solitude in the lounge bar. Our affection for each other increased and the days and weeks when we were apart were despairing. Occasionally I found excuses to return to London, once to receive the Military Cross from King George VI in Buckingham Palace. Liz was not invited with my parents to the Investiture but she was waiting to meet us outside the Palace, a lovely Jenny Wren anxious to see the medal.

'What did the King say, Tony?'

'He asked if I had recovered from my wounds and if my hand was all right. I was surprised he should have been briefed in such detail but I managed to reply: "Yes, thank you, your Majesty." He then said, "It was a remarkable escape, well done".'

We walked along the tree-lined Mall to lunch in the Savoy, my father immaculate in RAF Chaplain's uniform, Great War medal ribbons decorating his chest, and we celebrated my one medal with a meagre yet gracefully served meal, all that ration restrictions provided. It was a special day, with Liz and my parents.

I was posted to the staff of an Armoured Division. The invasion of Europe was bound to happen soon, so we met as often as possible, living in a frantic state of fatalism from day to day. making as much as we could of each moment left to us, not knowing if we would ever see each other again. I was falling more hopelessly in love with her each time we met. We discarded all caution, all conventions, just existed in a crazy world selfishly for each other.

The skies were full of aircraft day and night droning their way on missions into Europe. It seemed nothing could survive the immense onslaught and daily it meant that the invasion was closer. England became the greatest war operating base of all time, a coiled spring straining to be set free.

Then, suddenly, I had to go. I raced up to London in the early morning and rang Liz as she came off nightwatch. She rushed up at once. We had breakfast in my club and then walked in St. James's Park for an hour— perhaps our last one together.

16

Europe
Letter to Liz

I sailed from Newhaven in Sussex in a Landing Craft Tank and I was I dreadfully sick. It was the supreme climax in a world of superlatives: the greatest armada ever, the greatest amphibious assault ever, monumental bombardments, mighty forces, massive slaughter, enormous destruction. Everything was on an immense scale utterly different from the war in Hong Kong and Burma. Here casualties were evacuated quickly and rations with mail arrived daily. Provided you kept your head down, it was a lovely war.

In France I was not far from Liz, who wrote to me almost every day, letters that kept us together. A highly efficient Field Post Office succeeded always in finding me and a cheerful Post Corporal delivered her letters. Quickly he recognised her large handwriting and gave me the letter with such comment as, 'Another from the young lady.'

I wrote whenever I could or sent a field postcard when I could not. Liz kept all my letters. As the weather improved and the Allied armies began to advance, the volume of my letters increased. I was restricted by censorship from mentioning operations or place names and dates, but this rule was relaxed later. I did not keep a diary or camera—infantry soldiers were not supposed to keep either—so my sole record of the war in north-west Europe was restricted to the letters I wrote to Liz from ditches, slit trenches, cellars, Jeeps, of life at the front, written as if I was talking to her.

'I turn and talk to you so often and find you are not there. I wonder where you are and I miss you terribly; and I wish you were with me to share this great adventure. Life at the front would come naturally to you, a soldier's daughter, ever fearless. You would enjoy the excitement and thrill of battle and then despair bitterly at the awful slaughter and destruction, just as I do. I have been trained for war for many years and I accept and am accustomed to this existence. But I do not believe in the theory that I will not be hit, that it must always be the next man, so I take cover when needed, as a trained soldier should. I worry about the danger you face from buzz bombs exploding over London. You are in greater peril than me here at the front. I know that you had your baptism of fire as a small girl with your father in Canton and more fire when you were bombed in Singapore and London but please take special care.

I miss you perpetually. Separation adds to the dregs of war that seems to have lasted all our lives. But it will not last much longer; with the Americans there must be a million men in France armed with enormous quantities of war material.

Rain has turned the penetrating dust from roads ruined by tracked vehicles into mud but I am in a farm house, attractive with creeper-clad walls, though smelly inside. Our rations are better than the civilians receive at home. Cheeses like Camembert are plentiful. The French are well fed but are a sullen lot, happy only when selling calvados and cider, both of which I detest. The troops talk interminably of women but truthfully would prefer a bath and sleep, which I need also.

Goodnight my darling.

You must have read in the papers the news about Falaise. Prisoners in thousands have been taken, mainly dirty dishevelled Wehrmacht. The battlefield is sordid, the smell ghastly in this August heat. It's a great victory over a ferocious hard fighting army. I expect Paris will fall in a few days. Soon we will cross the Seine and be on our way to Berlin and the war will be over before Christmas—we'll have a marvellous Christmas together, won't we?

The weather improves as we advance. I spent a few days in the 1914-18 battlefields. I thought of you there with your father near the Menin Gate when you tripped over the tip of a bayonet buried in the ground, dug it up and kept it. I despair at the millions killed and wounded there, less than thirty years ago in a war to end all wars; yet we are still fighting. A pity we did not have Monty in command in the Great War. He's just been made a Field Marshal—good on him, as the Aussies say.

Brussels fell on 3rd September, exactly five years since the war started. The Belgians are as dull as the French and, as in France, all the pretty girls have fled with the retreating Germans, who only leave rubbish and ugly signs behind. In Brussels the people gave us a rousing welcome. I had an excellent meal in a restaurant hastily renamed 'Blighty Cafe'. It's awful not to be able to phone and talk to you. I miss your laughter, I keep thinking what you would say to all the things that happen here, what you would laugh at or hate. A great Sandhurst friend, Arthur Denaro, has been killed. You'll remember that wonderful night with him at Quags shortly before D Day. It's very sad.

It's regrettable we did not secure the Maas and Waal bridges after the drop at Arnhem, a brilliant inspiration, a valiant effort but sad to lose wonderful men, including many friends in 1 Airborne Div. I'm afraid the war will be prolonged, we will be bogged down for the winter but I will have more time to write. I will not be home for Christmas but don't let it get you down, darling, we'll make up for it at Christmas 1945 and have a glorious time.

Holland lacks so much of the beauty I like—no trees, no hills, few nice houses. The windmills are picturesque but dangerous—the Bosch fire 88 mm shells into them, knowing we use them as lookouts. I never want to see more rain or mud or sleep by myself again; and I'll never let you out of my sight when I come back. It's fortunate you are learning to drive 3-ton lorries. You can do all the driving, I'll need plenty of rest with you around.

I'm in the front line again, safe in a cellar under a roofless Dutch house in a small empty town. Communication trenches lead to the front line at the bottom of the garden where the MMGs are mounted to fire on fixed lines into no man's land of trip flares, barbed wire and minefields. The Hun shells us occasionally—you can hear 88s screaming towards you and instinctively you take cover—and patrols approach stealthily at night. The other night a patrol set off a flare and a man was shot. With difficulty the body was pulled in at dawn, a German officer with a bullet straight through his temple, a handsome fair-haired Saxon, very young. A sad waste of life.

A few weeks ago our Sherman tanks suffered horribly in a clash with Panzer Mark Vs and 88 mm. anti-tank guns. The fury, gunfire, the sight of tanks brewing up with their crews and the noise was terrific. Our artillery hammered the Germans, Typhoon fighter bombers swept upon them. During the conflict an officer in a slit trench wrote a poem describing vividly the horror. He says he can write only under stress. He gave me his copy, here it is. You will understand and cherish it. Please keep it for me.

> There is no peace apparent here, for all
> The air is filled with bitter tortured sound
> Of screaming noise as though the very wall
> For all the skies has burst; and all around
> These straggling woods are rocked, as spitting guns

Belch forth in ever louder din. And yet,
Above this monstrous pall of sound, there runs
The faintest air of gentle music, set
Sweet in pitch to earthly ears, and slow,
In solemn measure, sober and pure, the hope,
The music of the souls of men; the glow
Of splendid hearts that at this hour do grope
Among the agony of fearful might
For peace, in all its clear and shining light.

I watched our bombers returning from Germany. They looked like small flies high in the sky with grey bursts of flak round them. The fighters do a victory roll over us as they return. There is a huge glow in the sky as a German town burns. The fire resembles the dawn breaking—but not a real dawn which at first light destroys the danger that lurks in the darkness of the night, the light for which every soldier prays.

You are all I have to live for and I hate being away from you but I would not have missed this campaign for anything, even though you are not with me. I was brought up with soldiers and all my adult life I have been trained for war. The first experience in Hong Kong was tragic so it is wonderful to be on the winning side now. They say no man has lived his life until he has known privation, love and war. I have known all three.

Congratulations on passing your driving test. So now I write to HMS *King Alfred*, no longer HMS *Pembroke*, where I used to meet my Jenny Wren at the Ship's gate. You'll be healthier in your new job in Sussex by the sea. Your two long service stripes were well earned by all the thousands of enemy codes you broke.

I'm in reserve in a farm house with a large family. They are all speaking English with a Cockney accent now and even swearing. I hope they don't understand what the words mean. The German occupation of Holland was harsh and the people in this south-east corner suffered greatly. They welcome us as liberators, are far more cooperative than the French who resented us fighting on their land. In the Great War the French charged the British rent for the land we used to fight the Germans! The Dutch are always ready to help and provide shelter and straw for us in the farm buildings. My Middlesex soldiers like the Dutch and often give them things from our rations.

The Germans have been driven over the River Maas. I placed my Company Headquarters in an ice cream factory hastily vacated by them. It's warm and dry, we sleep in the refrigerators, deep inside, safe from shell fire. An Alsatian puppy was abandoned by the German soldiers who also left tin hats, water bottles, gas masks, but no booby traps, thank God. The poor little puppy is scared stiff, so used to being kicked. Now the tommies' food is given to it. He ate my supper and bit me three times. I discovered three American pilots in the factory and released them, much to their relief.

Twenty-six years ago today the Armistice was signed. I was four and you were two weeks old. How quickly the world forgot those torrid years. We are now living much like those men did then. I love the photo of you in MT gear, a navy blue shirt with your cap worn 'flat aback'.

I'm living in a rat-ridden cellar near the River Maas, a few hundred yards from the enemy. The frozen river and snow covered fields between us are a desolate waste of deathly frozen silence, no shooting, no excitement; just waiting and watching. Neither side will disclose their positions. At night German patrols cross the ice and are visible in the eerie light reflected from the snow. It's 100% stand-to all night; I have not undressed or taken off my boots for weeks, it's not worth the risk and against standing orders. From this same cellar a German patrol grabbed a Scottish officer who had just taken off his boots and trousers and dragged him barefoot and bare arse over the ice and snow. Ugh!

Yesterday I picked up a sniper in my field glasses and a man in the same trench aimed his rifle to shoot him but the alert German fired first and shot off the man's thumb. 'Look at me f…ing thumb!' he cried, and then, still feeling no pain, 'That's good old Blighty for me!'

I long for a bath. It's one of the things I hate being without. When I return I'll spend hours in a bath and the rest of my time in bed with you! Battalion HQ has a mobile bath in a trailer stolen in Normandy, marked with the army sign for 2nd Bn. The Middlesex Regiment and which is always accompanied by a fat pig wearing the flash of the 3rd British Division, a red triangle in a black triangle, and a tricolour scarf, since it is a French pig!

I had a letter from Arthur King, still a POW in Germany. It's astonishing he can write to me, very different from the treatment of prisoners by the Japs. And another from an officer in China. Kweilin has fallen to the Japanese, beautiful Kweilin with its grand mixture of old and new, the old Manchu Palace and modern city, the sparkling river threading through green valleys and fantastic limestone hills. The Japs are west of Luichow and on the way to Kweiyang and could cut the Burma Road, which will make all the work of opening the Ledo Road pointless and the lives the Chindits and my Lancashire Fusiliers gave just wasted. I am concerned for the Methodist Mission in Kukong, Constance and the Moores.

How exciting for you to be with Mary and Johnny and Laurence Olivier to
see the film of Henry V. It must have been marvellous. I have always loved
King Henry's speech before Agincourt. His words about St Crispian's Day
could easily be applied to D Day, 6 June 1944:

> And gentlemen in England now a-bed.
> Shall think themselves accursed they were not here;
> And hold their manhoods cheap, whiles any speaks
> That fought with us upon Saint Crispian's day.

A year ago at that meeting in London we met again and I began to live once
more. You looked so lovely in your WRNS uniform. I think I first loved
you then. I was lonely in a strange London after all those years in the East.
You have no idea what it meant to me to find you, how I appreciated your
kindness and how much I needed you. Perhaps I will write a book one day
about us, our love for each other—if you will help me.

I read your last letter by candlelight in yet another freezing cellar. I am
not upset or frightened of the future. We must both learn to live for the
moment and not worry about the future. Your letters are my Bible, my
faith, my hope. No woman could have helped her lover more than you
have, my darling. Even the shells kept away last night. We both know what
we mean to each other

Great excitement! Monty is giving his army a week's leave, so many to go at
a time. Everyone loves the Field Marshal. My battalion, 2nd Bn. The
Middlesex Regiment, has been under his command since 1936 when Monty
commanded the 9th Infantry Brigade and then the 3rd British Division,
which the press call 'Monty's Ironsides'. The soldiers talk of nothing else but
leave. One poor chap due for leave the second week in January is in an awful
stew because his wife has written to say that would be the one week in
which he simply must not return. The whole Company is offering advice
and many have written hurriedly to wives and sweethearts to ensure they are
not caught in the same unfortunate dilemma.

The battalion has been pulled back into reserve for Christmas. On Christmas
Eve I went to Holy Communion in a candlelit old Dutch barn held by an
elderly Padre who is so like my father. It was solemn and beautiful, like that
Mass in the Italian Mission in Waichow. I prayed for you, darling, and for
the men of the 1st Battalion, all prisoners. In the prison camp large numbers
of prisoners went to Communion, many old sinners who have never been
before. In strife man turns to God. We surrendered on Christmas Day 1941,
a terrible day; here in 1944 I have champagne, whisky and turkey and feel

abashed to take them when my real mates are dying of starvation. Why did fate choose me to be the only one of the 1st Battalion to escape? Here the officers had the traditional drink with the sergeants and they remembered the 1st Bn. and the fall of Hong Kong. I am the only man to have fought with both regular battalions. We shared our food with the local Dutch families who were very thrilled. I admire and respect these staunch people. Even back here we are still within range of German artillery.

The New Year arrived with an almighty bang. The whole Maas front blazed into activity as the Germans fired off all their weapons, shooting tracer and Verey lights into the air, producing a first class fireworks show. We did not reply until it became too much of a spectacle when our artillery opened up, silencing the nonsense. At first light fifty fighters came over flying low and attacked our airfields.

Thank you, darling, for 1944 and all you have given me in this year, the best and most wonderful year of my life; a year in which I have no regrets, a year for which I am terribly grateful. I love you very much—there can be only full and complete love for us. I like the photograph of you with the dark background and also the one in uniform—it's the Jenny Wren I love. Your pictures are on show and much admired.

It's cold, 'spring is a little late this year', but snow brings beauty to the Maas and with it an issue of white clothing for patrolling. I lost my cherished jeep during an attack; the clutch burnt out. A Sherman towed me and REME recovery replaced it with a brand new jeep, right in the battlefield!

After being fattened for an offensive for twelve pleasant days in the village of Lubbeck near Louvain, where in May 1940 this battalion with 3 Div first encountered the Germans, we are now in the fighting. I have not been able to write but I sent a field-postcard. I'm commanding a Company with the 9th Infantry Brigade in a big battle. A thousand guns fired a murderous barrage for hours on end. We took thousands of prisoners, in bad shape and dejected, sunken eyes and faces grey from sleepless days and nights of continuous fighting. When we made them put their hands above their heads they wept and pleaded for mercy, thinking we were going to shoot them, and then, assured that they would live, they confided that 'The war will end at 11 o'clock today!'

I could not help feeling sorry for the prisoners. They fought bravely through a terrible bombardment and many were so young, just sixteen and seventeen years old. The front line British Tommy treats the prisoners fairly, helping the wounded. There is somehow a strange fraternity among soldiers irrespective of race, we are all in the same boat, we face death together.

We had a lot of stuff thrown at us; the Germans must also have a thousand guns but the Nebelwerfer, a multi-barrelled mortar, caused the most casualties. It is called a 'moaning minnie', which is the noise it makes as it fires. I am expert at jumping into cover, once into a bomb hole full of water, also into a trench occupied by a German soldier who was terrified.

There is something stirring and thrilling about a battle, the terrific artillery barrage, the tanks roaring into the armageddon and the courage of the men, the determination on young English faces—it is one of the most wonderful things I have seen and it makes you realise with what 'a strength and majesty the British soldier fights'. I am proud to be in this magnificent Army of Monty's. As we came out of battle, having captured Goch and Cleves, some chaps cheered us—and that was very gratifying. I thought of you all through the Reichswald battle, thinking how you, with your fine ideals, would have admired the courage. I have not slept for endless days and nights and I'm dead beat.

I hope you are happy at HMS *King Alfred*, Hove and driving carefully. The news of a 1000-bomber raid on Tokyo is great; that will teach the bastards. The Russians are on the Oder; the end is in sight.

After the Reichswald I had a welcome spell in pleasant country on the west bank of the Rhine, living in a farm house, well fed by a farmer's wife. All the troops occupied fine houses. The people swear that none are Nazis but swastikas are everywhere. Later, under a smoke screen, the whole battalion together with other MMG battalions dug in to prepare to give covering fire for the crossing of the Rhine on 23rd March. The artillery started a counter-battery shoot at 1700 and at 1800 a massive bombardment began. An hour later we opened fire, increasing the rate of fire up to H hour at 2100, when the 51st Highland Division began to cross in buffaloes. The noise from the gunfire was tremendous and it was a really very exciting and historic moment. The Rhine Crossing, the entry into the German Homeland, is a decisive factor in the defeat of Germany. In the morning Churchill, who had been watching the drop of the airborne divisions, drove along the whole front with Monty, passing close to me; a smiling Churchill, triumphant in victory.

I crossed the Rhine at Rees which is smashed flat, every house shattered; just dead soldiers, dead horses, minefields. Civilians smile at us but it's relief from the bombardment or terror of us. My route took me back into Holland, into the textile town of Enschede, quiet and sinister. I soon found why: two

Panther tanks were aiming their guns at me. I swung the jeep round like a rearing stallion and shot out.

Later I returned with our tanks and then the whole city turned out to greet us. Bottles of Bols gin and champagne, secreted during the occupation, were brought out and we were feted, hugged and kissed by old grandmothers and lovely young girls alike. The tommies gave them rations, chocolate, cigarettes; children and women climbed into machine gun carriers, rode on tanks. It was a marvellous party. I spent the night there, sleeping on a soft bed, not daring to undress or remove my boots, not because I was frightened of amorous Dutch girls but that the Bosche were not far away.

Advancing into Germany gives me a wonderful sense of freedom after months on the Maas and in the Reichswald. The Guards Armoured Division is leading. They captured Nordhorn, were delayed by blown bridges on the Dortmund-Ems Canal and captured the bridge at Lingen.

With my company I am in command of five SP AT guns and a 4.2 mortar platoon to defend the left flank of the advance. It was great fun to be on our own. I drove into Holland again and luckily I stopped at the lodge gates of a castle where an old retainer warned me that German tanks were leaguered the far side of the castle, for suddenly a squadron of Panthers drove out fast from behind the building heading north towards Emden. We could not shoot as they were out of range. The retainer had saved us from being surprised and massacred.

Someone pinched my camp bed but I acquired a mattress, which with others is strapped on the roof of my wireless truck plus a crate of live chickens who lay eggs as we roll on. Jock Horrocks, 30 Corps Commander, saw the truck and told me to get rid of the loot. Shortly afterwards I passed Corps HQ and noticed that their vehicles were heavily weighed down with mattresses and other loot, so naturally I have retained my gorgeous mattress.

From a German house I acquired a large suitcase which contains all your letters. My batman hates the case, pulling it in and out of the overloaded loot-filled wireless truck, explaining its contents to everyone: 'More bleeding letters from the Major's young lady.' In your last letter you asked if you should wear uniform or plain clothes when I return on leave. I would prefer you to wear nothing at all.

3 Div has been switched to another front. We did a gigantic drive through Rheine and Osnabrück and northwards. Saw inmates from a concentration camp standing forlornly by the roadside, pathetic skeletons in striped pyjamas. We were forbidden to stop because our duty is to smash the German army as

Tony and Liz – WWII.

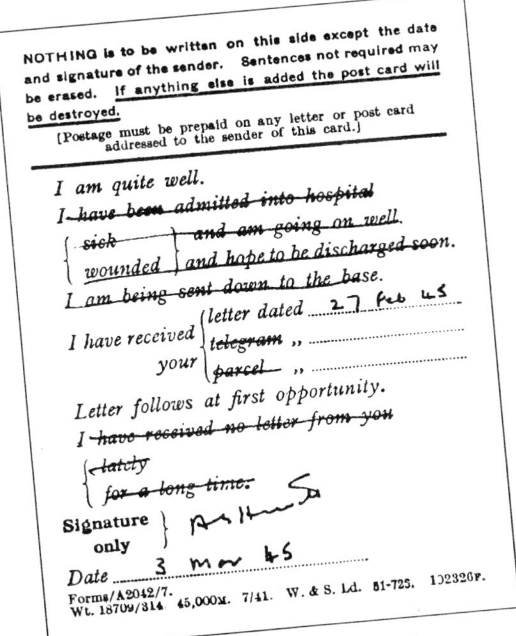

NOTHING is to be written on this side except the date and signature of the sender. Sentences not required may be erased. If anything else is added the post card will be destroyed.

[Postage must be prepaid on any letter or post card addressed to the sender of this card.]

Field Service Postcard—from Tony to Liz.

Wedding photo, outside Caxton Hall. (L–R) Tony, Liz, Juliet Mills, John Mills, Mary Mills.

Tony in The Gambia

A Drummer of the Royal West African
Frontier Force

Liz on the Zambesi in her
BOAC Uniform

Tony, with his Corporal Driver and Mark, in front of his Canberra house.

Discovering the Australian outback. Tony and anthill, Anningie Station N.T.

quickly as possible. This business of rushing through Germany is incredible: we never stop, we are very tired and lack sleep. Yesterday I took nine prisoners, mere boys, extremely frightened. Soldiers and civilians vow strongly they are anti-Nazi, some even say we are their liberators; and then I have Nazi salutes and Heils thrown at me and when I turn on them they are amazed. They seem docile and pleased to see us. I wonder if the British would behave in this way if we were defeated and occupied? I don't think so.

A week ago I was ambushed in a village. I was driving too fast to be hit and faster still after the shot—but the armoured car behind me was hit by a Panzerfaust. We fought back furiously and the Germans gave in to the hammering and surrendered. They were SS troops. I gave a cheeky SS officer a hard kick up the bottom.

I am now the Brigade Major of 185 Infantry Brigade commanded by Brigadier Mark Mathews. I miss the exciting gypsy-like front line life with my Cockney friends and find it strange to eat at a table, do staff work again, sleep under cover. You will have read that Bremen fell to us. With the Brigadier's articulate direction I wrote the operation order for the attack on the city. In succession the Div. Comd., Maj. Gen. Whistler, the Corps Comd., Lt. Gen. Horrocks and the Army Group Comd., Field Marshal Montgomery visited the HQ before the battle. Each one in turn climbed a windmill near the HQ to view the battlefield, much to the consternation of the staff, for one 88 mm. shell at the windmill could have wiped out any one of these brilliant commanders.

Monty, casually dressed, was extremely cheerful. He complimented me on the operation order, a kind gesture for he could only have had time to glance at a page. Most of the staff smartened themselves up—I even wore a tie—but the GS03, a Desert warrior, appeared in a scarf, corduroys, brothel creepers. Monty laughed: 'I see you adopt my style of dress.'

A thousand-bomber raid battered doomed Bremen on the night of 23rd April—I had a grandstand view. Next night the barrage opened at 2300 and continued for seven hours. We entered Bremen on 26th April. Every building is a wreck, knocked to hell, the city just a heap of rubble; astonishingly people still live in the ruins. Sixteen submarines were being built in the docks, some nearly complete.

My enterprising batman, with a huge smile, drove a large Mercedes Benz tourer into the HQ and shouted to me. 'Look what I've scrounged for you, Sir!' I was delighted but madly the MPs confiscated it. Later a similar model appeared as the Brig's staff car. Half my luck.

My temporary job as BM of 185 Bde ended when the usual BM returned from hospital. It was a valuable experience being in the planning and execution of a big battle. The hectic advance of the North German Plain and the Bremen battle have filled my letters with me but please do not think I am not interested in what you are doing. Frank Man could have faced a court-martial for taking you to sea in his MTB—but at last you are a seawoman! The open air life of driving is far better for you than code breaking during long night watches. Drive those trucks and ambulances carefully and don't back into any more taxis or run over another Naval dispatch rider.

Great news, I'm returning on leave, 26th May to 4th June.

```
                        M E S S A G E   F O R M
                        = = = = = = = = = = = =
                                                  Date-Time of Origin
                                                      081505 B

From:-        2 Mx.

To:   (For Action)  Os.C. "A" - "B" - "C" - "D" - "HQ" Coys - Tech Adjt - Q.M.

- - - - - - - - - - - - - - - - - - - - - - - - - - - - - - - - - - - - -
Originator's No.
  2Mx/40/31   (.)  Hostilities with GERMANY will cease w.e.f. 0001 hrs to-morrow
                   9 MAY (.)  Well done All Ranks


- - - - - - - - - - - - - - - - - - - - - - - - - - - - - - - - - - - - -
This message may be sent      Originator's Instrs        T.H.I. or T.O.R.
AS WRITTEN by any means       Degree of Priority
incl Wireless



            Lt.Colonel.
```

'Well, it's all over. Here is Joe Weston's nonchalant message. After nearly *six* years of war, surely he could have been more emotional than 'Well done all ranks'. When the message arrived I was dining with my Company officers, Bob Moberbly and John Milne, both Wykehamists, and a Canadian, Conc McConaghy. We tried to celebrate the momentous occasion with a champagne party, but none of us felt in a party mood. After so many years of strife it was hard to believe the war had ended; and the reaction after months of living so fast and so much on our nerves was disquieting. I kept thinking of those splendid men I had seen killed or terribly wounded and those courageous Die-Hards I had left in the prison camp. So much privation and hardship has happened and so much separation. It is extraordinary to even think that it is nearly all over; to think I have fought my last battle; and I never thought I would live through it as an infantry officer—though ever since I have been in love with you I have been convinced I would survive. You have given me so much hope and purpose for living. I hope you are happy it is over. You have suffered a great deal in this war; and you have done much to bring about victory.

Yesterday was VE Day. I cannot believe there will be no more shells, no more mines, no more dead or wounded. Do you think our whole outlook will change now? Do you believe that you and I will cease to live dangerously, fatalistically, not caring for the future, just living for the day? Will we be cautious, observe conventions, stop living selfishly in a crazy world only for you and me? I hope not; it would be very dull. We are not going to be dull on my leave, are we?

17

Britain

Drama

VJ Day, 15 August 1945, broke as the night ferry from Ostend berthed at Tilbury, where I disembarked. A few days later, when the tumult and shouting by rejoicing crowds in London died down, I met Elizabeth. On VE Day in May I had hoped that peace would not change us, that our wild and extravagant love would continue indefinitely, but three months of peace had sobered us, forced us to face the problems of the future.

Now the end of the war against Japan, which had raged for nearly four years, brought changes in our way of life: Elizabeth was demobilised from the Royal Navy and I became a student at the Army Staff College, Camberley. Our wonderful crazy wartime world had ceased.

There was now a more vital consideration, the possible return of Martin. I heard that Monkey Stewart had died in Japan in 1942 and that Noel Gudgeon had died on the Burma Railway on 15 June 1943 but there was no news of Martin.

Monkey's death was a terrible loss, a brave and much beloved Commanding Officer. Noel's death saddened me. Elizabeth was extremely upset. Although she had expected it ever since that psychic message she received in Cornwall in June 1943—almost on the day that Noel died—the confirmation distressed her. She could not believe that Noel, so animated, young and strong, could have died and yet, instinctively, she had known and accepted it for years.

At the end of September 1945 Elizabeth heard that Martin had survived the ordeal of prison camps in Japan and was on his way to England by sea. She understood the joy the news gave Martin's mother and she was glad for Mark who was only a few months old when he last saw his father but she foresaw great unhappiness. When she had sailed away from Hong Kong in 1941 with Mark and the amah, Martin had cut her off without money and had started proceedings to end the marriage. The war with Japan then intervened and she did not know if Martin still intended to dissolve the marriage.

Almost daily Elizabeth was plagued by her family to attempt to make a new start with Martin. They were completely insensitive to the situation and refused to accept that the marriage had actually ended. Eventually, because of Mark she succumbed to the pressure, thinking she had no alternative. I tried to comfort her but it was a time of distress and bewilderment, so different from our years of blithe adventure.

To prepare for Martin's arrival Elizabeth moved into a cottage in Buckinghamshire with Martin's mother, a gracious woman who lived a lonely life separated from her husband, a resident of France. She adored Martin possessively, which augured ill. Elizabeth realised she had made a mistake; she should have waited until Martin returned and should have stayed apart until the situation was discussed with him.

On 27 October Martin's mother received a telegram saying that he had landed in Liverpool and would arrive in London the next evening, which by an odd chance happened to be Elizabeth's twenty-seventh and Mark's fifth birthday. Making another mistake she went to Euston Station to meet him.

The troop train steamed into the station at 5.00 p.m. and hundreds of ex-prisoners burst out of the carriages. Elizabeth wandered along the platform searching in the excited milling crowd for Martin and asked a Middlesex man if he had seen him.

'There he is. You've just walked straight past him!'

Elizabeth did not recognise him and he did not seem to know her. He looked old and strange, dressed in an ill-fitting battledress and a dark blue beret, carrying a huge Samurai sword. In silence they stood and stared at each other. An appalling fit of emotional anguish swept through Elizabeth. Apathetically, she led him to a taxi, into the compartment of which he brought the sword, clutching it firmly. At the Savoy, where Elizabeth had reserved a room, Martin refused to permit the hall porter to take or even touch the sword and carried it defiantly into the bedroom. Elizabeth was beginning to dislike the monstrous weapon, the scabbard of which was elaborately engraved in Japanese designs and characters, but she appreciated that Martin was extremely attached to it. This was apparent when he brought it into the dining room and placed it on a chair beside their table, refusing the waiter's offer to deposit it in the cloakroom. He was confused, lost in a frightening new world, desperately grasping the sword, a link with his recent life, a symbol of revenge for the horror and suffering.

At his home the next day Martin received an emotional welcome from his mother and a friendly smile from Mark who was happy to have someone he could call 'Daddy' like other boys at school. Throughout the greetings the Samurai sword was still held by Martin. His mother took an instant dislike to it: 'Do put that horrible thing down and don't bring it into the house.'

Martin experienced great difficulty in settling down to a different way of life; he could not sleep, nightmares disturbed him, his nerves were on edge. No organisation came to rehabilitate him. There were just too many ex-prisoners and wounded for the authorities to cope with.

They were strangers with little common bond or interest, poles apart, with an empty void in their lives of five long years. The proximity of her mother-in-law in the same house added to the discord as did the Samurai sword. To Elizabeth it represented the horror perpetrated by the Japanese. Millions had been executed by Samurai swords, thousands recently in China and Malaya. The sword was an emblem of the violence and cruelty that had killed Noel. She hated it but understood she could not part Martin from the sword even if it forced them further apart. She hated all things Japanese and was sure her father, if he had been alive, would have approved the taking of a sword only in battle, not as a souvenir after the Japanese had surrendered.

They put Mark in a boarding school for a week and stayed in the Compleat Angler at Marlow on Thames to be alone and sort out their differences, but failed to resolve them. Elizabeth was sorry for Martin, she knew how inhumanly he had been treated by his Japanese captors. She realised this terrible experience had changed him and that it would change any man but he was so very different from the man she had married, the charming, reckless fun-loving young lieutenant. She was not in love with him and knew she never could be. She had been too long on her own.

Months later I was posted to the Directing Staff of the School of Combined Operations in Devonshire. Suddenly, out of the blue, Elizabeth rang. Martin was involved with another woman, she said, and the marriage was over. It was wonderful—the dawn had broken.

The way ahead was not easy. Having no income of any kind Elizabeth searched anxiously for a job as did two million unemployed persons. The cost of victory had crippled England's economy. Coal, electricity, food, drinks, shoes, clothing, almost every commodity was severely rationed. Thousands of the unemployed were ex-servicewomen like Elizabeth, highly trained, skilful and intelligent. For many the war had brought about a social revolution. Girls who would normally have stayed at home until they were married and then lived the rest of their lives as housewives were now reluctant to accept that way of life. Moreover, those who had served overseas in the forces wished to find jobs abroad and escape the gloom of a depressed Britain, the harsh conditions and rationing.

Thus, when positions for air-hostesses became available with British Overseas Airways Corporation two thousand women applied. Only ten were taken of whom Elizabeth was one. Her experiences in the Royal Navy and living in China and Malaya were invaluable and she loved the job immediately. When she was not overseas she stayed with her mother in London. As I was in Devonshire, we were far apart.

I was a member of the first Directing Staff to be appointed to the School of Combined Operations to develop the principles of amphibious warfare. One of the tasks given us was the preparation of a paper exercise of a seaborne landing in Italy for Field Marshal Viscount Montgomery of Alamein, then Chief of the Imperial General Staff, who presented it to the Army Staff College. He took a close personal interest in our proceedings and it became a lively and refreshing experience getting to know and working for the great master.

Many distinguished persons visited the School including Lord Mountbatten, who had been the first Chief of Combined Operations in the war. Shortly after his visit he became Viceroy of India, commissioned by Prime Minister Clement Atlee to fulfil the Labour Government's first major step in dismantling the British Empire.

Indian independence came at midnight 14/15 August 1947 and with it the partition of the sub-continent into Hindu India and Moslem Pakistan. Millions lost their land and homes and were slaughtered. The carnage and genocide of the poor pathetic people that I had loved saddened me: a terrible human tragedy. It seemed that time had reverted four centuries, that the Mogul invaders were driving infidels out of northern India, that the Hindus and Sikhs were forcing Moslem hordes back whence they came. All the benefits that the British Raj had brought to India had vanished on that August night; the legal, administrative and educational institutions, infrastructure and stability. Thousands of Britons had given their lives for India; earnest men had worked themselves to death for the people; all their endeavours had been swept away.

The ruined Residency at Lucknow with the Union Jack which had not been lowered since the eighty-seven day siege in the Mutiny in 1857 represented the endurance, bravery and suffering of the British. It was a shrine of the Imperial British Raj. I had driven past it when I had returned to India from China in 1942. I had known the story of the siege since I was a small boy and I hoped the flag would not be destroyed by Indian nationalists. In fact just before midnight on 14 August, British officers had themselves lowered the Union Jack, cut down the flag pole and saved the ensign from desecration. Later the flag was sent to King George VI.

Indian independence was the virtual end of Empire. It could have survived the fall of Hong Kong and Singapore but it was doomed when India, the cornerstone, was lost.

I wanted to see something of the remaining Empire before it dissolved so I applied for an appointment with the Colonial Forces. I was posted to the Royal West African Frontier Force, sailed to Freetown, Sierra Leone and joined the 1st Battalion The Sierra Leone Regiment.

Scarlet bougainvillea, frangipani and flame trees, made me feel at home. Perched on the Ridge below the 4 000 foot Lion Mountain, barracks, colonial servants' houses, Flagstaff House. Government House and the Hill Station Club completed a typical colonial scene. The Ridge was exactly like the cantonments of an up-country Indian station.

My soldiers were huge black Africans dressed in red fez's, scarlet zouave jackets, khaki blouses and shorts, long puttees but no boots. Feet were polished with boot polish and bare arms with rifle oil to make them shine. When an American lady visitor, attracted by these dazzling giants, enquired to whom they belonged, a humorist replied: 'To an army of white officers with black privates.' Spontaneously she replied. 'Oh Lordy, how gaudy.'

Meanwhile, Elizabeth was flying with BOAC in Dakotas, DC3s, to places like Lydda, El Adem in the Western Desert where German prisoners-of-war were still clearing the battlefields three years after the war had ended, Cairo, Khartoum, Juba, Nairobi—long journeys in small non-pressurised aircraft which were often thrown about by air turbulence.

In London the case for divorce was heard in the High Court of Justice before Mr Justice Lord Merriman in March 1948. Lord Merriman offered both petitioners the option of sharing Mark and settling financial matters mutually. Elizabeth and Martin agreed and a Decree Nisi was granted to each of them. Mary Mills, Elizabeth's sister, went to the court with Liz and after the case took her to stay at her house in Fulmer, Buckinghamshire. With the ever-vivacious John Mills they celebrated with champagne. Liz could hardly believe she was free—nine years of marriage had slipped away in the few minutes it took Lord Merriman to give his judgement. Immediately, she sent me a cable—a special 'golden' cable.

18

Africa

Triumph

A gravestone in Freetown, Sierra Leone, is inscribed tersely 'White Man's Grave', which is an apt description of the place. When I received that 'golden message' I felt free to escape from the white man's grave and trek up-country to learn about the homes and tribes of my soldiers, Moslems and pagans. I travelled north by train and bus to the end of the gravel road and then, imitating Livingstone, I walked eastwards into 'darkest Africa' on tracks through dense primeval jungle accompanied by six intrepid soldiers and thirty robust carriers who carried on their heads the coin, gin and medicine boxes, food, water and clothing.

For three weeks I walked up to twenty miles a day from village to village. sleeping in round palmleaf huts provided by village headmen. Tribal Chiefs welcomed me with gifts such as a goat, bananas, yams. I repaid the estimated value of the gifts in coin, ostensibly as a present to the Chief. Old soldiers greeted me warmly, saluting and showing old war medals, even one from the Ashanti War of 1900. I helped the sick with items from my medicine box—aspirins worked wonders. I gave sulphonamide tablets to a woman with pneumonia and I stayed all night in a small hut with her until she recovered. If she had died I would have been blamed for her death and I could well have been placed in the big communal cooking pot and stewed in palm oil.

A herd of migrating elephants delayed the trek while they smashed down the forest and a village; gorillas, baboons and other inquisitive monkeys were always close, leopards abounded, magnificent tropical birds of every description and beautiful huge butterflies enriched my march and an enormous boa constrictor denied approach to a drift crossing. Traversing fragile rope bridges spanning raging torrents, I climbed a mountain range on the border of Sierra Leone and French Guinea and found the source of the

River Niger from which it flows 2 600 miles to the sea in Nigeria. As I gazed across endless miles of undulating forests the immensity of Africa awed me and I wondered how it was with Elizabeth now flying over East Africa on the other side of the continent

Back in the Battalion I told the troops about the trek which they named 'The Big Patrol' and when I mentioned a village or Chief a soldier would jump to his feet and proudly exclaim, 'That be my home' or 'My Chief'. The Big Patrol developed a bond with the troops. They appreciated my interest in them and they trusted me. Soldiers would come instinctively to me with their personal problems. I became devoted to these amiable men.

And then Elizabeth wrote from Uganda saying she was on her way to South Africa flying in a Solent Flying Boat:

> We flew off from Southampton, lunched ashore at Marseilles slept in Augusta and with our 32 passengers visited Syracuse, a fascinating biblical city. After lunch in houseboats on the Nile at Cairo, we flew up the huge river to Luxor and went to the ruined temples in the Valley of the Kings, an inspiring sight. In withering heat we stayed in the so-called Grand Hotel at Khartoum and in the evening looked at the Omdurman battlefield. Up the White Nile to Lake Victoria, landing at Port Bell and staying in the Imperial Hotel at Kampala, Uganda's capital. It's a beautiful place and reminds me of Singapore, same trees and flowers and like Singapore it's bang on the Equator.

Two decades later after gaining independence this prosperous country declined into anarchy, fratricide and utter horror, its covetous hopes of freedom devastated.

Elizabeth loved her work as an air-hostess in Solent Flying Boats. Each five day journey from England to South Africa was an adventure in itself but extremely hot and turbulent in unpressurised aircraft flying low following the course of rivers. She enjoyed the remarkable sights of Africa from the air, especially herds of galloping wild beasts disturbed by the aircraft as it flew over Tanganyika, Nyasaland, Rhodesia. As it approached the Zambesi, the Victoria Falls could be seen and the roar heard miles away. When she descended from the Victoria Falls Hotel to the 'boiling pot' she was drenched in spray by the cascade rushing downwards. Finally the Solent landed on Vaal Dam near Johannesburg.

When the Decree Nisi was made final and absolute, I tried to persuade Elizabeth to join me in Sierra Leone. A large house overlooking mountains, forests and sandy beaches would be ours, with four servants and a car.

Amused with my naive persuasion, Liz replied she would be flying to

Accra on the Gold Coast in a BOAC York in charge of a planeload of children. She would be the first air hostess ever to arrive in Accra and the English schoolchildren the first children ever to fly to the Gold Coast for their summer holidays. She would be staying only three days and would be with her cousin, Lord Hemingford. the Rector of Achimota College.

Could I join her? I could stay with the Hemingfords.

Accra is over 900 miles from Freetown. The return airfare was £50, a great deal of money in those days. With acute lack of tact I cabled: AIRFARE FIFTY POUNDS IS IT WORTH IT? Furious, Liz retorted: DON'T BOTHER.

General Urwin, the GOC, kindly offered me a seat in his RAF aircraft but it was delayed and then it was too late. Liz had flown away. It was an abortive affair but Liz with her inborn craving for adventure and travel had enjoyed the flight out, flying low across the Sahara from Castel Benito in Tripoli and staying in Kano, Nigeria, which she described as 'something out of the Arabian Nights, a throbbing sinister city within an enormous wall, a feeling of mystery, fantastically dressed people, some in uniforms like Roman soldiers.'

On her return journey a baby chimpanzee destined for the London Zoo was placed in the York. The little creature whimpered and cried until Liz held his tiny had and stayed with him to the end of the journey. Unfortunately a malarial mosquito must have bitten Liz somewhere in West Africa and ten days later she was taken off the South African Solent run with a dangerously high temperature and placed in Kampala General Hospital where a quinine injection with a dirty needle caused an infected ulcer.

Mutiny broke out in The Gambia Regiment of the Royal West African Frontier Force at Bathurst, the capital of The Gambia. Five hundred miles north of Sierra Leone, north of the Portuguese and French Guineas, the British colony of The Gambia occupied a thin strip of land, running due east from the Atlantic Ocean for three hundred miles along the Gambia River and surrounded entirely by French Senegal. Wags called it the anus of the British Empire. Albeit, this diminutive colony was the definitive outpost of Empire: and the command of its Regiment was the most independent in the Empire.

The mutiny was quelled by riot squads of The Gambia Police. The Commanding Officer was removed and I was chosen to replace him. I was delighted to be granted this jewel of autonomous command but before I could assume command I heard that my father was seriously ill. I flew to England on compassionate leave.

By extraordinary coincidence Elizabeth returned from Uganda a few days before I arrived in England. If she had not been kept in hospital with malaria for two weeks at Kampala she would have been out of England on the South African run. An operation in London to remove the infected wound followed by sick leave retained her in England for the whole of the month of my leave. It was wonderful to be with her again, years of despair dissolved into vapour. We were free, ecstatic, rushing about London like young lovers, which of course we were, returning to our old wartime haunts, the Bagatelle, the Ritz and the Berkeley. We were in love just as we were in those crazy days before D Day. Mary and John Mills invited us with Mark to stay in their charming Georgian house, Fernacres, where Mark played with Juliet (Bunch) and Hayley—both future film and stage stars—while we were taken to the first night of Terence Rattigan's *Playbill*. That night we decided to be married as soon as possible and chose Saturday 18 September at Caxton Hall; oddly, the same Registrar had also married the Mills seven years previously.

Mary and Johnny, and Juliet aged six, came into the Hall with us and an officer on leave from Sierra Leone was my best man. As we came out of the Hall the press swarmed round us and took pictures which appeared in the *Evening News* and other newspapers with headings like 'STAR LOOKS ON . . . FILM STAR JOHN MILLS . . . PLAYWRIGHT MARY HAYLEY BELL'. It was pleasing to have suddenly acquired such a celebrated brother and sister-in-law even if our wedding was slightly overtaken by their fame. Waiting outside were a group of relatives including my sister Margaret and Dennis Hayley Bell, the gallant RAF fighter-pilot about whom Liz had worried so much during the Battle of Britain.

Johnny gave us a wedding lunch at the Caprice in Mayfair. With his natural charm and love of fun and laughter, Johnny turned the lunch into an uproarious party, playing the restaurant's piano and singing songs from plays in which he had acted. From Mary's own play, *Duet For Two Hands* he played the music of the 'Min River Boat Song' written by her father. Johnny's life-long friend Noel Coward then took over with a few of his ever-enduring songs and, addressing sharp quips about love and marriage directly at Liz and me, recited appropriately from *Private Lives*.

The honeymoon was spent in Claridges in the blissful luxury which only that wonderful hotel can provide. The first evening for sentimental reasons we dined and danced in Quaglinos and met many friends. The next night we dined at the United Hunts' Club and met Flash Chattey of my Regiment who had been with us in Singapore and Hong Kong. Without consideration for a honeymoon couple, our friends and Flash insisted on being shown our gorgeous suite in Claridges and sampling the exquisite room service. It turned into a wild party.

It was hard to believe we were really married at last. Many things had happened since I had first met the girl I liked so much in the primrose-coloured frock with large brown buttons running down the middle twelve years ago in Singapore. Our supreme happiness was marred, sadly, by the death of my father, a victim of the effect of long service in India, a terribly harsh campaign in Mesopotamia, gas poisoning in trench warfare in France and desert fighting in Egypt and Palestine.

Elizabeth continued flying with BOAC while she awaited approval of her request to resign. I sailed to The Gambia in the Elder Dempster Liner MV *Apapa* which stopped at Bathurst only because the Governor of The Gambia, Sir Andrew Wright, was on board. As soon as the ship anchored in the Gambia River the Governor's yacht came alongside with the Colonial Secretary and Attorney General aboard. The Governor invited me to go ashore with him. At the jetty a splendid Guard of Honour mounted by The Gambia Regiment, resplendent in scarlet zouave jackets, presented arms with a Royal Salute played euphonically by the Regiment's Drums and Fifes for His Excellency the Governor and Commander-in-Chief. I had arrived in The Gambia in style.

I prepared for Elizabeth's arrival by Christmas, the much delayed Christmas I had promised her so often. There were few better places on this earth than The Gambia to spend a Christmas and in our case a honeymoon. The climate was delightful, cloudless skies and warm sunshine; there were no shortages of food or drink, a paradise after rationed England in winter. The Colonial Secretary gave me a wooden bungalow near Cape St Mary surrounded by casuarinas, bougainvillea and flowering shrubs, with expansive views of the Atlantic Ocean and a private bathing beach.

The Africans were contented in this blessed plot that had been a colony for centuries. Independence was not to come until much later. The only discord was the mutiny which had occurred recently. My soldiers were fine proud men, all Moslems, by race Mandingos. To discover why such men should mutiny I held a *durbar* with the troops sitting round me under a large banyan tree, and I listened and listened.

The Governor agreed to abrogate fines which had been placed illegally on the troops, to settle the cost of damage the troops had caused in a village which had stolen an army woman and to build a Mosque in the barracks so that the Regimental Imam could impose Islamic law. I now had a happy Regiment. At every dawn the troops ran to the beach singing, 'Commanding Officer very fine man,' in repetition until they dived into the surf, a 'very fine' sight of hundreds of beautiful black shining bodies.

Each day the Regiment performed a ceremonial mounting of the Guard at Government House. It was a comic Gilbert and Sullivan colony, so small, yet with all the same trimmings of a large one. A few thousand people, ambulant citizens who wandered into the Senegal whenever they wished, were administered by an Executive Council and Legislative Council. The Executive met once a week, its function being to advise the Governor, who presided. It consisted of the Colonial Secretary, Commander Armed Forces (me), Financial Secretary, Attorney General and unofficial members such as the Police Commissioner and the Bishop of The Gambia and the Rio Pongas. The Legislative Council's primary function was the enactment of legislation and control of public funds, which was performed by the heads of departments: Health, Education, Public Works etc. Clearly a large body of officials were assembled to govern a tiny colony.

All over the Empire, colonies were administered in exactly the same manner. In The Gambia a genial administration offered stability and security for the inhabitants. It was into this prosperous and fortunate Colony that Elizabeth was now due to arrive, having placed Mark in a boarding school in Wiltshire and having made arrangements for him to fly out and join us for the Easter school holidays. The furnishing of my government house was delayed by the Public Works Department but fortunately the United Africa Company lent me a splendid UAC house, an enormous concrete structure with wide open arches in place of windows.

Elizabeth arrived at the airport, harmoniously named Yum Dum, in the dark at about half-past ten. We jumped into my car and I introduced my soldier driver, Sambujang Darbo, who drove off at speed to the huge white UAC house. We rushed in; at last we were together—our long vigil and odyssey had ended. We scrambled into bed and each other's arms. Hours later, as the African dawn began to break with a lambent flame, I heard a noise outside the bedroom's open archway. There, to my horror, just below the vaulted opening, was my car with the driver still in it. I told him to drive back to barracks.

Later, when she met Sambujong Darbo again, Liz asked why he had stayed in the car all night outside the house, why he did not go home.

'CO no dismiss me.'

'Who is CO, what is CO's name?'

'His name be darling!'

19

Australia

End of Empire

Great Empires end tragically or simply fade away. The greatest was fading, or rather dwindling to its end. A few protectorates, possessions and colonies remained but in reality the end of the British Empire came in 1948 with the granting of independence to India, Burma and Ceylon.

However, in 1949, there was still a small piece of the Empire left for Liz and me in The Gambia, where, during Easter school holidays, Mark, now eight years old, arrived to join our Gambian honeymoon. His pink-face, white knees and flamboyant school cap was greeted by the fun-loving Mandingo people with screams of laughter and joy. Mark was accepted immediately as a friend and he soon became brown, swimming in the warm sea and running with us for miles along pristine beaches, entirely uninhabited.

Liz loved The Gambia, its sub-tropical climate and its people, coupled with the happiness of our marriage. I rejoiced in the autonomy I held in my command of The Gambia Regiment, with no superior army authority within hundreds of miles, except the Governor, who was Commander-in-Chief. I was devoted to my fine Mandingo soldiers. There was no other command like it anywhere else.

But regrettably I was transferred to Sierra Leone as the Chief of Staff of the Army Headquarters in Freetown. We flew south to the Colony, overloading the DC3 with all our newly acquired possessions, and were 'marched in' to a modern concrete 'army married quarter' on a hill above the roaring breakers of the Atlantic ocean and just below the forested Lion Rock, a haven for leopards and millions of dazzling butterflies.

Intense heat, endless rain, malaria, yellow fever and a miscarriage suffered by Liz, destroyed any attraction the place may have held. In early days of the

Colony's history, when freed slaves from North America were being settled in Freetown, a succession of Governors died at their posts from tropical diseases. I did not wish to emulate those staunch characters and with much relief I was transferred to regimental duty in Germany.

With Liz, a car and all our worldly goods, I joined the 1st Battalion The Queen's Royal Regiment at Iserlohn, just east of the Ruhr. The battalion was a part of the 4th Infantry Brigade commanded by Brigadier Rohan Delacombe, who later became Governor of the State of Victoria, Australia. It was a joy to train seriously with the Queen's, the senior English Regiment of the Line, with infantry and armoured divisions and air forces to defend Western Europe from the menace and might of the USSR.

Liz was extremely happy. The Queen's had been her father's regiment and she had known them as a child in Hong Kong. Mark joined her for school holidays.

The 1st Battalion The Middlesex Regiment, rebuilt from the one I had fought with in Hong Kong, returned from Korea to be stationed in Austria at Zeltweg near Graz, where we joined them and from where we made frequent journeys to Vienna through the USSR Zone over the Semmering Pass, fraught with the danger of causing an international incident by infringing some petty Russian regulation.

In Vienna, divided into four international sectors, Liz and I attended each month ceremonial mountings of the British, French, Russian and American Guard at the Palace of Justice and receptions in one of the four Embassies. The romantic history of the city, its bomb-scarred beauty, the thrilling menace of Russians just across the Danube and the exceptionally friendly Viennese, endeared us to Vienna.

Adding to the ceremonies, the Coronation of Her Majesty Queen Elizabeth II was celebrated in June 1953 with a spectacular *Beating of Retreat* by the massed bands of the Cameron Highlanders, Green Howards and the Middlesex Regiment in the Gloriette of the magnificent Schoenbrunn Palace.

To replace the Colours lost at Hong Kong, new Colours were presented. As the only officer who fought at Hong Kong I received the Regimental Colour on which the words *Hong Kong* were emblazoned as a Battle Honour, which I acknowledged with emotion and with respect for our dead.

Off duty, Liz and I rode horses left at Zeltweg by the defeated *Wehrmacht*, dined in village inns, skied, climbed mountains, drove into Italy and Venice, Liechtenstein and Switzerland with ease; there were so few people about.

Europe was suffering terribly from the effects of the long war. Thousands were refugees, displaced homeless persons. Selfishly, for us in the Army of occupation, it was a good life; for me much better than 'bush whacking' in darkest Africa.

In November 1953 I was posted to HQ Allied Forces Northern Europe in Oslo, Norway, appointed "Chief of Exercise and Manoeuvre" and promoted Lieutenant Colonel. My task was to run manoeuvres to train joint service NATO forces in the defence of Northern Europe. Large scale manoeuvres were held annually, generally in northern Norway, 400 miles north of the Arctic circle, under the midnight sun in summer or pitch darkness in winter.

Americans outnumbered the remainder of the Headquarters Staff of British, Norwegian, Danish, French and Germans. We appreciated the vital importance of our task with huge Russian forces just the other side of the north-east Norwegian border, cooperated smoothly together and made lasting friendships.

I spent over three years in Norway with three long winters. Liz skied every day and I joined her at night on lighted trails. On Fridays we bussed to distant inns and skied back to Oslo in two days, sheltering at night in huts. We became disgustingly healthy. In spring and fall we walked in the mountains with Norwegian friends, in summer we sailed on the Oslo Fiord. Intrepid Liz shared with me the midnight sun north of the Arctic Circle, the beauty of which she has never forgotten. Mark skied with us on a spring holiday before I took him as a new-boy to Harrow School, his deeply sunburnt face contrasting strikingly with the other small new-boys.

When my tour of duty in Norway expired, I was ordered to return to the Royal West African Frontier Force in the Gold Coast, West Africa. Liz was flabbergasted, 'Not Africa again! Why you? You've served longer there than anyone!' It seemed incredible to me also, to be sent to the African bush after the knowledge I had gained in 3½ years of top level international staff work in NATO. But I went and Liz came with me, following the drum as she had always.

I flew to Kumasi in Ashanti, a state in the centre of the Gold Coast, and assumed command of 900 African soldiers, 25 officers from English and Scottish Regiments and a Regimental Sergeant Major from the Coldstream Guards.

Six weeks after my arrival, on 6 March 1957, the country gained independence and adopted the name of Ghana. At the Fort in Kumasi, where a British Governor had been besieged in 1900 by the warlike Ashantis, I witnessed with sadness the lowering of the Union Jack and the raising of the Ghana flag. The humiliation I felt convinced me finally that the Empire had ended, that Liz and I were its outgrown children. The Union Jack was sent to England as was the flag I saw flying at the Residency in Lucknow when I had just arrived in India from China in 1942.

Much was expected of Ghana, the first colony in Africa to become independent. It was a highly prosperous country with a flourishing cocoa industry and huge mineral resources but, under the leadership of Kwame Nkrumah, the first President, its wealth was squandered.

Kwame was educated by Liz's cousin, Lord Hemingford, the Rector of Achimota College. At a dinner in Accra, shortly after my arrival, he was extremely affable, saying he owed much to Dennis Hemingford; that when his country was free and independent, black and white people would work together: 'You can play a tune of sorts on white keys, a tune on black keys, but for harmony you must use both black and white'.

However, years later, when he dined in my officers' mess in Kumasi, he was less affable, angered at the Ashanti's hatred of him, in fear of his life, expounding, 'Your Westminster and legal system is useless. I cannot govern with an opposition arguing against me, I cannot allow clever lawyers to defeat just prosecutions—Africans want and respect strength like one party government and arbitrary justice. You British are too soft, too weak, you never tried to understand how Africans like strong rulers—no wonder you lost your Empire!'

My soldiers were now in the Ghana Army. The scarlet zouave jacket, red fez and cummerbund were considered imperialistic and replaced by a cap, scarlet tunic, red-striped blue trousers—similar to a Guardsman without a bearskin—highly imperialistic and ridiculous in the heat. We paraded in this fancy dress for a visit by HRH The Duke of Edinburgh. I don't think he was very impressed.

I was due for leave after the first 18 months but I wanted to go a month earlier to see Mark playing for Harrow against Eton at Lords in June. I asked the Commanding General, Victor Paley, an old Etonian, who replied at once, 'Of course, Tony, I'd be delighted to let you see Eton thrash Harrow'. Old school ties never die!

On our return from Europe Liz got poliomyelitis. She had been inoculated once but was hit before there was time for a second dose. Extremely ill, she was ordered by a South African surgeon, a polio specialist, to lie absolutely still in her bed in the Kumasi General Hospital with two young nurses caring gently for her. Gradually the paralysis relaxed; the effect of the first inoculation worked. She returned to my house in an ambulance. My orderly, John Grunshie, a huge strong soldier, carried her like a child in his powerful arms up the stairs, crying all the way. 'Why you cry John?' Liz asked. 'Because madam no fit to walk again'. He adored Liz, as did all the soldiers; for two years she had looked after their wives and children with great affection. But Liz did walk again and was well enough to travel to England for my next appointment. She had inherited her father's indomitable spirit, withstood danger and illness like Hayley on Shameen at Canton.

Sailing away from Ghana, I saluted my troops and the *Hausa Farewell*, a West African Force bugle lament, by gently casting my Ghana Army hat into the wake of the departing ship. It was hard to part from those amiable African soldiers, but I had learned to accept an army life of frequent transfers to different formations and countries.

Liz accepted and enjoyed this nomadic odyssey—she could never have submitted to a suburban parochial existence of living for years in only one town. And this move was enthralling, visiting interesting places like Casablanca, Tangier, Algiers and Majorca, disembarking at Marseilles to drive to Zurich and ski for months at Arosa during a long leave. Moreover, Mark was with us, having distinguished himself at Harrow by being *Head of School*.

I joined an infantry division in Lancashire, northern England. The Lancastrians are splendid people like those soldiers I knew in the Lancashire Fusiliers in India, but in their county it rained almost every day, coal dust from mines and soot from 'dark satanic mills' fell upon us—even the sheep were black—and it was cold. We longed for a transfer to a better climate.

Unexpectedly, the War Office informed me that I was to be the next Commander of the Caribbean Area in Jamaica. We played calypso records endlessly, arranged with the shipping company to include our Spaniel with our passage to the West Indies, waited on leave in Majorca for final instructions. Then, painfully, the Jamaican Government decided that the next Commander would be selected from Jamaican military forces, and that it preferred a black man.

Doomed to remain shivering, we watched a film being made of a book written by Liz's sister, Mary Hayley Bell, called *Whistle Down the Wind* with niece Hayley Mills in the star role. She was superb. And we saw Mark, now at Magdelene College, Cambridge University, playing for his *Blue* in the annual cricket match against Oxford University at Lords. Mark was a fast bowler.

Suddenly, I was appointed Military Adviser to the British High Commissioner for Australia at Canberra in the rank of Colonel. It was tremendous news, almost as exciting as breaking out of that wretched PoW camp, and a privilege to have been chosen for such an assignment, we were both absolutely delighted.

In October 1962, we sailed from Southampton in the Rotterdam Lloyd *Willem Ruys*, on a journey we had known well as outcast children of Empire. After Gibraltar, it was apparent that British "dominion over palm and pine" had definitely ceased. At Port Said the De Lesseps statue, signifying the opening of the Suez Canal which became the lifeline of Empire, had been demolished; Colombo, capital of Britain's once most treasured possession, had deteriorated into a unkempt city; and even Singapore, this 'naked island' of remaining Empire, was rapidly approaching independence. However, as a delightful surprise, John, Mary and Hayley Mills were waiting for us on the docks. Every cinema in town was showing one of Hayley's films The crowds went crazy about her, and we enjoyed an amusing family reunion.

As the ship ploughed southwards through the Indian ocean towards Australia, we anticipated that this was indeed the great adventure, that the free, independent Commonwealth of Australia would influence us tremendously. Liz and I were definitely outgrown children of Empire; the virtual end of Empire had come in 1948 and by 1962 the old impetuous romance of Empire had utterly expired. We looked forward to an entirely new life.

On the wharf a Scottish pipe-band and a large waving crowd welcomed the vessel to Melbourne, and virtually to Australia. Waving more frantically than most were two old friends who drove us to their property at Woodend, about 100 kilometres north, for lunch. The journey, after we had passed a long sprawl of nondescript houses, captivated us with the space of huge paddocks, seemingly unfenced, stretching far into the distance. Woodend's extravagantly wide street with small white houses and horses tied to wooden rails recalled Wild West American films. But what impressed us most was the sunshine, the deep blue cloudless sky and the enchanting spring weather in this state of Victoria.

Days later, in equally glorious weather the ship steamed into the amazingly beautiful harbour of Sydney. Met by a young Irish Guards officer, who was my Staff Captain, we disembarked. Leaving our heavy baggage, car and spaniel in his care, we flew to Canberra, staying in the Canberra Club near the University. From the Club we looked down on a golf course, a racecourse and a diminutive lake. With the surrounding mountains it was inspiring, as was the extraordinary sensation of living in a brand new city, immaculate but sterile.

The British High Commissioner, His Excellency Lieutenant General Sir William Oliver, greeted me warmly and said, 'get out of Canberra as often as you can, Tony. Go wherever the Australian army is stationed or training. See this wonderful country, take Liz with you. Don't spend too much time on the diplomatic merry-go-round here in Canberra'. I obeyed His Excellency's advice.

In a High Commission house allotted to us in State Circle close to the Prime Minister's Lodge we began the ghastly task of unpacking our trunks, boxes and crates—having no permanent home anywhere we travelled, like turtles, with all our worldly goods on our backs. Surprisingly, through the open door a handsome woman appeared holding a basket. 'I've brought you something to eat, I know how awful unpacking is.' she was the wife of an officer in the Australian Army Headquarters. Her casserole was delicious. Her kindness was characteristic of the universal friendliness we received from Australians.

We intended to drive to the Western District of Victoria to spend Christmas with friends, by what seemed from maps a reasonable journey on sealed roads, but friendly Australians warned us about the hazards of such a trip. 'Fit bull bars' they said, 'you're bound to hit a kangaroo, emu or stray cow'. Other kind helpers produced a large water bag to be carried in front of the radiator, 'It'll keep the water cool there'. 'Take three days rations, plenty of water, at least three crates of beer and an extra spare tyre. Never leave your car; if you break down someone will pick you up within a week'. Having a go at Poms was another Aussie characteristic!

Leaving Canberra at three in moonlight, well prepared for the rigour of Australian motoring, we sped along on superb roads at high speed. Liz, ex Royal Navy truck driver was the most reckless; Mark, who had just flown out for the winter vacation, the fastest; and me the most disciplined, drove in turns and arrived at our friends property in good shape.

Driving along almost empty roads with long open stretches between towns, so unlike congested roads in England and the Continent, the immense space elated me, arose a sense of freedom. The attractive countryside, screeching cockatoos high in the deep blue sky or eating the crops, pink and grey galahs swooping over our car, all added to our animation.

Our hosts were Bob and Liz Barr-Smith, owners of colossal Mount William Station. Their elegant homestead, set among trees of many kinds, expansive green lawns and rose gardens, equated an English stately home. Four daughters, superb riders, enlivened the happy household.

Liz Barr-Smith had served in the war in the WRNS with Liz in HMS *Pembroke*. Bob had joined the Life Guards straight from Cambridge University at the start of war, emulating his father's action in 1914. The only Australian in the 1st Life Guards, Bob fought tenaciously from Alamein to Tripoli, to Sicily and Italy. I met him in England before he rejoined battle from Normandy to the Rhine Crossing. Some say he was the only officer in the Household Cavalry who knew how to fix the engine of a vehicle, how to change a tyre, how to dig a deep slit trench—all learnt the hard way as a boy on Mount William. Bob certainly gave the impression that he could fix anything; which was the same impression that Australians were beginning to make on me. Bob and Liz were very special friends.

On Boxing Day, with Mark and an enormous crowd, we watched Australia defeat England at the Melbourne Cricket Ground in an atmosphere unique to Australia, remarkable for the barracking, hoots and jeers aimed at Aussies and Poms alike—and also for the humour and fairness displayed to both sides.

Queensland is a gigantic State, many times the size of the British Isles, even bigger than Texas. From books I had read, it had become the ultimate frontier that I must cross, rather like my obsession with the *Western Heaven* on my long journey through China, so we drove north through picturesque country along the New England Highway and the Great Dividing Range, stopping in motels, a new experience—there were none in England—run by friendly and helpful people. We crossed the border from New South Wales at little Wallangarra, nestling quietly in the hills, proudly informing us that we were entering the Sunshine State, and then descended to Brisbane, which retained a charming country town atmosphere. Joe Bonenti, the sprightly proprietor of the Bellvue Hotel, introduced me to a variety of Queenslanders, many of them graziers from huge properties out west, the men exceedingly big in stature and equally expansive in friendliness. Perhaps the enormity of their state made them so. The Commanding General, Mervyn Brogan, received me warmly and arranged a visit to a highly efficient infantry battalion and a jungle warfare centre—and the Gold Coast, its glorious long sandy beaches virtually empty of people.

One special day we lunched in Brisbane with Eddy Broad and his family. Pilot Officer Broad RAAF, as he was when Liz first met him in the *Arundel Castle* on the voyage from Cape Town to Scotland in 1942, was now a Judge of the District Court. Even as a sober Judge and father of five children, he was still like the lively young warrior who had invited Liz to dine by telegram— WALTZING MATILDA RITZ 1700 FRIDAY. She teased him about his early days in London, how her father, so rigidly British, took calls from Eddy, and never mentioned his name, reporting simply, 'That Australian called again'. Eddy mentioned the shocking casualties suffered by airmen from the *Arundel Castle* and how Australia had unselfishly given a generation of valiant young men to be slaughtered in bombing raids on Germany. When peace came, Liz had not known if Eddy had survived the holocaust until she saw his name in the Wallaby team to play against England at Twickenham. She and I watched the match and met Eddy afterwards.

Essentially, I worked on the diplomatic merry-go-round by attending functions as a duty. If you were in Canberra and failed to appear, your absence would be taken as an offence against the host country involved. Even if it meant going to a lunch, two cocktail parties and a dinner in one day, you must attend. Liz and I resented attending Emperor Hirohito's birthday reception at the Japanese Embassy, but we went, and I bowed to the Ambassador, remembering my last bow to a Jap in Shamshuipo camp and the kick I got for not doing it correctly.

We gave a drinks party and a lunch or dinner once a week. The merry-go-round was impersonal but interesting and valuable for the information you acquired and the people you met, including the politicians Gorton, Fraser, McMahon, Calwell, Whitlam and Prime Minister Bob Menzies.

At a dinner party given at the New Zealand High Commission by Luke and Anita Hazlett for Bob and Dame Pattie Menzies and Liz and me, the Prime Minister demonstrated his gift of diplomacy: 'High Commissioner, your country is the most beautiful country in the world', and after a pause turning to me, 'with, of course, the exception of the British Isles!'

Diplomatic entertainment was strictly taboo during weekends. This was when you met your real friends. Jo Gullett, horseman, soldier, politician, ambassador, author and Ruth became wonderful friends, inviting us often to the beautiful homestead on their farm *Lambrigg* by the banks of the Murrumbidgee.

Jo introduced us to Tony and Judy Chisholm who immediately invited us to visit their property near Central Mount Stuart, almost bang in the centre of Australia. We flew to Darwin, where I visited army and RAAF units, and then to Alice Springs.

I rang Tony. 'How do I get to you?' 'Drive 200 miles north up the bitumen, turn left at tea tree, then 56 miles down the dirt to the homestead. Bring crates of Swan beer'.

Hiring a car, we set off along the Stuart Highway, its verges lined with empty beer bottles chucked out of trucks carrying troops to Darwin in the war. As we came close to 200 miles on the clock, we searched frantically for a tea tree. In desperation I stopped at the first sign of human habitation, a shack with three horses tied up to the rails.

Inside were three large, deeply sunburnt men in wide felt hats, blue shirts, moleskins and high-heeled boots, leaning against a bar drinking beer.

They greeted me, in a slow drawl, 'G'day, mate, how're yer going?' 'To *Anningie*, I'm looking for a tea tree where I'm meant to turn off for Tony Chisholm's property'.

They roared with laughter, 'Jesus! This is it, mate, this is a place called *Tea Tree*, not a bloody tree'.

One of them broke the cap off a beer bottle and gave it to me. 'Here, you need this. Where're you from, mate? You don't talk proper, you must be a flaming Pom'.

I pleaded guilty and asked if they were cowboys. 'No, that's American, we're drovers, driving cattle'. They continued laughing at every word I said, saying they had never heard anyone speak like me. Liz came in. The drovers treated her with politeness like the gentlemen they were.

The homestead stood in a green oasis in startling contrast to the arid country burnt up by a seven-year drought. Water from a deep bore produced the verdant patch, which included modern quarters with running water for some five hundred Aboriginals but which were mostly unoccupied, the Aboriginals preferring to live in the bush.

Tony Chisholm ran this over-a-million acre property with one other white man, an ex-soldier engineer, and a large number of aboriginal drovers for the two hundred stock horses held in the home Paddock. Tony drove us 180 miles, still within his land, rolling and bumping past strange large rock formations jutting fiercely out of the earth, giant anthills, sad trees and bushes eaten as far as the starving lean cattle could reach, scraggy kangaroos and scrawny emus. He checked numerous bores, the only means he had of keeping a few of his cattle alive during the relentless drought. The vastness of it all was staggering and made both of us realise how enormous is the continent of Australia.

Judy, a very beautiful woman, worked in the homestead all day treating Aboriginals medically and calling the Flying Doctor for advice. She also ran a class for the School of the Air, and attended to clerical and administrative matters. Two Aboriginal girls dressed in long shapeless dresses helped her with the housework, but she could not rely on them entirely because of a habit of going *walk-about* without notice. When cattle were mustered forty miles or more distant, she accompanied Tony, living in a caravan, running the camp for the men and mustering on horseback herself when necessary.

As we left the homestead at dawn driving eastwards, the sun rose, filling the sky with a crimson aureole over Mount Stuart, a vivid vermilion circle of fire stoked with red dust from the prevailing drought stricken land. The beauty of it inspired us but its blazing fierceness symbolised the harshness of existence on this continent.

The visit to *Anningie* established for me that these graziers in outback properties were outstanding people possessing great courage endurance and ability to withstand the utter isolation and the demands made on them.

The lure of Queensland beckoned me again. I flew from Canberra with a group of Military Attaches to observe an infantry-tank exercise at Tin Can

Bay near Fraser Island, the largest sand island in the world. Monstrous Centurion tanks charged over the ground near Tin Can Bay in a deadly battles of pretence, smashing trees. plants and fauna, including rare Blackboys. It was not a pleasant sight, but quickly forgotten in perfect dry cool July weather in the illustrious Tin Can Bay Hotel, where I consumed quantities of delicious king-size prawns and XXXX-beer with all types of people, fisherman, farm labourers, artists, authors and weirdos. In company with the local policeman, a worthy Returned Soldier, this reckless mob flaunted, like good Aussies, their contempt for a law restricting service only to hotel residents and travellers on Sundays. My mates, which they became, loaded me with exotic fruits to take back to freezing Canberra—avocados, pineapples, pawpaw—which Liz accepted gladly.

We drove from Canberra to Adelaide by the Sturt Highway, a trip of over 1000 kilometres, along the valley of the Murrumbidgee as far as Hay, and then on long straight roads fading into the far circumference of the Earth. We saw no other vehicles, just miles of space except one rather sad Emu, gazing at us with disgust for disturbing his tranquil domain. The sky, always blue, seemed much higher than in any other country, perhaps to be consistent in proportion with all the space. The *mafoos* at *Bom Jesus* in Macau would have approved and called it good *fung shui*.

Possibly also Australia's good *fung shui* made her the lucky country. It was a rich, highly prosperous country with resources of all kinds. There was full employment, open for anyone to succeed if they wished.

In pleasant Adelaide, with its symmetrical streets and elegant churches, we watched Googie Withers and John McCallum in *Woman in a Dressing Gown* and had supper with them afterwards. Like me, Googie was born in India and Harry, her brother, was a contemporary of mine in the Army. A lasting friendship with Googie and John was established that night.

Leaving Liz in Adelaide, I flew to Maralinga where RN, British Army and RAF and Australian detachments were stationed. It was an extraordinary isolated camp on the verge of the great Victoria Desert, nowhere from anywhere. The dry desert breeze and smell reminded me of the Sinai Desert and Bedouin but here was a much cleaner smell for this desert kept very few people and fewer camels.

I was taken to the site of a nuclear underground explosion, a gigantic deep circular pit with the sides smoothly glazed by the intense heat of the discharge and with a clean pool in the bottom from recent rains, all still slightly radioactive. To me Maralinga was a sinister place, the troops hated it and their task of clearing up radioactive material. I had to visit it a number of times because the soldiers were a part of my command in Australia.

I was thankful to fly back to Adelaide and Liz and take her off to Woomera, where space rockets were launched. This was quite different from Maralinga, not so isolated, with lavish amenities for the people working there. The scientific jargon was meaningless to me, so we took off for the vineyards and wine towns north of Adelaide, the superb wines another example of Australian ingenuity.

In the three years, 1962 to 1965, that I served as Military Adviser to the British High Commissioner there were many activities with which I was involved.

In 1962 The Royal Ulster Rifles came to train with the Australian Army at Singleton NSW and take R & R in Sydney. The Ulster Rifles were the first British Regiment to come to Australia for a hundred years. They were well received, by the Irish in Sydney.

The next year a Military Tattoo was held in Sydney. The Household Cavalry Band (mounted on Sydney Police horses), Pipe Bands of Scottish Regiments, The Grenadier Guards Band and a drill Company combined with an equal number of Australian Army, Navy and Air Force Bands and troops. The Tattoo was a success because of the help I received from Gerry Fowke, my Sandhurst mate, retired from the Welsh Guards.

Liz and I went to Wellington, New Zealand and met Eddy Crossley's widow. Eddy died in 1956 aged 39. I told her and Eddy's children the story of the escape.

Every year Australian and British military attaches and advisers from India to Japan assembled in Singapore for a meeting at which the attaches reported on the countries in which they served, and thus provided valuable military and political intelligence. Liz came to Singapore with me for a lavish round of parties with the attaches and their wives.

Leaving Australia, again with the intrepid Liz, I visited Papua New Guinea, representing the High Commissioner with a speech on Empire Day (24th May) in Port Moresby and then flying all over the country in fixed wing aircraft and helicopters, calling on District Commissioners, meeting Patrol officers and The Pacific Islands Regiment, a splendid outfit.

And we continued travelling round Australia; to Tasmania to stay at Connerville, the oldest sheep property in Australia owned by the O'Connor family; to the south western district of Western Australia and handsome Perth where we stayed with the Governor of Western Australia, Sir Douglas Kendrew, an old friend; and many times to Melbourne, renewing our friendship from Germany with Sir Rohan Delacombe, the Governor of Victoria.

Perhaps one of our longest trips was back in Queensland again, to the army in Townsville, staying on gorgeous Magnetic Island, to Cairns and pretty Green Island. Then into the Cape York Peninsula, flying low in an old DC3 and stopping at isolated dirt airstrips to pick up or let down an amazing mixture of people, cattle-men, Catholic priests, merchants. At Weipa 'New Australians' or 'Refoes' as European migrants were called, left the aircraft to work in the bauxite mine at Albatross Bay in the Gulf of Carpenteria. We flew on to Cape York, crossed Endeavour Strait to Thursday Island and to the gaunt unkempt Grand Hotel, its interior full of Somerset Maughan types; rejected aspiring authors, pearl traders and divers, rogues and scoundrels. We experienced a hilarious night with the mob, drunken but amusing, who took an instant liking to Liz and her English accent.

Australia's respect for those who fell in defence of her at Anzac Day on 25 April each year impressed me greatly. I attended Anzac parades in Canberra, Melbourne and Sydney, accompanied by Liz, whose association with the Royal Navy in the war made her equally attached to Anzac Day.

With our closeness to the Snowy Mountains I saw much of the amazing project to harness the waters of the rivers in dams and to produce electricity. Two English Officers of the Royal Engineers were engaged in responsible projects living in the mountains with their wives and among the 'New Australians' working on the scheme, a variety of people for many European countries. Liz and I saw them frequently, especially when we were skiing at Thredbo.

In those three years we saw as much of Australia as possible. We revered it and the captivating people, the space and the freedom. Mark, who joined us straight from Cambridge with a law degree, worked for Shell Australia. He became an Australian citizen, which convinced us to make Australia our home. We bought a flat in Double Bay in Sydney as a base to return to after my next job in the army, which was to be in Singapore, a dreary British Army job with a host of pompous Poms!

I now felt rather as I did when I had escaped from the Japanese, that I relished my freedom and the adventure and hated the prospect of returning to authority and bureaucracy. I had enjoyed a great deal of liberty in my work in Australia; it had been a marvellous adventure in a beautiful land. And so, there could be no better place to end this saga of Elizabeth Hayley Bell and Tony Hewitt to end than our venture in Australia.

Epilogue

Born to be outcast children of the Empire, Liz and I saw much of it in peace and in war. The threat of war from the early 1930s and the Second World War itself caused considerable stress and strain and affected our behaviour immensely. The War brought about a strange feeling, unlike anything in our lives since, of a splendid carelessness which somehow held us together.

When Japan struck on 8 December 1941 Liz and I were thrown head first into a boiling furnace. In a terrible tragedy, during a ferocious eighteen day battle, the garrison of Hong Kong was overwhelmed by a stronger enemy. In his dispatch General Maltby described the heavy artillery and mortar concentrations of the Japanese as 'comparable to those in the Great War'. Air Chief Marshal Sir Robert Brooke-Popham said insensibly in a dispatch that 'Hong Kong was regarded officially as an undesirable commitment'. Churchill cabled that for every day we continued fighting 'you can win the lasting honour which we are sure will be your due'. The loss of life and the agony of imprisonment was a cruel price for valiant soldiers to pay for a cause without hope even though they won the *Lasting Honour*.

I was fortunate to escape from the POW camp at Shamshuipo after six weeks' internment. I hated leaving the staunch London soldiers with whom I had served for seven years but my Colonel wanted me to take out a list of casualties for the relatives and relate the performance of the Die-Hards to the world outside the barbed wire.

Horrifying memories have lived with Liz—the evacuation from Singapore, the parting from Noel and the burning city. When I arrived in Singapore as the Deputy Commander of the Military District, we stayed a night near Opium Hill, where a nightmare haunted Liz with the sound of battle, explosions of shells and bombs, screams and cries of the wounded and dying. The place was full of spirits of young men killed in the Battle for Opium Hill where Noel and the Malay Regiment fought bravely.

I served two years in Singapore. I found the senior British officers inflated and devious. A journalist visiting Singapore at this time saw them as obtuse as they were portrayed in 1941 in Braddon's *Naked Island*. Possibly, I had become too used to the Australians' direct candid manner of speech and behaviour.

We lived in a large comfortable quarter in much the same conditions as we had lived before the war, looked after by skilled Chinese servants ruled by the No 1, Ah Wong. Liz enjoyed it. We travelled throughout gorgeous Malaya, to Kuala Lumpur and the *Dog*, the Selangor Club; to Seremban, where Noel and I had played rugby against Hugo Hughes' team, and the Sungei Ujong Club. In Port Dickson we paid homage to the Malay Regiment War Memorial and Noel, the lists of War dead names augmented by those killed in the *Emergency,* the struggle against Communist terrorists. Harper's Bungalow had gone, destroyed by the Japanese, but Cape Rachado Lighthouse on the hill was there and revived poignant memories for Liz as did the sandy beach and the warm sea of the Malacca Straits.

In Singapore, I retired from the Army and stayed in Hong Kong, living on the Peak, the scene of Liz 's childhood. We did not ride in sedan chairs as she did or eat ice-creams in the Peak Hotel because it had been burnt down many decades ago. We did not go to Shameen to relive Francis Hayley Bell's heroic stand on the bund against the Chinese Nationalists because foreigners were unwelcome in the People's Republic of China during the Cultural Revolution.

From Australia we often returned to Hong Kong, where I told the story of the Battle to serving officers of the garrison and took part in making a documentary video of the Fall of Hong Kong. Frequently I met ex-prisoners-of-war who had fought with the Hong Kong Volunteers, now old Chinese gentlemen who found it difficult to understand how Britain could relinquish the Treaty of Nanking of 1842 at which the Government of China had handed over the Island in perpetuity. Poor Hong Kong and its many Hong Kong Chinese citizens, it awaits the end in nervous anticipation.

In contrast to Hong Kong, Singapore is a flourishing Republic. We returned in 1992 on the 50th anniversary of its fall to the Japanese and paid homage to those, including Noel, who fell in defence of freedom. And, of course, I remembered my first meeting with Liz in Singapore in 1936—that lovely eighteen year old girl.

We settled in Australia, living gratefully under blue skies and a warm sun. We came as outgrown children of the Empire, former citizens of a demised Empire and became citizens of the Commonwealth of Australia.

Index

★